The American Vagrant in Literature

For Stella

The American Vagrant in Literature
Race, Work and Welfare

Bryan Yazell

Edinburgh University Press is one of the leading university presses in the UK. We publish academic books and journals in our selected subject areas across the humanities and social sciences, combining cutting-edge scholarship with high editorial and production values to produce academic works of lasting importance. For more information visit our website: edinburghuniversitypress.com

© Bryan Yazell 2023, 2024

Edinburgh University Press Ltd
13 Infirmary Street
Edinburgh, EH1 1LT

First published in hardback by Edinburgh University Press 2023

Typeset in 11/13pt Adobe Sabon by
Cheshire Typesetting Ltd, Cuddington, Cheshire

A CIP record for this book is available from the British Library

ISBN 978 1 3995 0671 7 (hardback)
ISBN 978 1 3995 0672 4 (paperback)
ISBN 978 1 3995 0673 1 (webready PDF)
ISBN 978 1 3995 0674 8 (epub)

The right of Bryan Yazell to be identified as the author of this work has been asserted in accordance with the Copyright, Designs and Patents Act 1988, and the Copyright and Related Rights Regulations 2003 (SI No. 2498).

Contents

Acknowledgements	vi
Introduction: Who Was the Tramp?	1
1. The Internationalism of American Vagrancy: Mark Twain and Josiah Flynt on the Tramp	30
2. Vagrant Nationalism: Jack London and W. H. Davies on the Super-Tramp	60
3. Tramps in the Machine: Interwar British Vagrancy	92
4. Steinbeck's Migrants: Families on the Move and the Politics of Resource Management	123
Epilogue: Tramping's Afterlife	151
Works Cited	166
Index	178

Acknowledgements

First and foremost, I owe a debt of gratitude to John Marx, my doctoral advisor, who has read virtually every page of this book over a period spanning several years. Such generosity (and patience) is legendary. Special recognition is also due to Mark Jerng and Hsuan L. Hsu, who guided me through the long process of first writing a dissertation and then turning those early scribblings into a coherent monograph. Alongside my faculty supervisors, support from the graduate student community at UC Davis was a critical factor in completing this book. Thanks to Matt Franks, Gina Caison, Pearl Bauer, Ryan Wander, Kristin George Bagdanov and Jasmine Kitses (among others) for their feedback and comradery during all stages of this project.

Since arriving in Odense, I have benefited immensely from the assistance provided by my colleagues at the University of Southern Denmark. Klaus Petersen, Rita Felski, Anne-Marie Mai and Peter Simonsen provided the guidance necessary for me to see this book through to completion. My postdoctoral term at the Niels Bohr Professorship Program gave me the freedom to work on this book at my own pace, an especially fortunate circumstance for a new researcher. Special thanks are due to Emily Hogg, Anita Wohlmann and Ella Fegitz for reading (and re-reading) chapter drafts as this book neared completion – and for their all-around encouragement. I am lucky to be in their company. Sophy Kohler's thoughtful editing and impressive command of the English language was invaluable in getting this manuscript finished. Thanks to Patrick Fessenbecker, Alastair Morrison, Mathies Græsborg Aarhus, and my colleagues at DIAS and DaWS for expanding my sense of how to approach the study of literature.

Financial support from the Danish National Research Foundation (grant number DNRF127) played no small part in allowing me to complete this project. Research related to the John Steinbeck chapter, including a visit to the Steinbeck archives, was supported by the University of California Humanities Research Institute. I would also like to thank the attendees and organisers of conferences where I presented samples of this work, especially the 2017 'Out of Place': Vagrancy and Settlement conference in London and the 2016 Asilomar Conference in Pacific Grove, California. Material from Chapter 4 previously appeared in *Modern Fiction Studies* 63.3 (2017), and portions of Chapter 1 in *Journal of Transnational Studies* 8.1 (2017).

This book has travelled with me for a long time and across two continents. I could withstand the turmoil implied in that timeline only due to the assistance of those around me. I am grateful for the work done by Michelle Houston, Susannah Butler and the rest of the staff at Edinburgh University Press to produce this book during a period of lockdowns, office closures and general uncertainty. Finally, thank you to my friends and loved ones – from the West Coast to the *Fynske kyst* – who have given me the emotional support to pursue this work amongst the twists and turns that a career in academia entails. Thanks to Ziggy, my constant writing companion and sometime office mate. Dana, my gratefulness for your support and companionship extends beyond what this small page can contain. I can say without any hint of exaggeration that I could not have done this without you.

Introduction: Who Was the Tramp?

In *Social Problems*, published in 1883, economist and social theorist Henry George assesses the various threats plaguing the United States during the fraught period now known as the Gilded Age. Many of the dangers he decries will look relevant to the modern reader's eyes. Among them, environmental collapse due to industrial waste and trenchant poverty are at least as pressing to Americans now as they were in the nineteenth century. However, one of the most severe problems among these social ills may appear out of place to readers today: the 'tramp', the wandering vagrant type that confounded legal authorities near the turn of the century. Indeed, to George, tramps stand out as not one problem among many but the pre-eminent threat to democratic society. 'Consider this terrible phenomenon', he observes, 'an appearance more menacing to the Republic than that of hostile armies and fleets bent on destruction' (179). George continues in his text to outline an origin story for tramps that highlights their close relation to the tumultuous social context of the Gilded Age more generally. 'In the beginning', he writes, '[the tramp] is a man able to work ... but who, not finding opportunity to work where he is ... [is] driven by those imperative needs to beg or to steal' (179). Although George saw job shortages as the underlying problem, he understands tramps to be imminent threats in their own right. Forced onto the road, the tramp 'becomes a vagabond and an outcast – a poisonous pariah, avenging on society the wrong that he keenly, but vaguely, feels has been done him' (179). In this presentation, the tramp is an agent of destruction. George was hardly alone in figuring the tramps as 'hostile armies', however. According to Richard Wrigley and George Revill, by the time *Social Problems* was published tramps had already become 'the moral panic of the nation'

(262), distinguishing them from among the larger population of the poor that swelled in late nineteenth-century America.

By far the most influential American economist of his time, George is but one prominent voice among many clamouring for a solution to the so-called tramp problem.[1] For readers in the twenty-first century, however, the tramp may appear to be a poor representation of the problems attending both migration and homelessness. After all, to speak of tramps in the West conjures a very specific image of shabby, solitary and typically white men on the road or stowing away in rail cars. For observers like George, the tramp's perverse embodiment of liberal autonomy – his rejection of authority and boundless mobility – posed a clear danger to the nation state. The disappearance of this tramp type as a pre-eminent social threat, moreover, reflects a sustained refiguration of vagrancy over the course of the past century, a move undergirded by a changing public perception of itinerant homelessness and its attendant social policies. For Americans today, for instance, the threat of single white men on the road pales in evocative power compared with the threat of undocumented labour and migration from the global south. If anti-migrancy rhetoric remains broadly similar over the past century – evident in the appeals to 'hostile armies' of roving people battering down the gates of healthy society – the specific targets of these screeds shift according to the intersecting discourses of labour and policy at a given moment. The case of the tramp is exemplary of this discursive project: the figure's rehabilitation in the public imagination occurred over several decades, against a historical backdrop encompassing successive economic crashes, on the one hand, and rapidly expanding welfare institutions, on the other. By reconstructing this history, *The American Vagrant in Literature: Race, Work and Welfare* locates the vagabond figure among the prevailing political turmoil at the turn of the century. More importantly, it also makes a case for placing tramping texts at the forefront of the social and cultural debates that precipitated the rise of the welfare state in the twentieth century.

The interdisciplinary efforts to define the exceptional vagrant figure for the purpose of rehabilitating him are, as this book stresses throughout, critical precedents to the widescale reforms that occur in the mid-twentieth century. Bringing the wide array of sources contributing to this project into focus requires moving beyond the borders of any single literature or national context. Rather, the discursive project that connects tramping literature to the construction of the welfare state involved parties with at times vastly different understandings of their texts' readers and their potential impact. During the turbulent years near the turn of the century, in particular, ideas for addressing the social problems associated with unchecked industrial capitalism – poverty, homelessness, slums and the like – abounded in both North America and Europe (Rodgers 28). As historian Daniel Rodgers explains, it would be a mistake to claim that the various activists, policy makers and writers who pushed for various social reforms during the nineteenth and early twentieth centuries all worked with the goal of creating something called the welfare state, a term coined by the New Deal's opponents only well after the peak of its legislative power (28). In this light, the references to welfare and welfare reforms that appear in this book apply to sources that call for, or otherwise anticipate, a statist model for relief that at once identifies among its population the specific groups in need and then administers support to them. Ultimately, *The American Vagrant in Literature* stresses the continuities between vagrancy reformers in the US and the United Kingdom as well as between pre- and post-welfare-state policies for addressing the problem of out-of-work citizens.

In addition to supplementing existing accounts of the development of welfare policies, *The American Vagrant in Literature* offers critical insight into the process by which a distinct demographic group – in this case, the singular tramp – can become the cause célèbre for public debates about social policy. The claim throughout this book, inspired by scholarship on the subject of governmentality, is that the disappearance of the tramp as the pre-eminent social problem by the mid-century does not mean that the conditions generating homelessness no longer exist – indeed, as figures from the past decade show, quite the opposite is true.[2] Rather, the disappearance indicates that the figure no longer does the work it once did to inspire fear or adulation in audiences. As the final chapters of this book attest, the tramp's estranged familiarity becomes rather mundane in works such as Jack Kerouac's *On the Road* (1957), which looks to people of colour to perform the kind of dangerous itineracy that the white vagrant once enacted. The literary history that connects criminologists, ethnographers, novelists and travel writers together reflects the coterie of sources that placed tramping and the tramp at the intersection of larger debates about race and social policy. As Peter Miller and Nikolas Rose explain, the 'activities of the minor figures' are most demonstrative of the science of governance, without which states could not 'govern at all' (5). As one historical version of vagrancy, tramps are a case study in how governmental institutions and, as will become clear, cultural sources create, administer and refigure specific demographic groups.

George's vilification of the tramp as public enemy number one should indicate the extent to which this particular type of unemployed person bespeaks the larger economic, social and political events in the US at the time of *Social Problems*. After all, even though homelessness and unemployment were far from new phenomena in the nineteenth century, social commentators at the time saw something unmistakably distinct in the problem posed by the tramp. The tramp type that George decries comes into being, according to Tim Cresswell, after the crash of 1873, when publications such as *The New York Times* popularised the term to identify specifically the growing population of unemployed migrants in the US (48).[3] As we will see in Chapter 1, the speed with which the tramp moved from this specific coinage to the forefront of political discourse is suggestive of the sweeping social upheaval of the period. Indeed, the boom-and-bust era of the Gilded Age was inaugurated by the greatest financial collapse in US history at the time, the Great Depression of 1873. Historians now refer to this economic crash as the Panic of 1873, a designation that, as Michael Bellesiles points out, fails to account for the unprecedented scale of the market downturn, surpassed only by the second Great Depression, which began in 1929 (1). Indeed, the scope of the 1873 collapse encompassed not only the US but much of Europe as well, including Germany, France and Britain (Reti 62).

As this historical framing already suggests, tracking the development of the tramp as a popular figure requires an international frame of reference. This book therefore covers not only the period between the two monumental depressions, but also – like the itinerant tramping subject – a vast geography, drawing from sources not only in the US but in Germany and Britain. To be sure, scholars have extensively documented the respective dramatic shifts in governmental policy and popular culture after each economic depression and the social unrest that followed. Rather than treat these literatures as discrete bodies, however, *The American Vagrant in Literature* reads them together to reveal the political and cultural linkages that extend across the nineteenth and twentieth centuries and connect the US to Europe. In fact, it is impossible to discuss at length the origins of the tramping archetype without elaborating on the wider social transformations that occurred during this period. As Michael Denning explains, the 1873 crash and subsequent labour strikes inaugurated nothing less than 'the new phenomenon of unemployment' in the

US (*Mechanic* 149). The codification of tramping unfolds against a backdrop of dramatic expansion in the science of government and the technology of criminal enforcement as well as developments in media and entertainment. Faced with a curious public, government officials and popular authors together considered the same problem – namely, how do we make tramping pay?

As this last point indicates, literature was hardly a bystander in this endeavour, but rather provided some of the key texts in a long process of articulating state interest in tramp mobility. In the years between 1873 and 1929, the discourse surrounding tramps – as the subject of both popular texts and anti-vagrancy ordinances – travelled on an international stage before becoming normalised within welfare institutions such as workhouses and labour camps. In view of this timeline, *The American Vagrant in Literature* follows the course of two narratives. One treats the US as a place of origin for the modern tramp, a specific embodiment of mobile labour whose viability is always in question. The tramp as a cultural type, the centrepiece of popular memoirs and dime-store novels, moves from the US to Britain and becomes naturalised, so to speak, among the long-standing vagrant codes and vagrant groups that exist there. While tramp literature travels from the US to Europe, the narrative concerning labour and vagrancy codes moves in the opposite direction. As the first half of *The American Vagrant in Literature* especially demonstrates, the legal codification of vagrancy involved importing governmental codes from Britain (and Europe, more generally) to the US. If widespread and enduring poverty became an overriding problem for rapidly industrialising states across the North Atlantic after 1873, the tactics for responding to this problem evolved over the course of the early twentieth century. By singling out vagrancy as one highly specific version of homelessness – in the person of the tramp, especially – this book scrutinises how discourses involving labour, welfare and moral responsibility attach to specific archetypes that extend from the vaudeville stage to governmental reports.

A product of its time, the tramp archetype embodied the social unrest and moral panic associated with the threat of unending economic turmoil. The years spanning the 1870s saw the US in the throes of what numerous historians have identified as a veritable 'tramp scare', a populist reaction against the supposed threat vagrants posed to small communities unequipped to control them (Bellesiles 111).[4] While the public largely saw the general population of poor as chronically indolent, Bellesiles explains, they saw the tramp as 'an all-purpose supercriminal, seemingly capable of every transgression' (117). In everything from scholarly studies to newspaper accounts and sensationalist fiction, tramps were said to organise themselves with the aim of plundering communities across the country (Cresswell 9–10). Unlike the notion of the downtrodden poor, tramps embodied all manner of threats facing the healthy functioning of society. While the recently unemployed factory worker might seek the means to re-enter the workplace, the reasoning goes, tramps aggressively seek what they need in order to stay *outside* the factory floor or the family home. Owing to this perception, Americans understood tramping as a crisis in need of innovative solutions, even as they became accustomed to the idea of long-term and widespread poverty, more generally.

As *The American Vagrant in Literature* stresses throughout, the policies enacted in response to the tramp panic set the groundwork for the welfare codes created after 1929 in several ways. Most immediately, one sees in this public debate an emerging consensus that stresses the need to rehabilitate tramps on the basis of their potential labour. For many observers, the tramp's exceptional mobility was evidence of an underlying talent that could be directed towards the social good. To be sure, for many Americans the tramp posed a problem that could be solved not by rehabilitation but by all-out elimination. As Cresswell points out, many editorials at the height of the 'tramp scare' called for simply removing – through deportations or mass murder – tramps as a population entirely (9). But more consequential were the newspaper editorials offering a range of methods for rehabilitating tramps, from poorhouses to rural labour camps meant to build good character (Wrigley and Revill 262). For instance, reformer Edmond Kelly's 1908 *Elimination of the Tramp* decries 'the man whose *soul* breaks down' and consequently moves to commit any number of unsocial acts, from 'innocently stealing a ride on a freight car' to 'assaulting our women, corrupting our youth, and breeding disease' (4–5). According to this reasoning, the problem of the tramp could be solved only when these vagrants found a productive outlet for their exceptional – if illicit – form of movement.

The campaign to regulate tramping also brings into focus the international network of exchange – between authors, legislators and social scientists – that facilitated the development of early welfare codes in the US and Europe. For example, the labour camps Kelly promotes in order to combat social breakdown in the US are modelled on extant institutions in Switzerland and other European states. The obstacle to implementing these camps, Kelly continues, derives from an overarching social dynamic that both the US and Britain share. 'Singularly enough it is the two nations – England and America – in which charity is the most lavish and most highly organised, that have most resolutely refused to adopt the obvious solution to this problem', the labour camp (3). For Kelly, the extensive and complex networks of charity institutions stand in contrast to the streamlined simplicity of state-mandated rehabilitation. Solving the tramp problem therefore requires not only a concerted effort on the part of government to identify vagrant populations; it must also involve directing the state's resources towards rehabilitating, in addition to just containing, individual delinquent labourers. As Kelly's text further indicates, international comparison helps to define not only the global circulation of the tramps but also individual state responses for treating them.

Of course, Kelly and like-minded activists distinguished one group among a larger pool of marginalised people by singling out the tramp as a demographic in need of reform. When speaking of the tramp, Kelly stresses at once the singular and masculine characteristics associated with this identity. In his view, the tramp is a man whose aptitude for hard work has broken down but can be repaired again. In other words, this form of vagrancy refers to a person whose features are eminently familiar: young men of European extraction who proudly express their autonomy. These features are also evident in reporting from government agencies tasked with controlling the vagrant population. For those who wrote anti-tramp laws, 'tramps were male by definition' (Cresswell 88). At the turn of the century, 'at least 85 per cent of vagrants' in the UK 'were demonstrably adult men under sixty-five years of age', a fact that compelled state agencies to pay little attention to women, children and elderly people also living in a state of vagrancy (Vorspan 60). Writing at nearly the same time in the US, tramp sociologist Nels Anderson remarks that women and children are the least visible segment of vagrant populations, writing that 'men of the road . . . monopolize the benches and crowd the shady places' wherever they go (34).

The tramp's vexed embodiment of masculinity and whiteness is critical to his cultural currency as the archetypal problem child of liberal democracy during the late nineteenth century. From the beginning of the 'tramp scare', journalistic accounts were early contributors to the tramp's racial and gendered connotations. News coverage of Coxey's Army, the organised march to Washington DC to protest mass unemployment in 1894, foregrounded the figure of the male malcontent. A contemporary article in *The New York Times*, for example, describes 'hard-looking people' (described as 'tramps' in the article's subheading) among the 'force of men' who marched in military-style regiments ('In Dreams'). Jack London similarly foregrounds the most masculine aspects of this tramp movement in his own recollection of his time with Kelly's Army, the western wing of the march to the capitol. 'Across the wild and woolly West, clear from California, General Kelly and his heroes had captured trains', he explains, 'but they fell down when they crossed the Missouri and went up against the effete East' (*The Road* 94). London's brief summation of this episode juxtaposes the hardy characteristics of the tramps and the 'wild and woolly' regions they inhabit, both of which contrast with the 'effete' forces that obstruct them. In London's case – and as Chapter 2 discusses at length – masculinity is a fundamental attribute of the tramp and a crucial component of the figure's heroism in London's writings and for sources inspired by his popular accounts of vagabondage.

The uniform description of the tramp's identity across sources and national borders brings into focus the overriding discourse involving autonomy and mobility from which these texts draw. The vagrants that appear in this book therefore had a visibility in the public discourse that was not accorded to any number of women or non-white people who lived in a state of vagrancy at the turn of the century. The US is instructive of this last point. In the South, for example, government officials from the colonial period to Jim Crow used anti-vagrancy ordinances to deny African Americans entry into mainstream society (Ranney 17). Likewise, non-white migratory workers might have shared the road with tramps but were absent in the popular imagination of vagabondage. As Mae Ngai points out, labourers from Asia and Central America have historically been welcomed to the US for the purposes of migratory work but thoroughly denied pathways to civil inclusion. The shifting legal designations around who is worthy of citizenship, just as the debate over who is or is not a vagrant, thus reveal much about how 'the nation has imagined and constructed itself over time' (Ngai 6). These cases make clear the ease with which ordinances nominally universal in scope operate in practice as weapons for the persecution of specific groups.

The public fascination with tramps after the 1870s warrants renewed scrutiny as it helps to clarify how a specific demographic comes in and – more importantly – out of the popular consciousness as a social threat. Over the course of several decades, writers on the subject of tramps advocate not for expulsion but for incorporation and rehabilitation – at least, for the privileged few. As Chapter 3 in particular discusses, the push to first discipline and then rehabilitate tramps around the turn of the century is emblematic of larger shifts in governance that Michel Foucault diagnoses in Western Europe. The coexistence of policies meant to eliminate certain demographic groups while rehabilitating others reflects what Foucault deems the 'paroxysmal point' of modern biopower that reaches its zenith in fascist states, but which exists 'in the workings of all States' (*Society* 260). The focus of this book adds to important accounts of racial exclusion like Ngai's by examining an under-discussed aspect of this governing logic: while vagrancy laws were once understood as a way to remove people from the public eye, they are retooled in the wake of 1873 to bring certain people back into the civil fold. The fact that this latter group consisted largely of single men of European descent demonstrates the extent to which racial categories informed early, nominally colour-blind welfare codes determining who was eligible for institutional support.

The racial subtext to tramping draws in large part from the conceptual framework of whiteness studies in the US, which has expounded on the social-constructedness of whiteness as a racial category as well as specific histories of racial making for different ethnic groups within the working class. Prominent studies such as David Roediger's *The Wages of Whiteness* and Noel Ignatiev's *How the Irish Became White* make the case that race- and class-consciousness go hand in hand; to separate one from the other ignores the extent to which specific demographic subjects both create and sustain this intersection. These influential accounts, however, largely limit their comparative analysis to labour movements involving the working class.[5] Specifically, both Roediger and Ignatiev identify the process by which immigrant white ethnic groups differentiated themselves from Black populations in order to associate themselves with the cultural capital or privilege that attended white identity in the US.

Meanwhile, recent studies have begun to uncover how deeply vagrancy literatures reflect larger anxieties around not only class and labour but also racial identity. For example, Alistair Robinson's study of British vagrancy in the Victorian era reveals the deeply racialised thinking around the subject, which expressed fears regarding racial contamination and degeneration against the backdrop of imperial expansion (8). Likewise, Sal Nicolazzo argues that sources as far back as the seventeenth century understood vagrancy as a 'racializing' category that demanded the development of a modern police force to detain and discipline (29). *The American Vagrant in*

Literature expands the scope of these comparative studies to consider new demographics that are excluded from the working class but afforded the privileges associated with whiteness.[6] Rather than chart the upward mobility of white subjects in the US, this book elucidates the myriad ways in which governmental and popular writers of vagrancy draw from the discourse of whiteness (and its connotations of autonomy and mobility) in order to manage the subclass of vagrants. The whiteness of the tramp – as well as his masculinity – provided a lifeline to welfare states tasked with distinguishing the so-called deserving poor from groups occluded from this nascent support system. Even while tramps shirked labour and domestic responsibilities, governments and authors alike stressed their potential for reform largely on the basis of race and gender.

At the same time, the tramp's vexed embodiment of whiteness is also crucial to explaining this subject's prominent spot in political debate and literature. Popular accounts from the turn of the century suggested to their readers that tramps almost look like 'us' – the white, male citizens constituting the voting populations in the US and Britain – but not quite. Instead, the tramp eschews the confines of work and home in favour of homosocial communities along the road among fellow wanderers. According to this thinking, the tramp is a grotesque reflection of the ideal subject in the Anglo-American liberal societies at this time: white, male and staunchly autonomous. As the first chapter explains, this conceit is in part what colours Twain's satirisation of rich tourists in *A Tramp Abroad*, published in 1880, which puts affluent thrill seekers into close rhetorical proximity to tramps in order to stress their similarities. In Twain's case, the aimless wanderer is a privileged observer of society, one whose movements overseas bring into focus the mores and customs of a given state by means of a sustained comparison with foreign examples. The notion of the vagrant as a vehicle for social commentary is, as the pages that follow elaborate, essential to many different accounts, from the work of ethnographers such as Nels Anderson and Josiah Flynt to Twain's travelogues, the novels of John Steinbeck and Charlie Chaplin's iconic Little Tramp films. According to these depictions of vagrancy, incorrigible tramps deserve not expulsion from society but greater incorporation into it. The prospect of saving the tramp therefore involves convincing him to re-enter the domestic spaces he elected to leave.

Tramp Writing and International Exchange

As these cases make clear, the minute facets of who is included in – or, more importantly, excluded from – the category of vagrancy assume different forms in different political and cultural systems. Rather than offer a comprehensive overview of vagrancy in all forms, therefore, I focus on its most popular or mass-marketed form during the final decades of the nineteenth century and the first decades of the twentieth century. There are several consequences of delimiting my sources along these historical and literary lines. Most immediately, I am better equipped to trace the discursive thread linking US and British sources on their shared preoccupation with a single figure, the tramp, and its potential for rehabilitation. Furthermore, these sources provide critical insight into the shape and direction of the popular debate regarding welfare reform, in particular, and the morality of poverty, in general. Vagabond accounts such as those of London and Orwell were all popular in their day, thereby exposing the arcane world of vagrancy for the benefit of a middle-class audience hungry for these reports.[7] In other words, such narratives were crucial both in shaping the public perception of the poor and also in influencing representations of vagrancy in other written accounts. The popularity of these sources is, moreover, indicative of the type of audience these authors intended to reach: the travelogue in the case of Twain and the investigative exposés of Orwell and London were aimed at wide audiences. As I have been suggesting, tramps are a useful case study in governance because they appear in these writings to be so closely associated with the same implicit values that characterised the ideal liberal subject, albeit to such a dangerous degree that it called for discipline and control.

The persistent emphasis on who can or cannot be considered a tramp provides more than just an echo of the more familiar question of who can or cannot draw benefits according to welfare policies. In both cases, as I argue throughout this book, the distinction often rests on the subject's proximity to whiteness and the performance of masculinity. During this historical period, non-white populations were more likely to suffer from anti-vagrancy legislation but were largely invisible in the pages of popular tramp fiction.[8] This disparity has only begun to register within literary criticism. For example, Hsuan Hsu sees evidence in Twain's depiction of white and mobile tramps in narratives such as *Huckleberry Finn* – and the comparative absence of non-white vagrant types from these same texts – of governmental policies that historically 'enabled uneven policing and enforcement along racial lines' (54). In the British context, vagrant classifications similarly played out along entrenched ethnic lines. As Robinson explains, such thinking in the Victorian period led to dramatically different receptions (and policing) of vagrant groups in Britain, since 'hawkers' and 'itinerant pedlars' were 'less susceptible to racial construction' in the popular imagination at the time than were members of the Gypsy, Roma and Traveller communities (35). Although the complex histories implied in this last example extend outside the boundaries of this text, I refer to it here to highlight how the project to expand (and racialise) 'the lexicon of vagrancy' unfolded on both sides of the Atlantic (Robinson 3). Acknowledging points of convergence between American and British versions of vagabondage, *The American Vagrant in Literature* brings into focus the international framework that surrounds canonical versions of the tramp type in culture.

To view these sources together also elucidates the international perspective that informed not only tramp writing and anti-vagrancy codes but welfare legislation, more generally. Henry George's reference to 'hostile armies' of tramps articulates the sense that vagrancy poses a problem for the health of the nation state inasmuch as tramps move back and forth across borders (179). The consensus that marks the tramp as a seditious agent, in other words, also identifies the international nexus in which both this figure and the policies designed to contain him would come into being. In this context, observers of tramping as well as tramping authors themselves would develop the trope of vagabondage in order to stress its most transnational characteristics. This construction is far from static over the course of the late nineteenth century. Rather, it is the subject of a dialogue that develops over time and across the North Atlantic, from American sources such as the works of Twain and London to literature by the poet W. H. Davies and Orwell in Britain.[9] As I argue throughout, the comparative imagination that fundamentally informed tramping narratives is on display in these canonical works. *The American Vagrant in Literature* places the comparative tradition in tramp writing, on display in these canonical examples, outside a purely literary context and connects it to the governmental developments unfolding at the same time on both sides of the Atlantic. The period corresponding to the 'tramp scare' in the US also encompasses a time of profound international influence on the level of policy making. As Rodgers points out, between the 1870s and World War II, 'American politics was particularly open to foreign models and imported ideas' unlike any period before or after (4). During these years, ideas regarding progressive social reform circulated back and forth on a map stretching from San Francisco to Berlin (Rodgers 4). But this internationalist moment has largely been forgotten in the US, where the popular understanding of welfare stresses its distinctiveness from its European counterparts. A study of tramping literature reaffirms the formative role that international comparison played in US welfare history while also stressing the part that literary authors played in contributing to the governing discourse of unemployment and welfare relief.

For their part, US government officials likewise understood tramping as a problem to be solved with reference to overseas policies. The British Vagrancy Act of 1824, in particular, provided lawmakers later in the century with a model for new laws authorising the arrest of vagrants. Concerned with the '[p]unishment of idle and disorderly Persons', the British law greatly expanded the power of the state to incarcerate subjects on the basis on their occupation of public spaces (Vagrancy Act Preamble). In effect, the original law concerned itself first and foremost with giving definition to the otherwise vague category of the unproductive class:

> every Person wandering abroad, or placing himself or herself in any public Place, Street, Highway, Court, or Passage, to beg or gather alms, or causing or procuring or encouraging any Child or Children so to do, shall be deemed an idle and disorderly Person within the true Intent and Meaning of this Act. (Vagrancy Act s. 3)

Written in the period following an influx of unemployed and disabled veterans at the end of the Napoleonic Wars, the 1824 law targeted specifically the rising class of homeless within England, the political and industrial centre of the British Empire (Beier and Ocobock 22).[10] At its crux, the law defines vagrancy by tying labour to the spaces where labour is performed. The very spectacle of idleness becomes illicit once public spaces – any street, highway or inhabitable space – become sites that only productive bodies can occupy. In 1876, New Jersey passed an anti-tramping bill that nearly duplicated the sweeping language of the British code, defining tramps as people who 'shall be found going about from door to door, or placing themselves in the streets, highways or roads, to beg or gather alms, and can give no reasonable account of themselves or their business in such places' (qtd in Kusmer 53). Borrowing from British sources, the New Jersey law in turn served as the model for anti-tramp legislation passed in various other states over the course of the following decade (Kusmer

53). Granting local governments sweeping authority, these retooled laws also reflect the international basis for vagrancy codes in the US.

The sense that the tramp can only be understood and contained via reference to foreign states extends from ethnographic and governmental sources to journalists, novelists and poets writing about their experiences as vagrants. Indeed, an underlying comparison between the US and the UK runs throughout much of poet W. H. Davies's 1908 *Autobiography of a Super-Tramp*, a text that would establish him as one of the most popular examples of the British tramp. Throughout his writings, Davies calls into question the value of Britain's regulatory policies in view of the relatively laissez-faire environment in the US, where the tramp thrives in comparison with his less autonomous British counterpart. In *Beggars*, published the year after his autobiography, Davies writes that the British public should have an interest in 'how well or ill their own nation is represented by beggars' across the Atlantic (1). With this claim, Davies is careful to link specific versions of vagrancy back to the international nexus in which they operate. However, the movement of these types to and from the US provides Davies with the opportunity to compare national types rather than legal systems. If Davies represents himself as the archetypal 'Super-Tramp' in Britain, he suggests that this moniker has value only as it relates to the US, the 'most important country' for all the world's vagrants (1). In all the preceding cases, vagrancy is both exceptional and relational. On the one hand, policy reformers decry the uniquely dangerous vagrants in America while advocating for European-style policy reforms. On the other, tramp-writers such as Davies proclaim their singular talents while admitting that these talents thrive less in the UK than in the US. Both sides agree that the tramp needs to be approached comparatively, even if they disagree as to the value or origin of tramping in the first place.

As the above cases indicate, to follow the discursive movement of the tramp reveals an interdisciplinary effort to delineate and categorise distinct populations of people from among the growing class of unemployed and homeless. The categorisation of the tramp threat stands against innumerable other attempts at ordering vagrancy and its subgroupings. Sources both in and outside of government were more than willing to participate in this effort, even if these sources disagreed on how to approach the problem of vagrancy. The work of Ben Reitman, the American anarchist and physician, is yet another example of how non-governmental sources write to separate and distinguish among vagrancy. Famous for his activism alongside Emma Goldman during the first decades of the twentieth century, Reitman is about as far removed from the operation of the state as one might imagine. Yet he provides a demographic division of the vagrancy classes in his categorical description of 'hobos who work and wander, the tramps who dream and wander, the bums who drink and wander' (qtd in Anderson and Rauty 3). Reitman distinguishes hobos from 'bums', in his words, on the basis of their unwillingness (or inability) to work. Reitman being an outspoken advocate for the poor, his description of tramps as a class of dreamers is indicative of more sympathetic accounts of vagabondage during the early decades of the twentieth century.[11] At the same time, his categorisation implicitly arranges subgroups of vagrants into a hierarchy based on the implicit value of their labour – or lack thereof.

Nels Anderson mirrors this assessment in *The Hobo*, his 1923 study of vagrancy drawn from his participant-observation of vagrants. For Anderson, the tramp's 'romantic passion' to 'gain new experience' stands out from the population of wandering homeless: he is a 'specialist', an 'easy-going individual who lives from hand to mouth for the mere joy of living' (94). Even as Reitman and Anderson understand tramps to be a subgroup of vagrants, they describe them in language that highlights their singular, idealistic talents. To be sure, the exact lines separating these subgroups were subject to revision and disagreement among even the most dedicated ethnographers of homeless people. Robert Park, Roderick McKenzie and Ernest Burgess's influential sociological study of urban space, *The City*, effectively collapses Reitman's distinction between the idealistic tramp and the hobo. For these sociologists, 'the hobo is the bohemian in the ranks of common labor. He has the artistic temperament' (160). The gap between this account and Reitman's classification of the artistry among vagrants – all written, it should be noted, in view of the Chicago urban landscape – is less a contradiction than further evidence of the archetypal tramp's proximity to larger questions of artistry, labour and budding state infrastructure (as in the case of the urban space) during this period.

Normalising Vagrancy within the Welfare State

The responsibility of documenting and codifying the tramp did not fall to any single discipline. Rather, a collection of sources – both sympathetic and antagonistic to tramps themselves – resorted to the language of taxonomy and demographic sorting in their accounts of vagrancy. It should come as little surprise that the disappearance of the tramp archetype from headlines, which the second half of *The American Vagrant in Literature* relates in detail, came as the result of medical as well as legal intervention. In 1909, for example, French psychiatrists Alix Joffroy and Roger Dupouy proposed to treat vagrancy not as a crime but as evidence of disease. In *Fugues and Vagabondage*, they link vagrancy to the medical phenomenon of the fugue state, characterised by the total failure of self-government in afflicted individuals. Writing one year after the publication of Davies's popular memoir, Joffroy and Dupouy understand vagabondage as 'the fact of wandering without the power or the will to return to a fixed domicile' (qtd in 'Pathology of the Tramp' 999). A review of *Fugues and Vagabondage* in the *British Medical Journal* at the time emphatically underscores the larger cultural implications of this medical explanation of vagrancy:

> Most writers have explained the inextinguishable love of freedom and the hatred of the yoke of settled employment of [true vagabonds] by assuming in them ancestral instincts and by regarding their vagabondage as an atavistic phenomenon, an hereditary archaism of ethnological rather them [sic] of pathological significance. The glamour of this romantic history vanishes, however, under the cold scrutiny of Professor Joffroy and Dr. Dupouy. For them the vagabond is a 'psycho-path,' ego-centric, 'autophile,' extrasocial, often antisocial; in a word, a paranoiac! ('Pathology of the Tramp' 1000)

As archetypes for freedom, tramps represent extreme cases of individualism that must be studied, monitored and treated. According to Joffroy and Dupouy, the vagrant or vagabond is at once a product of modernity (rather than a symbol of a 'romantic history') and a threat to modern society. Ultimately, they figure the tramp's inability to settle into the fixed spheres of home and labour as a disability inasmuch as it places the freedom of the individual (or in this case, the 'paranoiac') ahead of the collective health of society. This framing of vagrancy in terms of social well-being is emblematic of the interlocking interests of the state and medical institutions: the tramp needs rehabilitation for the benefit of the public health because his refusal of 'settled employment' harms the body politic as much as it does the vagrant's physical body.

There is a stark split in the example above between the distinctly literary or 'romantic' history associated with vagrancy and the emerging sense of the pathological threats that vagrancy poses to the national hygiene. The biological framing here reflects a shift in public perceptions of the problem of tramping. By 1909, the tramp persona is no longer new in the way writers such as Henry George presented it in the final years of the nineteenth century. As the *British Medical Journal* notes, the tramp's apparent hostility to settled employment has already been the subject of ethnographic study. By considering the tramp as a pathological case, however, these sources unlock new tools for treating vagrants that draw from advancements in both medicine and welfare infrastructure. This intersection distinctly calls to mind the 'discourse of power' that Foucault outlines in *Society Must Be Defended*, which uses biologically inflected language to place into tension 'the race that holds power and is entitled to define the norm' against 'those who deviate from the norm ... who pose a threat to the biological heritage' (*Society* 61).

The nineteenth century is crucial for both Foucault and my account of vagrancy because it is during this time when medicine, law and governance converge in order to substantiate the state's role in protecting the integrity of the nation – or, in more blatant terms, the 'purity of the race' (*Society* 81). Accounts of the consolidation of the welfare state in the UK and the US exemplify the more prosaic operation of the governing dynamic Foucault describes. As Miller and Rose explain, in the first half of the twentieth century both states developed tools – for crafting policy and developing a governing ideology – for bringing the citizen into closer relation to the state as an agent for the public good. The ideology that emerges demands that both individuals and society sacrifice some level of autonomy in exchange for improving the collective whole (48). At the same time, it also implies that citizens embrace a dual identity as both autonomous individuals and constituent members of a manageable demographic. Failing to contribute to the social good along these lines therefore signifies a failure on the individual's part that warrants a swift and collective response.

As a case study, the tramp is especially useful for understanding the demographic logic that is so critical for the state's treatment of public health in the twentieth century. George Orwell's influential account of his time on the tramp in *Down and Out in Paris and London* (1933), for instance, diagnoses this governing science at a key moment of transition. Specifically, Orwell shows the material consequences of Britain's Vagrancy Act in the form of the British workhouse – or 'spike', as it was known. 'Under the Vagrancy Act', he writes, 'tramps can be prosecuted for smoking in the spike – in fact, they can be prosecuted for almost anything' (*Down and Out* 153). Throughout, Orwell recalls his exposure to extreme squalor and humiliation at the hands of the spike's administrators (*Down and Out* 146–8). His claim that the spike used the letter of the law to thoroughly debase vagrants brings to light an especially disturbing instance of what Miller and Rose mean when they describe the 'mutual claims and obligations' between citizens and the welfare state. The spike offers minimal substance and shelter in return for state-sanctioned labour. But the spike's viability as a site for controlling vagrant populations works only inasmuch as all other spaces are denied to them. Orwell notes that the law prohibits people from sleeping in public areas such as the park or the railway station. At the same time, the official explanation for the law rests on protecting the health of the people who seek shelter there. The code is particularly offensive to Orwell because its distinction of public from private space, along with waking from sleeping hours, belies the fact that a homeless person exposed to the elements 'is going to die of exposure . . . asleep or awake' (*Down and Out* 208–9). Rather than threaten punishment, the law appeals to the individual's sense of self-preservation.

As the chapter concerning *Down and Out in Paris and London* will argue, Orwell's tramp writing scrutinises the moment when Britain normalises vagrancy as one of multiple – and therefore administrable – demographics.[12] Implicit in the case of the shelter is the intersection of both individual self-management and large-scale demographic ordering: the law at once proscribes the category of vagrancy on the grounds of the public's welfare while also imploring individuals to protect their own health. Vagrants are not cast out of public spaces as they once were; they are steered from one type of public space (such as the Tube station or the park) to another type, the casual ward. The spike exemplifies the dual meanings of public at play in this governing regime: it is not public in the sense that it is visible or in the open but in the sense that it is an expression of the public interest. The operation of state power in this context is visible in the sites themselves as well as on the bodies of the people who pass through them. Foucault alludes to this overlap of power mechanics in his description of the 'utopian' geographies of the European working-class estates built in the nineteenth century. In these towns, the very space of the home involves 'disciplinary mechanisms that controlled the body, or bodies, by localizing families (one to a house) and individuals (one to a room)' (*Society* 251). At the same time, these individualised spaces operated under 'rules on hygiene that guarantee[d] the optimal longevity of the population' as well as pension plans and communal health-insurance systems (*Society* 251). These sites at once inculcate individual acts of self-government while also managing the community at large in terms of public health and population regeneration.

The tramps who enter the spike are likewise faced with a power structure that immediately disciplines their failure to self-govern. But just as important for the operation of the welfare state is the fact that the spike also makes vagrants a population subject to management and medical scrutiny. As Robinson likewise notes, the intent behind the casual-ward system conforms to a Foucauldian 'biopolitical narrative', wherein state agencies categorise and monitor the general population in the name of health (103). The spike thus fundamentally alters the autonomy popularly associated with tramping, in more ways than one: whether or not the disciplinary structure of the spike results in rehabilitation, the very instance of entering the spike translates vagrants into aggregate data transferrable to medical and police authorities.

Orwell's focus on governance is not anomalous; rather, this emphasis is a feature of how prominent vagrancy narratives scrutinise the consequences of greater governmental oversight over its most vulnerable and mobile populations. The comparative investigation of vagrancy that Orwell embeds in his text, which is divided between his time in the UK and France, gives him a vantage point for decrying local governmental policies. From this perspective, he delineates the regulatory growth of the British welfare state well before the introduction of the National Health Service (NHS) after World War II. To read Orwell's familiar works alongside the relatively obscure sources that I assemble in this book reveals the precedents not only for his performance of tramping but, more importantly, for his understanding of the tramp as a privileged observer and critic of policy. Decades before Orwell, Davies took exception to the excessive regulations and codes that made tramping unappealing in the UK in relation to the US. The spikes that both Orwell and Davies encounter in their memoirs resemble something more akin to a prototype for Britain's modern welfare state as opposed to something incompatible with it. In the case of the US, vagrancy texts likewise opine on the operation of government even as the governing regime no doubt differs from its British counterpart. Whereas Britain constructed its welfare state in fits and starts over decades, the onset of the 1929 Depression called for quick and meaningful reform in the US. The popular concern for the so-called Okies, who were typically white American farmers displaced by the Depression and environmental collapse, illustrates this last point. John Steinbeck famously took up the case of the displaced Okie in *The Grapes of Wrath* (1939), which dramatises the major social upheaval that follows when this large population, losing their homes and family farms, become vagrants overnight. As Chapter 4 claims, Steinbeck's representation of homelessness in terms of the family rather than of the individual is the culminating act in the longer push to rehabilitate tramps and vagrants on the basis of their familiar characteristics. Steinbeck's vagrants are social outcasts who yearn to re-enter the home and work on the farm.

Reading Steinbeck alongside prior tramp-writers provides fresh insight into the otherwise familiar split between the US and Europe on the subject of welfare administration in the twentieth century. If states such as New Jersey looked to British precedents to pass anti-vagrancy laws, the federal initiatives passed under the Franklin D. Roosevelt administration created welfare programmes that were by design distinct from their European counterparts, thus ending decades of Americans looking primarily abroad for legislative inspiration (Rodgers 410). President Roosevelt made this distinction especially clear in his 1935 address to Congress, which outlined the moral foundation of the government's anti-poverty policies. Roosevelt acknowledges that 'every Nation' after the Depression has made 'social justice ... a definite goal'. As a result, he argues, 'the American people do not stand alone in the world in their desire for change'. At the same time, he claims that the 'dependence upon relief' is not only 'inimical to the dictates of sound policy' but, more importantly to him, a 'violation of the traditions of America' (Roosevelt). Here, Roosevelt acknowledges the welfare institutions coming into being across the Atlantic while also asserting the necessity of a distinctly American version of welfare relief. His reasoning sustains an implicit comparison of domestic and foreign welfare codes in a number of ways. Most immediately, it emphasises the global foundation for more robust regulation of public health. At the same time, it maintains that the international movement towards welfare reform should only redouble the state's interest in maintaining policy that conforms to nationalist 'traditions'. In other words, the global dimensions of poverty and poverty laws counterintuitively call for a more trenchant protection of local forms of identity.

The tramping literatures collected in *The American Vagrant in Literature* anticipate Roosevelt's logic to the extent that they couch their appeals to welfare reform in what is essentially nationalist rhetoric. Such appeals become gradually clearer as one reads from Twain to Steinbeck, with Steinbeck reimagining uprooted migrants as agents for the nation state. If the spectre of single white men on the road threatened society with grotesque versions of the ideal liberal subject, Steinbeck's writings imagine ways of locating these wayward subjects back within the productive boundaries of family and work. In other words, he sees families displaced by the Dust Bowl not as a threat but as a force that will invigorate the nation state along the lines of racial and ideological purity. In *The Harvest Gypsies*, a series of journalistic essays written in 1936, Steinbeck plainly outlines the appeal of the white migrant in the case of the Dust Bowl farmer. In contrast to the 'earlier foreign migrants [who were] invariably ... drawn from a peon class', he writes, 'the new migrants ... are small farmers who have lost their farms, or farm hands who have lived with the family in the old American way' (*Harvest* 22). Although Steinbeck's version of vagrancy is hyper-specific, his reasoning brings to the foreground the latent racialisation of tramping from at least the nineteenth century. For example, in 1899, Josiah Flynt's influential tramping ethnography, *Tramping with Tramps*, had called for better methods for integrating tramps into the mainstream of civil life. The 'talents' tramps possess, Flynt argued, would make them productive members of society if only they could 'realize its responsibilities and take advantage of its opportunities' (*Tramping* 5). For Flynt, the state should use the tools at its disposal to help tramps recognise the benefits of productive labour and civil life. Steinbeck's representation of vagrancy in works such as *The Grapes of Wrath* and *The Harvest Gypsies* effectively inverts this proposal: white migrant farmers are already knocking at the door of productive society, if only the state would recognise this opportunity and let them in. The empathic appeal to whiteness in this latest example should come as little surprise, given how thoroughly Steinbeck has normalised vagrancy in the case of the Dust Bowl farmers, who now embody the 'old American way' (*Harvest* 22).

The process by which tramps emerge in riotous rebellion against civil and economic responsibility only to be contained in the state's drive to protect public health is explored over the course of *The American Vagrant in Literature*. The first chapter, 'The Internationalism of American Vagrancy: Mark Twain and Josiah Flynt on the Tramp', establishes the comparative framework that is essential to writings about tramps from their emergence in the late nineteenth century. Despite their clear differences in genre and intended audiences, Twain's *A Tramp Abroad* and Flynt's *Tramping with Tramps* both stage tramping in Europe as a way to consider the problem of idleness back home. In his travel narrative, Twain equates economic self-governance with civil responsibility. The tramp in Europe separates what he sees as productive Americans from their idle counterparts; the shrewdness of his overseas travel sheds a critical light on the wasteful materialism of the American tourist. An influential sociological account of tramping, Flynt's *Tramping with Tramps* takes up Twain's comparative approach nearly twenty years later and encodes it in a work that proposes to contain vagrants as a criminal class. Overseas tramping in this case is a vehicle for evaluating not Americans abroad but the governmental policies of foreign states. Ultimately, what had appeared in Twain as a critique of wealthy Americans at play is put to use in Flynt against those at the other end of the social spectrum. Taken together, these texts bring into focus the comparative framework, hinging on the relation of the US to Europe, in which tramps and anti-tramp policing codes come into being.

Chapter 2, 'Vagrant Nationalism: Jack London and W. H. Davies on the Super-Tramp', expands on the comparative framework Flynt develops by locating a similar internationalism encoded not only in tramping ethnographers but in tramping texts that celebrate vagabondage. The most famous British tramp-writer in the early twentieth century, W. H. Davies is a crucial figure in this process; he takes the tramping archetype developed in the US and localises it, so to speak, in Britain. In *The Autobiography of a Super-Tramp*, Davies valorises the individualism of the American tramp and the ruling institutions of the US that, in his telling, allow tramps to thrive. In doing so, he measures the individualism of British society in relation to what sees as the American ideal. I read Davies's work in view of Jack London's own US–British comparison in *The People of the Abyss* (1903), which stresses the exceptionalism of American tramps to the detriment of their British equivalents. For both writers, the distinct features of vagrancy in a given context directly reflect the characteristics of that society as a whole. But unlike London, Davies, with his description of himself as a British tramp thriving in the US, takes up the concept of American vagabond mobility and makes it flexible and adaptable rather than an expression of inherited identity. In doing so, Davies considers the extent to which the features of vagrancy spring from an essential national character or the environment in which they are generated. In short, vagrancy in these cases sheds light on the characteristics of not only individuals but entire nations of people. Ultimately, this discourse links to the contentious modern debate over migrant forms of identity – specifically, whether or not migrants change or are changed by the society that hosts them.

Chapter 3, 'Tramps in the Machine: Interwar British Vagrancy', contends with the decline of the exceptional tramps that are at the forefront of Davies's narrative, who disappear in the wake of the Great Depression among the throng of unemployed workers. This transformation, I argue, indicates the extent to which social reforms in both the US and Britain had contained the exceptional form of mobility that the tramp had enacted. Orwell's *Down and Out in Paris and London*, in particular, elaborates on how governmental oversight brought an end to unregulated mobility in Britain. His vagabond text foregrounds the physical decline of the tramping population, as well as the specific policies and institutions that guided this disappearance. Alongside Orwell, this chapter looks to Charlie Chaplin's final portrayal of the Little Tramp in *Modern Times* (1936), which navigates the economic and political forces that generate poverty. I argue that growth in the institutional power of the state directly refigures the conception of vagrant mobility in these sources: in both cases, vagrants are citizens rather than outcasts, and they suffer as a direct result of their incorporation into governmental institutions such as the casual ward. Recalling the treatment of plague victims in Foucault's *Abnormal*, the situation of vagrants within the spikes exemplifies a system of governmental power based on the close incorporation of formerly deviant subjects into society, rather than their exclusion from it (46). As my reference to Foucault further suggests, Orwell's description of the physical deterioration of this population anticipates more modern critiques of population control associated with biopower.

The final chapter, 'Steinbeck's Migrants: Families on the Move and the Politics of Resource Management', considers more fully the extent to which governmental and literary interventions together shift the social politics around vagrancy. In Orwell's case, the state had come to an impasse in its fight against vagrancy: state policy had successfully contained this population but did not know how to redeploy their labour into productive outlets. Steinbeck provides an answer in the US to the problem Orwell identifies in Britain. Like Orwell, he decries the bloc of institutional forces that effectively preclude certain members of the population from fruitful labour in both *The Grapes of Wrath* and *The Harvest Gypsies*. In tandem with cultural projects emanating from the Works Progress Administration (WPA), Steinbeck transforms the public's understanding of vagrancy by focusing not on solitary vagrants but on itinerant families. With this formulation to hand, Steinbeck offers an explicit roadmap for moving whole populations of workers across the country to where their labour will most benefit the nation state. As a result, Orwell's ambiguous sense of the big state disappears from Steinbeck's explicit push for greater governance of cultural, economic and demographic modes of production.

The American Vagrant in Literature closes with a brief consideration of what I term the afterlife of the tramping archetype in the US in the post-war era, which is largely devoid of the dangerous connotations that characterised tramps near the turn of the century. After World War II, one is most likely to encounter references to tramping in literary works by romantic road-trippers and anti-establishment writers such as Jack Kerouac. In Kerouac's *On the Road* (1957), little remains of the vigorous social debate over the tramping problem that concerned writers from the preceding century. Rather, tramping signals the author's romantic (and in his telling, masculine) pursuit of anti-establishment ideals, his rejection of the conventional workplace, and his restless wanderings. In short, tramping still connotes the rugged individualism of the preceding decades, but the social and political situation has changed considerably. Whereas the initial chapters show how authors such as Twain and Steinbeck wrote in favour of including tramps and vagrants within the scope of fledgling welfare society, this final section argues that the tramp signals for Kerouac his own restlessness within the post-war Fordist welfare state. As in the preceding century, the tramp here is highly specific in terms of characteristics even as the larger socio-economic implications of these characteristics have changed. In short, white vagabondage is distinctly less dangerous in the popular imagination, a turn that Kerouac extensively laments. The rehabilitation of the white vagrant type that this book as a whole considers spotlights literature's role in defining specific demographic types, directing attention to this group and making them the subject of wide concern. Ultimately, this literary analysis of vagrancy brings into view the lines of influence and social concerns that tie together ostensibly disparate literary sources from Steinbeck's fiction and Chaplin's films to nineteenth-century ethnographies.

The Legacy of Vagrancy Narratives and Racial Visibility

The collection of writers all inhabiting, celebrating or otherwise representing the subject of vagabondage is vast – indeed, too large for any single project to cover with appropriate depth of study. Rather than try to account for every tramp text published in the timespan roughly covering the Depressions of 1873 and 1929, I have chosen to analyse specific works that exemplify the type of interdisciplinary and international focus that is, I argue, the crucial feature of tramping literature during the period. In each of the preceding cases, the intercontinental mobility associated with tramping encourages authors to better scrutinise governmental institutions and practices in a number of domestic cases. The cultural, political and transatlantic exchanges that allow us to move from Twain's version of tramping to Orwell's – from an example where actual tramps remain in the subtext to a case that foregrounds the imminent disappearance of tramping – are the objects of this study. This delimited focus gives a clear perspective on how different political entities respond to a common problem with a shared archetype in the form of the vagrant, even as the local conditions driving homelessness and poverty assume different forms in each state. The tramp persona that emerges in the nineteenth century, as I have indicated, is coded masculine and white; he travels across the Atlantic as he pleases; he resists incorporation into both the domestic sphere and the industrial wage-labour market. At the same time, the tramp is emphatically local in his presentation. Travelling across the Atlantic on a whim makes Jack London and W. H. Davies, for example, feel more rather than less tethered to their respective countries of origin.

Underlying this study is the apparent disjunction between the growing population of non-white migrants to the US and Britain at the turn of the century and the uniform whiteness of tramp-writers during this same time. Of course, the exclusion of non-white authors from mainstream publishing during this period is not, on the surface, a surprising state of affairs. Still, this specific construction of the tramp is telling of how literary sources struggle to visualise the movement of labour from, for instance, Asia and the Pacific – a crucial driver of industrialisation for both Britain and the US (Lye 9). Scholars elsewhere have remarked on a similar dynamic present in other literary narratives from the nineteenth century and on. For example, Carolyn Lesjak argues in *Working Fictions* that the absence of manual labour in the foreground of Victorian novels does not mean that the social problems related to industrial labour are absent from those pages. Rather, Lesjak claims that the lack of labour at the forefront of, for example, the narratives of leisure associated with Oscar Wilde should be seen as an act of misdirection: readers of such texts can, in fact, recognise 'the presence of labor' by its conspicuous absence (11). Her reading provides in the case of Victorian fiction a way of distinguishing labour in narratives that explicitly divorce themselves from any so-called realistic depictions of work, a dynamic that registers 'the problem of visibility at the heart of capitalism', more generally (11).

Vagrancy texts as detailed here involve a similar sleight of hand, one in which so many of the issues related to international migrancy – immigration quotas, racial scapegoating, renewed scrutiny of the deserving poor – inform the subtext of narratives about hyper-visible tramp types. The features associated with the tramp gloss over the less visible forms of migration occurring within and between states by relocating the danger associated with these foreign cases to familiar, if incorrigible, cases of white men. But these narratives do more than substitute this specific figuration of white vagrancy for these other, less familiar forms; they are acutely aware of the different types of vagrancy that exist in other states or regions of the US and Europe. Rather than whitewash all categories of homelessness, these narratives stage prolonged discussions about *which* homeless populations are most useful for the state. Simply put, it is not the case that these tramp-writers believe that they represent all forms of poverty; rather, they represent the most useful or socially adaptable one. The turn towards regulating the movement of vagrants in the nascent welfare programmes of the US and UK therefore represents the logical conclusion for writers who detailed the talents of tramps near the turn of the century.

While the white tramp represents in these texts the last bastion of individuality among growing populations of poor citizens, it nevertheless engages in demographic work of its own. By way of concluding, I turn again briefly to Davies's *Autobiography of a Super-Tramp*, which gives a glimpse of how the tramp's exceptionalism operates on the assumption that some members of the impoverished classes are more deserving of civil inclusion than others. As outlined above, Davies's tramping enables a comparison between his British origins and American society on the basis of how each country treats its poor populations. In one instance, he pauses in his description of travelling down the Mississippi River to describe the collection of both white and Black out-of-work labourers he encounters along the way:

> Unfortunately the ill feeling which invariably exists between these two colours came to a climax on the first day of our arrival. The negroes, insulting and arrogant, through their superiority of numbers, became at last unbearable. On which the white men, having that truer courage that scorned to count their own strength, assembled together, and after a few moments' consultation, resolved to take advantage of the first provocation ... The negroes, whose

favourite weapon is the razor, produced these useful blades from different parts of concealment, stood irresolute, waiting for a leader, and then came forward in a body. (*Autobiography* 131)

The brawl leaves one dead and several injured, all of which Davies reports with a dry tone that is characteristic of his writing. But despite presenting himself as an outsider in this instance, Davies is nonetheless quick to discern the 'truer' worthiness of the white men in contrast to their Black counterparts. He further describes the Black labourers in terms that stress their lack of individuality: they are a swarm that moves in lock step, benefiting from 'superiority in numbers' but suffering from a lack of individual resolve in the form of a 'leader'. If Davies is in this instance reiterating a familiar, prejudiced picture of Black Americans in the era of Jim Crow, he does so in a manner that emphasises the tramp's exceptionally scrutinising eye as a social critic. He has no problem separating the valour of one impoverished people from another because this demographic sorting is, after all, at the core of all of vagabond narratives.[13] In this instance, Davies's love of freedom from oppression, which so thoroughly informs his 'Super-Tramp' persona, does little to help him sympathise with systematic anti-Black oppression in the US. Rather, the imperative to distinguish the deserving from undeserving, the able-bodied from the disabled, and white from Black via the perspective of the tramp supersedes any universalising sense of identification with the poor.

I conclude with reference to this scene from Davies because it so adeptly showcases the counterintuitive position in which tramp-writers often found themselves: their celebration of autonomy did not always mean that they considered themselves apart from mainstream society. Davies is, after all, the Super-Tramp whose mobility and autonomous expression separates him from any number of travellers who express in his eyes something less than staunch individuality. Against the backdrop of urban migration and global decolonialisation movements, writers from Davies to London and Steinbeck to Orwell decried the injustice facing a particular portion of the population living in poverty. Scrutinising these accounts reveals much about how specific literary types clarify otherwise unwieldy debates regarding migration, social policy and public health. The way the tramp archetype simultaneously takes on and sublimates the racial question inherent to migrancy into one involving individualism and liberal subjectivity finally points to the aspects of this rhetorical strategy that are still so visible today.

Notes

1. George's widespread and international popularity both in and outside the academy on matters of economic policy and social reform has few parallels in American history. His 1879 book *Progress and Poverty* sold millions of copies worldwide. George's influence extended into Europe as well. His speaking tours in Britain, for instance, drew large audiences and indelibly shaped the Fabian movement there (Rodgers 70).
2. As of 2019, the homeless population in the US has been on the rise for three consecutive years. A similar trend is visible in England over the same period of time. For the US data, see the Department of Housing and Urban Development's press release; UK data comes from *The Guardian* – see Busby.
3. Cresswell identifies the 6 February 1875 issue of *The New York Times* as the first appearance in print of 'tramp' as a term to refer to a specific type of vagrant (48). However, Bellesiles claims that the first appearance of the tramp in print may have occurred as early as 1872 (324).
4. Among studies of American vagrancy, Todd DePastino, Cresswell and Bellesiles all use the term 'tramp scare' to denote the moral panic near the end of the nineteenth century that, while hinging on the stereotype of the tramp, reflected a greater anxiety about industrialism. For the gender politics underpinning the literature spawned by the 'tramp scare', see Cresswell's 'Gendering the Tramp' from *The Tramp in America*. DePastino's 'Great Army of Tramps' in *Citizen Hobo* locates this national panic among larger concerns about industrialism and the rising middle class.
5. In 'Whiteness Studies and the Paradox of Particularity', Robyn Wiegman reflects on, and subjects to critique, the field of whiteness studies that followed Roediger's and Ignatiev's publications. Writing in the wake of these texts, Wiegman suggests that 'labor history' has 'become installed as the governing disciplinary apparatus of whiteness studies' (136)
6. In addition to the previously mentioned texts, other recent works that spotlight the contributions of tramping literature and related forms to popular understandings of race and inequality include Luke Lewin Davies's *The Tramp in British Literature, 1850–1950* and Hannah Lauren Murray's *Liminal Whiteness in Early US Fiction*. The appearance of these works, which includes *The American Vagrant in Literature*, points to an emerging consensus regarding the relevancy of largely forgotten texts from the nineteenth century to the pressing social problems that persist in the present.
7. Immensely popular in his lifetime, London reached a global audience. Indeed, Orwell himself acknowledged London as a key source of inspi-

ration (Shelden 121). For his part, Orwell would also find widespread success following the publication of his tramping narrative. John Rodden points to the sixpenny Penguin edition of *Down and Out in Paris and London*, which sold especially well during the war years, as the 'landmark event' that 'signaled the beginning of Orwell's popular career' (44).

8. In addition to Hsu, Erin Royston Battat foregrounds the racial politics behind popular understandings of hobo culture during the 1930s.
9. To be sure, the term in the British context draws from a romanticised legacy of the highwayman, a specific figure that – owing to its lengthy history in Europe – should not be too easily conflated with any historical counterpart in the US. In addition to Robinson in *Vagrancy in the Victorian Age*, David Brandon outlines this specific English legacy in *Stand and Deliver!*. However, the rise of the tramp in the late nineteenth century alters this term to apply less to the armed highwayman and more to the wandering vagrant in a manner that, as I have claimed, bridges both US and British popular culture.
10. Indeed, the law takes pains to establish that its regulations apply only to the state of England among all of the British Isles, stating 'nothing herein contained shall ... apply to *Scotland* or *Ireland*' (Vagrancy Act s. 22). As this statute makes particularly clear, the Vagrancy Act was concerned with the protection of English territory at a time when British colonial possessions extended across the globe.
11. Reitman's lifelong dedication to radical causes should already indicate the level of sympathy he evinces for the 'dreams' he associates with tramps. Reitman himself co-founded the 'hobo college' in Chicago, a place that facilitated the intellectual exchange of ideas among the vagrant class (Shumsky 24).
12. The reference to multiple demographics assumes a racial subtext, which is important to acknowledge given Britain's colonial administration at that time. Partha Chatterjee's *Politics of the Governed* argues that this governmentality originates in colonial Southeast Asia, although he identifies its central role in Anglo-US governance as well. Robinson's *Vagrancy in the Victorian Age* brings this colonising discourse to the foreground of British vagrancy literature in the nineteenth century. Finally, the concomitant rise of welfare-administration policy and heterogeneous populations within the US and Britain is the subject largely of Miller and Rose's *Governing the Present*.
13. The administrative or demographic mindset I describe here is also evident in Davies's *Beggars*, which (as I alluded to earlier) opens with the argument that vagrancy reduces people to the essential cores of their respective national identities.

Chapter 1

The Internationalism of American Vagrancy: Mark Twain and Josiah Flynt on the Tramp

In the winter of 1879, Mark Twain was in Germany finishing the manuscript of what would later become *A Tramp Abroad* (1880), a travel narrative detailing his experiences in Europe. Twain's time abroad shaped his understanding of tramping in ways that extend beyond the pages of his own travelogue. In a letter written to the Hartford *Courant*, for instance, he draws on observations in Germany to comment on vagrancy measures in the US. As his letter makes clear, travelling abroad provided him the vantage point not only for understanding tramps – whose illicit travels spanned state lines and crisscrossed the Atlantic Ocean – but for containing their movement. Twain's letter notes the implementation of strict anti-tramp codes in his adopted home of Hartford, Connecticut, and praises the 'good news' that the city 'at last ceased to be the Tramp's haven'. The correspondence cites approvingly the editor's call to halt 'giving at doors' to beggars since, according to Twain, 'any community which will allow tramps to be assisted by its citizens will be sure to have a plentiful harvest of tramps' ('Hartford' 113):

> We have a curious proof of this fact here in Munich. You are aware that when our ingenious Massachusetts nobleman, Count Rumford, took high office here under the Bavarian crown in the last quarter of the last century, he found Bavaria just what Hartford has been for years, – the Tramp's paradise. Bavaria swarmed with beggars. Count Rumford applied the same remedy which you have lately found so effectual: he provided work for all comers, & then shut square down on all forms of begging. His system has remained in force here ever since. Therefore, for three-quarters of a century Bavaria has had the reputation of being the only country in Europe uncursed by tramps. I have lived here two months & a half, now, & have walked a mile

to my work & a mile back again, every day during that time, through a densely populated part of the city, yet I have never once been accosted by a beggar. ('Hartford' 114)

While tramps appear fleetingly in Twain's famous works, as this chapter will demonstrate, this letter elaborates his understanding of tramping in several ways. First, it recognises vagrancy as a problem for local governments that nonetheless applies to a global scale. At the same time, he also shows sympathy for tramps and their talents. Elsewhere, Twain's letter recalls vagrants who, in the act of soliciting charity, use a 'peculiarly deep & sagacious bit of diplomacy' to win over their audiences ('Hartford' 116). Although Twain rails against legal systems that encourage 'tramp-breeding', he nonetheless refers to the creative tools associated with this population. Indeed, he further suggests that they possess talents that society is still unable to fully appreciate: 'I wish an experienced tramp would reform; & expose the means by which tramps acquire their surprisingly minute & accurate information about the inside affairs of families' ('Hartford' 114–15). In this telling, there is concrete social value – evident in the tramp's 'diplomacy' and circulation of 'information' – in incorporating vagrants into the social fold.

In a scant few pages, Twain's letter articulates a version of the tramp problem that connects to contemporary efforts to define and control this population. First and foremost, Twain stresses the value of international comparison for American observers wishing to understand tramps – their origins and movements across states – and to produce policies for controlling them. In his telling, Munich is a useful case study for potential new laws in Hartford because tramps are dispersed across Europe and North America alike. At the same time, tramps are tractable enough in response to strict legislation in local contexts. Indeed, Twain further suggests that regulating tramping along these lines poses benefits to society as a whole. If Bavaria offers a model for legislation, there is more to be learned about what reforming tramps would mean in the context of the US. This last point relates to Twain's other significant contribution to tramping discourse in his writings: the emphasis on the tramp's potential usefulness as an artist or diplomat. As Peter Messent points out, Twain had already begun to equate literary artists with tramps before the publication of his *A Tramp Abroad* text. In 1877, for instance, Twain delivered a speech in Boston in which he imagined 'three rough and boozy looking tramps' assuming the identities of Emerson, Holmes and Longfellow to prey on the generosity of a miner in the Sierra foothills (Messent 139). After these literary giants proceed to eat the miner out of house and home, the miner complains that he 'ain't suited to a literry atmosphere' (qtd in Kaplan 209). Although delivered for laughs, Twain's depiction of these pillars of American literature as hungry hucksters nonetheless puts on display the author's own concerns over the kind of worthwhile labour that the literary establishment provides for society.[1]

This underlying equation of tramping with an artistic form of work is essential to this chapter's presentation of Twain as an early, if unacknowledged, contributor to efforts to rehabilitate actual tramps. When Twain himself takes up the titular role of *A Tramp Abroad*, it suggests that his earlier approximation of tramps with literary authors was anything but a glib remark. Rather, his representation of vagrancy in this text, as well as in his Hartford letter, brings into focus his overarching equation of tramping with artistry: the author is akin to the tramp to the extent that both are constantly at work, exchanging their artistic labour for literal forms of support from their respective audiences. In the case of *A Tramp Abroad*, Twain himself enacts this understanding of artistry and work: as the pages that follow explain, he turns to this particular narrative mode – travel writing and narratives about tramps both being in high demand at the time – for the financial succour it provides. At the same time, his figuration of the tramp-writer works the other way as well, imagining the tramp as capable of performing worthwhile labour in a manner akin to artistry.

Travel abroad is crucial to Twain's formulation of the tramp-as-artist because, as *The American Vagrant in Literature* argues throughout, international comparison provides the means for scrutinising different forms of labour outside of their local cultural and governmental institutions. By presenting *A Tramp Abroad* as a text about tramping, I am less interested in how literal vagrants are depicted in this text than how the work conceptualises and also rehabilitates this subject position by distinguishing it from 'less worthwhile' travellers: American tourists. In Twain's text, travelling overseas allows the author to assess Americans as they travel. From this vantage point, Twain's tramp observes American behaviour in order to distinguish between producers and consumers – and to treat the latter as a scourge. The tramp's mobility grants him the ability to compare his countrymen and women with their European counterparts, and thus identify a specifically American form of indolence that must be disciplined. Ultimately, this understanding of productivity articulates a rationale for regulating vagrancy that will be taken up more explicitly later in the nineteenth century.

By presenting Twain in this light, I am not arguing that *A Tramp Abroad* alone transformed the policing of vagrancy but that its framing of tramping around international comparison reverberates long after its publication. After approaching Twain's travel narrative via its depiction of mobility and work, the second half of this chapter considers the text's afterlife in the social sciences. If the travel narrative of *A Tramp Abroad* invites governmental intervention, then the early American ethnographer Josiah Flynt accepts the invitation. The 'first and most famous tramp ethnographer' (DePastino 162), Flynt is located at the intersection of literary, scientific and legal efforts to make the vagrant amenable to the state's regulatory institutions. Flynt's ethnographic study, *Tramping with Tramps* (1899), was the era's definitive account of this new vagrant type. As his title makes clear, Flynt studied his subject by way of participant observation, tramping in the US and – more crucially to his study – in Europe. Like Twain, Flynt approaches international travel as a means for understanding domestic subjects. But while a shared narrative structure links Flynt to Twain, Flynt adds an explicit policy agenda when he re-enacts Twain's tramping voyage. Flynt elsewhere makes his debt to Twain clear: he reports in his autobiography that he 'had been diligently reading' *A Tramp Abroad* during his days on the tramp in Europe (*My Life* 203). In his own travels, Flynt sees no distinction between the realities that face him as a vagabond in Europe and Twain's depiction of travel. Rather, he looks to Twain's book for the 'ideal' forms that Americans and Europeans alike should assume (*My Life* 203–4). This underlying reverence for Twain's text has consequences, I argue, for Flynt's criminology as well. Discerning criminal forms of vagrancy in his ethnography, Flynt adapts Twain's critique of dangerous idleness. While Twain's travelogue and Flynt's ethnography use the figure of the tramp to different ends, together they testify to the significance of an international context in defining vagrancy in the US.

Ultimately, Twain and Flynt reflect two prominent points in an intertextual dialogue that first defined the tramp's features for a curious public and then proposed tools for disciplining this subject. By linking these otherwise disparate authors in this way, it is also possible to relate their efforts in the case of vagrancy to the larger project of welfare-state construction occurring at the turn of the century. While neither Twain nor Flynt speaks of social-welfare policies to the extent that John Steinbeck or George Orwell do in the twentieth century, when read together they showcase an undoubtable transformation in the state's approach to social problems such as vagrancy. The final pages of this chapter expand on this last point with reference to the shared depiction of German society in Twain and Flynt, which both see as an ideal stage for observing the behaviour of Americans. At the same time, they offer distinctly different versions of Germany. In Twain's text, Germany and other European states provide the backdrop for his critique of American tourists abroad. In contrast, Flynt is interested in the workings of the German state's disciplinary institutions – such as its policing codes and the administrative oversight of its population – and the potential for applying these back home in the US. For Twain, the American tramp in this setting is the subject of cultural critique, while for Flynt he is the subject of public policy. The shift in the figuration of both vagrancy and Europe from one author to the other indicates the degree to which the tramp had become, by the time of Flynt's writing, more clearly embedded in a transnational legal discourse. Instead of challenging the state, the tramp makes legible the international framework in which local administration comes into being. Underlying Twain's account is the sense that tramps make clear how every citizen participates in the circulation of ideas about governance. By making tramps the target of public policy, Flynt makes the case for a government that is better equipped to reach even its most marginalised citizens – on the basis, of course, of their potential value to the state. That this transformation occurs as the result of international dialogue between America and Europe makes it easier to place the US among an emerging network of welfare states, while making it more difficult to treat the tramp as a uniquely American phenomenon.

Rethinking American Vagrancy

The literary and governmental development of the tramp figure as the target of reform runs parallel to, and intersects with, the early consolidation of welfare institutions in the US. In order to make this point especially clear, it is necessary to first revisit the history of the tramp and the cultural politics that attended his emergence – and then codification – as a governing problem. As explained in greater detail in the Introduction, the specific character of the tramp once captured the imagination of Americans. Indeed, the end of the 1870s saw the rise of a veritably national 'tramp scare', a populist reaction against the supposed threat that tramps posed to local communities (Bellesiles 114). Within only a few years of the modern coinage of 'the tramp', national newspapers overflowed with grisly headlines detailing all manner of murders, arson and assaults attributed to tramps.[2] By 1880, tramps had begun to saturate American popular literature even as the widespread fear of this roving underclass was terrorising Americans across the country. The same industrial infrastructure that fostered economic development in the US – in particular, the rapid expansion of the railway system – also created a new mobile class able to traverse the continent. Put simply, this specific representation of homelessness became the personification of the forces of economic boom and bust (Photinos, 'Figure of the Tramp' 995). Much has been written on the subject of the American railway system's role in consolidating the literal and figurative viability of the US as a functioning nation state. For example, Tim Creswell explains that the railroad dramatically uprooted the relationship between the local and the national; the same system that helped to build a strong 'national economy within a global system' also ensured that erstwhile local vagrants could move in and out of towns on a national stage (24, 28). Of course, to suggest that the tramp is a product of the railroad (or any single industrial infrastructure) risks ignoring the wide range of literary sources that also moved the figure to the forefront of the national consciousness. In general, tramps appear in these writings to reflect the modernity of the state by dramatising its limitations: these subjects represent nothing less than direct antagonists to the modern economy, refusing fixed income and eschewing the confines of the domestic sphere at all costs.

Given the terms of this persona, tramps appeared in starkly different roles in literature from the period, posing as either the villains or the folk heroes of the industrial era.[3] Twain specifically took care to cultivate an aura of ambivalence surrounding the figure, populating some of his most famous literary works with tramps in addition to taking on a tramping persona of sorts for himself as the narrator of *A Tramp Abroad* in 1880 (Hsu 73). As Hsuan Hsu points out, the character of Pap in *Huckleberry Finn* (1884), undoubtedly among Twain's most famous works, gestures to his sustained interest in the subject of tramping and its complex embodiment of whiteness and mobility. Appearing in what Hsu suggests is the novel's 'most haunting scene of vagabondage' (61), Pap evinces a disdain for freed Blacks and the governmental policies that attempt to enfranchise this class. Looking to this violent characterisation, Hsu concludes that Twain dramatises the process 'whereby nonwhite vagabonds were intimidated (often by poor whites), disciplined, and rebound to the land, while white tramps were relatively free to move throughout, and beyond, the South' (61–2). Even in the face of criminalisation, white tramps benefit in a relative sense from the more diffuse cultural attitudes that underlie and shape the enforcement of the law. In this light, the tramp is best understood as a discursive formation inasmuch as his characteristic features are dispersed across the intersection of racial, gender and juridical discourses. Twain's own appropriation of the tramping mantle in *A Tramp Abroad* further underscores the kind of ambivalence that marked the figure in his writing. For Twain, the tramp represents a figure of the moment: an implicitly white subject, his material abjectness tied to his relative freedom of movement reflects the legal and cultural attitudes that shaped the politics of the US in the second half of the nineteenth century.

But if the tramp speaks to social developments in the US, the scope of this transformation encompassed much more than any single country. To be sure, the mythical status of the tramping vagabond – white, male and totally free from convention – is closely aligned with, and parodies, larger myths regarding the 'American Dream' (Seelye 553). More recent scholars on the subject of homelessness in the Gilded Age, however, are re-evaluating the national romance surrounding narratives of the tramp. One such study, Michael Denning's *Mechanic Accents*, deflates the mythical status of the tramp in twentieth-century accounts of the American Gilded Age. Rather than being a 'myth or symbol' of rugged individualism, Denning insists, the tramp is instead 'a category constructed in the wake of the 1873 depression and the 1877 railroad strikes' to designate nothing less than 'the new phenomenon of unemployment' (*Mechanic* 149). Foregrounding these social transformations, Denning helpfully identifies how the tramp (as the subject of literature) links to debates over the role of governance in response to unemployment in a historical moment that helped to consolidate the welfare state. This account of the tramp's creation is limited to an American cultural context – in particular, to the variety of documents written in response to the railroad strikes of the 1870s. At this time, however, the face of vagrancy was undergoing a revision due to forces outside the control of any single nation state. Indeed, the stock-market crash of 1873 was itself a response to overseas events, specifically the speculative boom in the price of silver after the end of the Franco-Prussian war (Metzler 27). Further, the US was only one of several Western states (along with France and the UK) to endure an economic depression after the initial stock-market crash (Reti 62). The 1873 Great Depression, the formative moment in the creation of the tramp in America, serves as a lesson in the type of global networks operating during the period. To suggest that the social construction of the tramp serves the interests of the US state in isolation would therefore miss this larger context. Twain's account is especially useful for approaching how domestic social concerns intersect with international phenomena. In fact, Twain implies, it is by tramping overseas that Americans can better scrutinise themselves.

Twain's Tramp: Idleness and Civil Responsibility

In this light, even the title of Twain's *A Tramp Abroad* broadcasts its intent to intervene in a subject that resonated across the US and Europe. By taking on this subject of tramping, Twain is drawing from an especially lucrative well of support, given the public's interest during this time not only in travel writing but also in narratives detailing the exploits of tramps. Little studied today among Twain's works, *A Tramp Abroad* was a commercial success in the US – and his bestselling text in England during his lifetime (Messent 139). Of course, Twain had already established himself as the single most successful travel writer in the US with the publication of *The Innocents Abroad* in 1869 (Steinbrink 62). That success also established Twain's literary alter ego as the innocent American tourist who, in this previous book as well as in *A Tramp Abroad*, cuts through the highbrow charms of the Old World with his indelicate worldview (Messent 138). Of course, Twain's popularity in the US did nothing to obscure the extent to which his travel texts subjected his fellow Americans to intense scrutiny and critique. As Larzer Ziff argues, the American voice that emerges first in *The Innocents Abroad* encapsulates an 'adolescent outlook' exemplifying the 'provincial, flag-waving American middle-class – even while he [Twain] satirizes it' (190). After the success of this book and the subsequent publication of a prequel in the form of *Roughing It* (1872), Twain was under immense pressure to produce a third entry in the travel series. In contrast to his previous journey, Twain approached his second European expedition with little direction from outside sources. But by all accounts, the apparent freedom to set his own itinerary – which would take him through Germany, the Alps and into Italy – only made the manuscript's production more onerous for the author. Charles Neider's introduction to a reprinted edition of the book claims that Twain's second European narrative reflected 'his labors and uncertainty' as a writer, while *The Innocents Abroad* depicted instead 'the author's joy in writing' (x). What makes *A Tramp Abroad* distinct from Twain's previous travel text, in short, is the narrative's account of travelling largely bereft of pleasure. In *A Tramp Abroad*, travel is work: it entails organisational labour that the author doubts his capacity to perform as well as writing labour in which he takes no joy.

This sense of work and production is visible, I argue, in Twain's own ambiguous performance of tramping in the text. To be sure, his appropriation of the tramp persona for his second European travel narrative is undoubtedly tied to economic realities from which even he was not immune. In 1877, he wrote to his close confidant, the novelist William Dean Howells, that he intended to 'fly to some little corner of Europe' in order to save money and flee 'business responsibilities' (Neider xi).[4] While Twain contemplated a trip abroad to save expenses, American workers were finding their status redefined in light of the 1873 stock-market crash and the subsequent depression. In this context, the rise of Twain in the role of the tramp dramatises what historians understand as a turning point in social welfare in the US. As Michael Bellesiles points out, the 1873 crash left a large swathe of Americans out of work and beyond the safety net. Facing the harsh realities of long-term unemployment, 'the middle class was in the process of constructing an ideology that blamed the poor for their poverty as a moral failing', a rationale that prompted many Americans to 'lash out at the easiest target, the homeless' (113). Out of this global economic depression emerged a consensus that the poor and working class must be made accountable for the public good.

From the very beginning of *A Tramp Abroad*, Twain plays up the social relevance of his tramping text. He playfully suggests that his book serves the public good: 'One day it occurred to me that it had been many years since the world had been afforded the spectacle of a man adventurous enough to undertake a journey through Europe on foot', he announces in the text's early pages. 'After much thought I decided that I was a person fitted to furnish to mankind this spectacle. So I determined to do it. This was in March 1878' (1). Twain broadcasts the usefulness of his travel text – it benefits not only fellow tourists but all of 'mankind'. On another level, this opening passage is also indicative of the kind of role Twain crafts for himself as the tramping narrator of *A Tramp Abroad*. Taken with the title of Twain's text, these early lines broadcast the multiple significations present in his depiction. To the extent that Twain (as the narrator of the text) undertakes the European journey 'on foot', he plays on the ambiguous semantics of 'tramp', mirrored in the nominative and verb forms of the term that appears in the book's title. Along these same lines, his opening depiction of his trip conflates tramping with the tramp as a subject position.

Already, when seeing this initial conflation, one gets the sense that Twain is less interested in literal tramps than in their currency in the public imagination. To be sure, the only tramp that appears in the book is Twain himself. But as numerous critics of Twain's work have pointed out, the text further encodes this tramping persona in almost every aspect of its construction. As mentioned previously, here Twain wanders from place to place in Europe without a set itinerary in mind. In line with these extemporaneous travels, he adopts a loose narrative structure – picking up and dropping storytelling threads as he sees fit – that embraces on a formal level the notion of the rambling tramp (LeMaster and Wilson 743). In this light, one sees that tramping serves not only as a mode of travel but also as a model for textual production.[5] While intentionally overstating his contribution to all of 'mankind' with his efforts, he nonetheless lays out the stakes of his international travel in terms that reverberate across literary as well as social lines.

From this basis the narrative as a whole links overseas movement to issues of distinctly national importance. While Twain travels across international borders, his account concerns itself primarily with the lives of Americans. At one point, he lampoons a tourist in Switzerland for his ostentatious display. The tourist reaches out to Twain on the assumption that their common nationality places them in a shared community. 'You're an American, I think – so'm I.' Twain quickly sizes up this 'specimen' of Americans abroad:

> He wore a low-crowned, narrow-brimmed straw hat with a broad blue ribbon around it which had a white anchor embroidered on it in front. Nobby short-tailed coat, pantaloons, vest, all trim and neat and up with the fashion . . . Projecting cuffs fastened with large oxidized silver sleeve-buttons bearing the device of a dog's face – English pug. He carried a slim cane surmounted with an English pug's head with red glass eyes. Under his arm he carried a German grammar – Otto's. (*Tramp Abroad* 136)

The tourist's insistence on finding Americans like himself abroad – 'I know an American as soon as I see him' (*Tramp Abroad* 137) – is belied by the European trinkets with which he surrounds himself.

But, for Twain, this consumption serves to ironically make the tourist recognisable as an American type. The juxtaposition of the tourist's preoccupation with American identity and the European trappings in which he presents himself underscores the narrative's central critique – namely, that these affluent tourists (through their eager appropriation of European culture) demonstrate a form of American exceptionalism that is itself merely the product of overseas consumption. The American identity that resides at the centre of this hotchpotch cosmopolitanism would risk getting lost in translation, Twain implies, were it not for the critical eye of the tramping author.

Twain expands his examination of the tourist type by placing it within a larger class of idle consumers. In the portion of the text entitled 'The Grandson', Twain presents archetypes for what he describes as 'Young America' (*Tramp Abroad* 215). As in the previous encounter with the 'specimen' tourist, Twain sardonically highlights in this latter portion of the text the extent to which European travel for the wealthy American is a self-conscious construction:

> His hair was short and parted accurately in the middle and he had all the look of an American person who would be likely to begin his signature with an initial and spell his middle name out. He introduced himself, smiling a smirky smile borrowed from the courtiers of the stage, extended a fair-skinned talon, and while he gripped my hand in it he bent his body forward three times at the hips as the stage-courtier does. (*Tramp Abroad* 212–13)

In this instance, the provincial voice otherwise characteristic of the narrative falls to the side in the face of his overt critique of the 'Grandson' figure. Specifically, Twain dismisses the tourist by knowingly highlighting the hollow artificiality at the heart of his pretence to high culture. A key component of this façade is the tourist's representation of himself as an 'old traveler', one who would have his fellow tourists believe his cosmopolitan disposition is anything but a front: 'I am as much at home in the palaces of Europe as you are among your relatives', the Grandson explains (*Tramp Abroad* 215, 214). Twain's demystification of the political underpinnings of this form of cosmopolitanism is already apparent in his consistent description of himself and his travelling ilk as 'tourists', a term whose negative connotations are intended to amplify the shallowness of people like the Grandson (Ziff 13). Twain's tramp persona may also be a self-conscious construction, but it is one that serves the public interest (as the book's opening pages suggest) by subjecting Americans abroad to scrutiny.

In Twain's figuration, the contrasting images of the tramp and the Grandson gesture to the problem of American cultural identity as an increasing number of Americans begin to travel globally. Next to these idle consumers of culture and luxury, Twain reasons, the tramp resembles something more akin to a productive member of society. Soon after his run-in with the Grandson, Twain makes this last point more directly: 'I have not purposed to misrepresent this boy in any way, for what little indignation he excited in me soon passed and left nothing behind it but compassion. One cannot keep up a grudge against a vacuum', he explains (*Tramp Abroad* 215). He concludes this aside with the suggestion that both this tourist and 'the innocent chatterbox whom I met on the Swiss lake are the most unique and interesting specimens of Young America I came across during my foreign tramping. I have made honest portraits of them, not caricatures' (*Tramp Abroad* 215). The appeal to accuracy here comes not coincidently at the same time he foregrounds his own role as one 'tramping' across Europe: while Twain is at work documenting his travels, the tourists he encounters persist in ignorance of their own idleness. Twain's knowing references to the stage in the passage above therefore not only call into question the tourist's social pedigree but also make the reader keenly aware of the kind of work inherent in the travels of tramp and tourist alike.

Ever the satirist, Twain flips the conventional understanding of idleness on its head. As Mark Pittenger points out, Twain's interest in resuscitating the image of the 'downwardly mobile' extended to his fictional narratives as well, which by the 1880s frequently featured 'aristocratic characters' – as in *The Prince and the Pauper* (1881) – who can only 'realize their submerged democratic tendencies' once they experience life in the social margins (10). Along similar lines, in his travel narrative the tramp is not the picture of obscene idleness, the American tourist is. Twain in turn castigates the American tourist in part by drawing parallels between their luxurious trips abroad and the incorrigible travel that the tramp enacts. At the same time, Twain's critique of these indulgent Americans echoes the moralising call for productivity that undergirds the 'tramp scare' movement. Twain's figuration of the tramp is opposed not to modernity per se but rather to the indolence that manifests itself in especially affluent sectors of society. His tramp is the antagonist to the comfort-seeking tourist, inasmuch as the latter romanticises travel while downplaying the huge expense that enables tourism in the first place. Always on the move, the tramp provides a point of intersection with these other travellers while still decrying their idle materialism. In effect, Twain's critique of tourism valorises the tramp's mobility. The tramp becomes the locus of literary production, the vehicle for extensive critique and the source of opposition to more feckless touristic counterparts on the road.

However, Twain's underlying interest in the tramp's potential labour is largely absent from critical accounts of his travel writing. Twain's sharp critique of 'Young America' no doubt informs prevailing interpretations of *A Tramp Abroad*, which understand it as primarily interested in posing a critique of modernity in general. According to these readings, Twain contrasts Europe's pre-modern traditions favourably against the sterile modernity associated with the US. Messent echoes this idea in his overview of the text, which argues that Twain praises the 'unhurried relaxation of his time in Europe' with a depiction of idle tramping, which ultimately produces 'an implicit critique of modernization and the normative (American) business world in favour of forms of freedom and vagabonding, wherever and however they may be released' (141, 153). To be sure, Twain's interest in satirising the modern American tourist is clear. But if Twain is suspicious of the governing ideology behind this consumerism, he intentionally avoids suggesting that an escape from the scene of modernity exists. Rather, his own exploration of the tramp identity makes clear the links – literal and figurative – that tie the US to the European continent. The picture of America's cosmopolitanism becomes more visible, the narrative implies, when one steps outside its consumer culture. From this vantage point, Twain implies, one recognises the level of production or work that goes into even the idlest displays of leisure. Although Twain adopts an ironic posture throughout *A Tramp Abroad*, his text (as well as his Hartford letter) expresses a keen awareness of the need to approach what might appear to be American problems – whether its bumbling wealthy class or its wily tramps – from a comparative perspective.

What informs the conventional line of criticism on Twain's text is the abiding misconception of tramping as an inherently pre-modern subject position and consequently at home within the antique institutions of Europe. Although it is apparent that Twain lampoons the Americans he encounters abroad, it is less obvious on the text's surface how his tramping persona informs this critique. For these critics, Twain distinguishes the attractive idleness of the cities he visits abroad from the bustle of modern American life at home. Further along this line of reasoning, Twain sees America as a country 'primarily' concerned with modernisation; what interests him in Europe is the lingering relics of a positive, 'pre-modern' culture

(Messent 142). Accordingly, the tramp's personification of idleness would assume not an American character but a distinctly European one. However, such readings of Europe as a site of pre-modernity for Twain simplify the type of cultural exchange and appropriation that *A Tramp Abroad* displays. Likewise, to suggest that the text turns to some alternative to modernity would involve placing both Europe and the tramp as a depiction of vagrancy outside the realm of the modern. Rather, the text proposes instead the folly of looking for a space outside the realm of the modern in the first place.

Of course, Twain was not the only writer in the US who vilified the materialism of the tourist. During this same period, Henry James, to name one prominent example, produced numerous works that similarly decried 'vulgar' American tourists and the tourism industry, more generally (Pearce and Moscardo 121).[6] While Twain may agree with this overarching point, his critique hinges less on vulgarity than on idleness. As I have argued, his tramp identity allows him to separate productive Americans from their idle counterparts. This figuration draws from the public discourse concerning vagrancy but redirects its suspicions away from the tramp and towards his purported betters. By making the tramp an arbiter of productive Americans rather than an icon of criminality, Twain reverses the terms of the ongoing debate over how to make vagrants useful members of society. On another level, his depiction of tramping overseas also marks the tramp as a transnational figure, able to track the proliferation of Americans across international borders. In the role of the tramp, Twain stands on the margins of American consumer culture in order to get a better view of its proliferation. Foregrounding the lives of wandering tourists, he suggests that the US and Europe, far from being at opposite ends of the spectrum, are indelibly linked by a system of cultural and economic exchange. His representation of the tramp is able to do what other overseas tourists cannot – namely, negotiate the relationship between the US and Europe. While the latter travellers are transformed by this exchange, this tramping figure curates it.

Although Twain avoids policy recommendations in *A Tramp Abroad*, his ambivalent presentation of tramps – and, more implicitly, the value in rehabilitating them – should not be read in isolation. Instead, it is worthwhile to recognise Twain's contributions to tramping discourse, especially given both the widespread popularity of his writing in his time and the timeliness of his tramping text in relation to public interest in the subject. In the context of British vagrancy literature, Alistair Robinson likewise argues that it is difficult to overstate the role of cultural sources in steering the public understanding of vagrancy (11). Whatever their basis in fact, these fictionalised or non-scientific accounts nonetheless exerted real force outside their respective genres. By stressing Twain's timely engagement with his readership, I adapt Denning's formulation regarding popular fiction: because texts like Twain's so keenly imagine and address a specific audience, they contribute to the 'symbolic forms' that define these readers while also attempting to 'police and reform' them (*Mechanic* 4). If vagrants themselves are not Twain's anticipated audience, his appeals to productive work and denigration of idleness nonetheless speak to his middle-class readers. The extent to which Twain informs a wider consciousness about vagrancy becomes apparent when he is read alongside Flynt, who writes nearly twenty years later. Although Twain makes use of the tramp to satirise tourists, this specific use affects other treatments of the vagrant. Twain's text participates in the normative construction of modernity inasmuch as it contributes to the elaboration of the vagrant as a subject position.

Flynt's Government: How Europe Shaped American Vagrancy

An ethnographic study of vagrancy, Flynt's 1899 *Tramping with Tramps* has more in common with Twain's travelogue than their disparate genres might otherwise suggest. As the pages that follow argue, the way Twain's text frames the subject of the tramp – which takes his powers to negotiate foreign societies as evidence of his potential value – resonates beyond the pages of travel writing. Indeed, the appeal of Twain's tramping subject to writers working across genres should not be minimised. As is the case now, as it was then, the distinctions between the literary genres practised by Twain and Flynt – fiction, travel writing and ethnography – are themselves contested and permeable grounds. To recall James Clifford's axiom, ethnographic texts such as Flynt's are 'not above historical or linguistic practices'; instead, they share the same 'constructed' and 'artificial nature' as their fiction-based literary counterparts (2). By pairing Twain's text with Flynt's, I stress their shared contributions to the popular understanding of tramping as it enters the twentieth century. In fact, Flynt is a critical figure in extending the implicit understanding of tramping embedded in Twain's comedic writing to scientific accounts of tramps and vagrant groups.

By the end of the nineteenth century, Flynt did more to define the figure of the tramp in the public eye than any other source of the day. Beginning in 1891, his essays and illustrated articles on the subject appeared in popular outlets such as *The Atlantic Monthly* and *Century Magazine* (Cresswell 60). Within a few years, Flynt had become the 'nation's premier expert on tramps' after publishing this work in 1899 as a collected volume, *Tramping with Tramps*, the era's authoritative account of the vagrant population in the US and abroad (DePastino 49). After the text's publication, Flynt became synonymous both with tramps and also with the type of undercover investigation methods he pioneered in the US, which he used to gain trust from a population otherwise unwilling to divulge their stories to outsiders (Pittenger 14). His sustained interest in tramping is also apparent beyond his social-scientific work. His only published novel, *The Little Brother: A Story of Tramp Life* (1902), extends this fascination in the form of a fictional account of a young boy's travels with tramps and vagabonds. As this last point suggests, Flynt's work reflects in a singular case the interdisciplinary preoccupation with the lives of tramps during this era.

Unlike Twain's idle tourists, Flynt was overseas not for pleasure but to conduct research on the tramping problem in the US. Born Josiah Flynt Willard, Flynt took to tramping to escape what he saw as the 'feminine atmosphere' of his urbane and religious upbringing (DePastino 162). The masculine and individualistic features associated with the tramp figure gave him an outlet for rebelling against this upbringing while also distinguishing him from his aunt, Frances Willard, the co-founder of the Women's Christian Temperance Union and a famous suffragist (DePastino 162). His ramblings away from home put him in close contact with vagrants and nurtured talents that would later benefit his work as an ethnographer – namely, a penchant for the type of 'impersonation and performance' necessary for participant observation (DePastino 163). His early interest in tramps solidified during his doctoral term at the University of Berlin, where he began studying in 1890. Flynt's German education was far from anomalous, but rather reflected a larger trend of the time. Beginning in the 1870s, German universities became the primary point of contact between American studies of politics and economics and European social institutions (Rodgers 76). In this context, Flynt was one among an entire generation of reform-minded postgraduates whose time studying in Europe would influence their progressive and reformist campaigns back in the US (Rodgers 76).

The details of Flynt's life and research are helpful for locating tramp-writers and anti-tramp reformers among larger developments in social politics at the end of the nineteenth century. At this time, sources in and outside of government were also looking to the European continent in order to understand and contain tramping in the US. Flynt's text in particular captures the extent to which observers of vagrancy at this time resorted to international comparison in order to broaden the disciplinary power of individual states. Further examples of this trend include John James McCook and his 'Tramp Census' in 1893 as well as Edmond Kelly's *Elimination of the Tramp*, published in 1908, which advocated for rehabilitative labour camps modelled on existing sites in Switzerland. By tracing vagrant movements overseas, reformers like Flynt, McCook and Kelly were in turn inspired by the social programmes they observed there.[7] In nurturing this international dialogue, they also envisioned substantial changes in the regulatory power of the state. As Daniel Rodgers points out in his study of early welfare policy in the US, the concept of adopting European-style labour colonies to address crime was popular among Progressive thinkers more generally. Reformers saw these sites as powerful tools to contain vagrancy as well as – more optimistically – powerful opportunities to instil among the population values associated with 'cooperative social life', such as temperance, physical fitness and standardised education (Rodgers 215). As the final section of this chapter will elaborate, the push to address vagrancy appears in this light to be a pilot programme among the larger Progressive reforms of the era.

Flynt's text assisted these efforts inasmuch as it identified vagrancy as an international social problem that can nonetheless be brought to heel within specific states. To appreciate the distinct features of American tramping, Flynt reasons, one must see how the tramp varies across different societies. A prefatory note from Andrew Dickson White, then-US ambassador to Germany, opens *Tramping with Tramps* with an explicit acknowledgement of Flynt's contributions to this end. Here, White argues that the rise of the tramp population in the US reflects the government's inadequate powers of oversight when it comes to migration and labour. While White sees tramps as a pressing problem for the US in particular, he looks to Europe for guidance. 'We are allowing a great and powerful criminal class to be developed', he cautions, 'while crime is held carefully in check in most European countries' (Flynt, *Tramping* viii). 'So well is this coming to be known by the criminal classes of Europe', White concludes, 'that it is perfectly well understood here that they look upon the United States as a "happy-hunting ground," and more and more seek it, to the detriment of our country and of all that we hold most dear in it' (Flynt, *Tramping* viii). In his role as an observer of European policy, White makes a strident case for using Flynt's ethnographic writings as a resource for revising US legal codes regulating this illicit form of migration. A co-founder of Cornell University and its first president, White personifies the major role that research institutions, alongside government agencies, played in developing the codification of tramping in law and culture.[8] Speaking at the intersection of law and education, White suggests that both governing bodies and the reading public should envision vagrancy along the lines of what Flynt's ethnography provides. The narrative model that Flynt produces in this case – hinging on the subject of the tramp and overseas travel – facilitates this appropriation for official governing bodies.

Sharing with Twain an interest in tramping, Flynt also situates his non-fictional work on an international stage. *Tramping with Tramps* unfolds across four distinct sections: his studies on the tramp persona and its distribution across the US; a description of his travels as one among tramps across Europe and the US; intimate 'sketches' of tramp life; and finally, a dictionary of tramp jargon. The bulk of the text, however, is split between his studies of the tramp population and his travel writings – a juxtaposition that evokes the type of international framework in which Flynt's tramps come into being. The travel writing that Twain helped popularise in the US is relevant to Flynt's own travels because, as Ziff puts it, this genre is fundamentally concerned with measuring one's 'national traditions . . . against the manner in which other societies met the problems of living the daily life' (7). In other words, travelogues by definition create an international frame of comparison in which to consider (what the author perceives as) the strengths, weaknesses or characteristic features of a given nation. While *Tramping with Tramps* appears on its surface to engage little with this popular legacy, it nonetheless replicates this model in theme and structure. Like Twain, Flynt presents travel as an activity that has less to do with appreciating foreign culture than with scrutinising how cultural and legal institutions shape national identity. Twain's travels in *A Tramp Abroad* take place in Europe but 'develop primarily American themes' and observe American subjects (Hellwig 85). The cultural institutions he finds in Europe are therefore helpful for distinguishing between (and passing judgement on) different types of American travellers. Flynt's more evident aim of understanding his subjects likewise compels him to evaluate them in foreign lands. In pursuit of American tramps, he moves not only across the US but also to England, Germany and Russia. The extensive scope of Flynt's travels is, he assures his readers, a critical aspect of his project of living as a tramp in order to demystify this class to his readers. 'My purpose in seeking out [tramps] was to learn about their life', he explains in the book's opening pages, 'and I soon saw that, to know it well, I must become joined to it and be part and parcel of its various manifestations' (*Tramping* 3).

Travelling across Europe in the guise of the tramp affords Flynt an ideal perspective from which to evaluate the governing regimes of the states he visits and, more importantly, the potential usefulness of these institutions as models for policy back home. While his text looks out for governmental policies suitable for appropriation, it must also keep in mind the distinctly American policies it is interested in creating. The kind of comparative framework that governs the text is perhaps most apparent in the text's careful construction of the American tramp as a distinct figure among the tramping classes of the world. Among the English 'moochers', for example, Flynt recalls that he is made keenly aware of the distinct features that separate him from his surroundings: 'They proclaimed our nationality wherever we went. Never in my life have I been so bothered with stares' (*Tramping* 234). Up to this point in the text, Flynt has indicated that British tramps have 'long been an object of curiosity' for him, owing in no small part to their cultural proximity to their 'American cousin' (*Tramping* 229). Once Flynt moves among these British tramps, however, he is overcome with a sense of the British vagrant's relative shabbiness. Unlike the American tramp, Flynt explains, the 'English moocher ... dresses in a way that in America would be thought indecent and in Germany criminal. He is too lazy to clean up, if he had the chance, and harbors vermin as if he liked them' (*Tramping* 238). Given the long history of English vagabonds in literature and legal documents, Flynt's dismissal of these tramps assumes a rather ironic subtext: although he envisions a veritably global class of vagrants, he is eager to distinguish American tramps to the detriment of their most similar cultural types.

However, for Flynt, whose audience consists of readers in the popular sphere as well as in government, it is imperative that he make the body of the vagrant the subject of public appraisal. The distinction of the American tramp to the detriment of the English moocher, while paying homage to an underlying sense of American exceptionalism, also makes it clear that Flynt is delineating a specifically American brand of vagrancy (and, of course, anti-vagrancy legislation) even while these concepts take shape overseas. To this end, Flynt's account of his overseas travels allows him to confront the most far-reaching aspects of state regulation even as he addresses a reading public contained largely in the US. In Flynt's pages, the American tramp is the template against which the British and German equivalents serve as contrasts: in only a brief descriptive passage, Flynt quickly distinguishes among these three types and alludes to their respective societal norms. In relation to his fellow vagrants, the American is more self-respecting than the English moocher but less subject to self-control than the German, whose presentation reflects the German 'criminal' system that polices cleanliness (*Tramping* 238). Balancing local colour with his more legalistic concerns, Flynt sets up an international, comparative model that nonetheless primarily describes a local demographic – the American tramp – as it circulates within and across borders. It is only by first treating the tramp as a global figure that Flynt is able to locate a distinctly American type of vagrant.

The discursive link between Twain and Flynt that this chapter has been developing highlights how tramp writing dramatises the emergence and then codification of a figure that pushes the limits of pre-existing understandings of labour, value and citizenship. In this context, Flynt's observations of American tramps should be understood as part of a larger, cross-disciplinary dialogue between sources writing on a shared subject. Flynt's own empirical work, in fact, was undertaken in full view of Twain's earlier narrative. Specifically, Twain's *A Tramp Abroad* appears prominently in Flynt's autobiography when he recalls his tramping days in Europe. Twain's travel narrative not only guides Flynt across the continent but also pre-emptively shapes his expectations of what he will find, and how he should present himself, while there. Flynt outlines the extent of this influence in a passage recalling his time in Switzerland:

> Eventually we got into the Rhone Valley, and at Visp, or rather at St. Nicholas, midway between Visp and Zermatt, we stumbled upon our ideal of a mountain guide, or, rather, on the ideal that the 'Tramp Abroad' book had conjured up for us. We had seen other guides before, dozens of them, but there was something in the 'altogether' about the St. Nicholas discovery that captured us completely. (*My Life* 203–4)

Flynt is initially unable to distinguish between the depiction of travel in Twain and the realities that face him as a vagabond in Europe. Instead, he understands *A Tramp Abroad* to be at once descriptive and prescriptive. For Flynt, Twain's text is not only describing Europe, it is also shaping the reader's experiences. He continues, 'I wanted to make sure that our guide was the real thing, a la "A Tramp Abroad"' (*My Life* 206). Flynt's reverence for Twain highlights Twain's prominent role in giving shape to Europe for an American audience. Like other readers of the time, Flynt sees in *A Tramp Abroad* an experiential framework for understanding European travel. In the guise of an actual vagabond in Europe, moreover, Flynt bridges the gap between the implied sense of vagabondage in Twain and the literal, ethnographic accounts that then appear in *Tramping with Tramps*.

Latent in Twain's work, the desire to reform tramps is at the forefront of Flynt's book. According to Flynt, tramps are able to reform and lead conventionally productive lives – if only the state can inculcate in them the 'responsibilities' attending civil participation and help them 'to take advantage of its opportunities' (*Tramping* 5). Flynt outlines this objective in the earliest pages of *Tramping with Tramps*. By making the vagrant an object of study, he declares, the juridical system can better develop tactics for incarcerating criminals of all types:

> Human justice recoils from a severe treatment of the man who, though an outbreaking sinner, bears evidence of being sinned against as well as sinning; and yet, before we can safely fall in with this view, we must carefully consider the theory on which it is based, and its claims to a scientific foundation. (*Tramping* 2)

Accordingly, Flynt argues that studying vagrants offers investigators a look at criminals 'in their own habitat' (*Tramping* 3), before they have been subject to the deleterious conditions of the penal system. As this statement makes expressly clear, Flynt sees his writing as a crucial component of the regulatory state. By delineating an otherwise diffuse population with specific demographic data, he makes the case that his work does nothing less than revise the 'distorted view of the criminal . . . in penology' (*Tramping* 3).

Specifically, Flynt ties this deficiency back to the theories of Cesare Lombroso, the Italian criminologist whose theories of criminal anthropology widely influenced American legal authorities. Lombroso held that criminality is an inherited trait; serious criminals consequently exhibit 'atavistic anomalies' – such as oversized ears, a pronounced brow or enlarged incisors – that physically mark their natural propensity to crime (Cordella and Siegel 7). Although Lombroso's theories had little currency in Europe by the end of the nineteenth century, they were highly influential with social scientists in the US, who embraced his views and their underlying notion of biological determinism (Siegel 142). If Flynt avoids any extended critique of the eugenic underpinnings of this line of reasoning, he nonetheless identifies the shortcomings in its categorisation of the criminal classes. Most immediately, this approach fails to identify vagrants as a specific demographic in the first place. Flynt explains, 'Lombroso and other investigators classify the cases they have studied as political, instinctive, occasional, habitual and professional; but, so far as my finding is concerned, only one class is of any great importance – the professional' (*Tramping* 3). Although Lombroso attempts to account for all classes of criminal, Flynt argues, the modern tramp confounds his system. The ineffective classification schema in turn generates further misinformation regarding vagrancy. Simply put, Lombroso's schema fails to account for what Flynt actually observed during his time on the road: 'Contrary to a more or less popular opinion, I must also say that the criminals I am acquainted with are not such because they are unable to keep body and soul together in any other way', he explains (*Tramping* 4). Rather, 'they are above their environment, and are often gifted with talents which would enable them to do well in any class' (*Tramping* 5). As this excerpt makes clear, Flynt sees his collection of data on vagrants as an essential tool in bringing about more effective policing of vagrancy.

At the same time, underlying Flynt's appeal to accuracy is an embedded sense that tramps are not merely one among many criminal classes but are instead diamonds in the rough. Rather than being the 'scum of their environment', the tramps Flynt observes possess 'talents' that would make them productive within 'any class' – but only if they 'realize its responsibilities and take advantage of its opportunities' (*Tramping* 5). Pittenger notes that Flynt's fervent critique of Lombroso's hereditarian model stands at odds with Flynt's own careful attention to taxonomising the vagrants he observes, which calls to mind 'an entomologist poring over his specimens' (36). The benefit to this taxonomy, Flynt explains, lies in its ability to monitor all vagrants more effectively, identify particular sub-demographics in need of the state's attention – and to remove this group from the general population lest their inclination to vagabondage spread. He makes the practical benefits to this effort especially clear in his discussion of 'penal conditions' for reforming 'the children of the road', the youngest among the tramps, before they become accustomed to vagabondage (*Tramping* 64, 29). In order to improve the state's regulation of vagrancy, Flynt contends, rehabilitation centres for these youths should be established on the basis of 'a humane and scientific separation of the inmates':

> Sex, age, height, and weight are not the only things to be taken into consideration when dealing with erring children. Birth, temperament, habits, education, and experience are questions of far more vital importance, and it is no unreasonable demand upon the State that careful attention to each of these points be required in the scheme of such institutions. (*Tramping* 64)

Flynt's ethnography is an attempt to provide the state with the very details it needs in order to better rehabilitate the most amenable members of the vagrant class, offering not only physical descriptions of tramps but accounts of their habits and temperaments as well. In doing so, Flynt imagines vagrancy less as an in-born atavism (as in Lombroso's model) and more the result of environmental factors (Pittenger 36). Habit, education and experience can turn a juvenile love of wandering into something more dangerous, the ethnographer contends, unless the state can identify these tendencies in their infancy.

The push to document all aspects of vagabondage as it appears in the US moves Flynt outside the borders of that country and into the international sphere in which vagrants circulate. But if Flynt's narrative valorises the mobility of tramping in this sense, it nonetheless evinces an overriding interest in the kind of state policies responsible for bringing the tramp (and the population of homeless in general) into the fold of the state's disciplinary apparatus. To this end, Flynt characterises the societies he visits on the basis of their respective approaches to eliminating vagrants through state policy. Germany serves for Flynt – as well as for Twain and White – as an origin point for the type of state reforms that would become an essential component of Western social democracies in the twentieth century. Before the unification of the German Empire in 1871, the Prussian state had hoped to offset the worst consequences of the factory economy, as it saw unfolding in England in particular, with a more proactive form of state administration (Beck 55).

After unification, the new nation state under the direction of Otto von Bismarck further extended this model of governance to the rest of the empire, which had become the 'pioneer in social insurance' among Western states (Esping-Andersen 22). By the time of *A Tramp Abroad*, Germany already had a first-of-its-kind compulsory insurance programme in place to cover workers who were unable to work due to injury or old age (Hennock 91). In view of Germany's pioneering role in social-welfare reform, both White and Flynt treat the German model as a useful test case for expanding the state's control over working and non-working citizens alike. As Rodgers puts it, Americans who travelled to Germany to study state policy 'found themselves spectators of the most wide-reaching state culture in Europe' in the final decades of the nineteenth century (84). In the case of tramps, the German welfare reforms provided the kind of administrative logic that, while not eradicating vagrants completely, attempted to subject these errant individuals to oversight.

The contrast between Twain's German sojourn and Flynt's is especially telling of how the latter frames tramping abroad in terms of governmental intervention. While Twain's account of travelling in Germany begins with an overstatement of his own exploits – 'the spectacle of a man' (*Tramp Abroad* 1) – Flynt's first impression of Germany points in another direction, to the singular figure embodying governance:

> William II of Germany is the ruler of about fifty millions of people. A small fraction comprises the nobility, while the great majority are commoners, and the rest, about one hundred thousand, are roving beggars. His Imperial Majesty is probably well acquainted with his nobles, and he thinks that he understands the commoners, but the tramp who passes his castle now and then is a foreigner at home. Yet he is found in every city, town, and village, and there is hardly a home in the empire which he has not visited. (*Tramping* 169)

Flynt introduces the idea of government regulation from the very first lines of his account of German society. But even in the face of this relatively expansive state, he still sees tramps as a problem that must be solved in terms of even greater state oversight. The German system of governance is a point of departure for Flynt, one that proposes a template for state regulation but still calls out for correction. The movement of 'roving beggars' poses a nuisance for the state inasmuch as these figures remain inscrutable in the eyes of the law: the wandering vagrant moves relentlessly through city and countryside while the government (embodied here by no less than the Kaiser) struggles to envision this portion of its population in the first place. Interested in the 'real facts' regarding the lives of these tramps, Flynt finds little help from extant government agencies: 'I called the Bureau of Statistics, hoping surely to find here carefully tabulated statistics of vagrancy; but I was disappointed' (*Tramping* 170). If Twain wrote at least partly in jest that his own tramping expedition was framed around a pressing social need, Flynt makes the same claim in all seriousness. He writes, 'I finally decided to give up these fruitless investigations, and to become a tramp myself in order to achieve my ends' (*Tramping* 171). To the extent that Flynt sees his own tramping as something that must be done in order to inform the public, he further draws from the figurative depiction of tramps (and the tramping author, in particular) in Twain's work. But while Twain's irreverent presentation intentionally overstates his text's usefulness as a travel guide, Flynt is careful to address himself directly to those legal authorities who would benefit from his account.

Flynt takes on what Twain depicted as the tramp's adept reading of international forms of cultural exchange and puts it to work importing governmental techniques. Even as he describes vagrants as 'human parasites' throughout his text, he works not to expel this population but to bring it within the fold of the civil sphere (*Tramping* ix). Flynt strives to make tramps visible, in terms of the demographic data that the state calls for, as a first step towards making them accountable. His account of travelling in Germany therefore provides American readers with a clearer sense of what they can appropriate from states with relatively long-standing welfare bureaucracies. Although vagrancy in Germany, like German unemployment relief programmes, predates any American equivalent, Flynt is nonetheless careful to scrutinise the habits of German vagrants through a decidedly American lens. From this perspective, he quickly finds faults with the German system he is documenting. As his encounter with the Bureau of Statistics previously indicated, Flynt's recollection of his travels in Germany points to governmental unwillingness to recognise the features of the tramp – whether in the US or abroad – as the great obstacle to containing vagrancy in a given state.

If authorities in the US failed to see vagrants as they actually appear, the German state refused to distinguish vagrants as a social group in the first place. Accordingly, its system for distributing unemployment relief made no distinction between unemployed labourers and what Flynt sees as the professional tramp, who 'prefers begging to working' (*Tramping* 171). According to Flynt, the 'voluntary vagrant' confounds even an expansive welfare system so long as this form of governance assumes all unemployed citizens are actively seeking conventional forms of paid work (*Tramping* 198). To respond, the scale of the state's intervention is less crucial than its tactics and strategies of application. Thus, while Flynt dismisses the German welfare system of taxation and poor relief as 'even more inanely generous than its counterpart in the United States' (*Tramping*

198), he proposes making the US system more adept at identifying all types of work within a given social system – even in its illicit forms.

Tramping and the Early Welfare State

The preceding pages have made the case for locating cross-disciplinary depictions of the tramp at the centre of larger, and more familiar, movements for social reform. The intertextual dialogue that connects Twain to Flynt reflects the sustained development in the way readers in and out of public office understood tramps as a class worth rehabilitating. In addition, these sources should be located among social reform movements of the time, which reassessed the relation between the US and Europe. As outlined above, the push for greater governmental oversight of social practices placed not only Flynt but also McCook and Kelly at the forefront of the Progressive Era in the US, whose activists campaigned to modernise the country's legal institutions from roughly 1890 to 1920. The interdisciplinary training and investigations that these sources all pursue is, in fact, a characteristic of the Progressive movement in general, which was largely middle class in composition and dominated by experts in fields such as medicine and education (Courtwright and Miller 94).

The circulation of statistics and demographic data, as is evident in the tramping sources above, also reflects a larger trend in Progressive politics, which likewise turned away from overtly moralising rhetoric to language coded in scientific observation (Courtwright and Miller 100). In this context, Flynt's landmark *Tramping with Tramps* did not appear out of the blue but rather emerged alongside a bevy of works dedicated to understanding the poor and working classes using the methods of observation and undercover social investigation. Pittenger thus locates Flynt's tramp writings alongside other American undercover writers during the Progressive Era, who 'crossed the class line' and reported on their findings to their readership (1). In addition to Flynt, writers of the period who shared an interest in bringing empirical observation to depictions of the poor included Walter Wyckoff, a seminarian and economist, the naturalist writer Stephen Crane, and Margaret Sherwood, a writer and professor of English (Pittenger 14–15). At the same time, it is important to note that this turn to scientific observation as the basis for policy had the effect of reinforcing several social prejudices.[9] More apparent manifestations of this scientific racism in the case of tramp writing will appear later in this book, as American authors like Jack London and John Steinbeck develop the subject's exceptional characteristics in relation to other non-white or foreign cases.[10] Suffice to say, socially ingrained assumptions regarding, for example, the racial superiority of white people and the intellectual superiority of men found new outlets in the dubious findings of reform-minded social scientists and medical researchers at the time (Schuster 256).

Flynt's emphasis on rehabilitation as well as criminalisation should also call to mind the nineteenth-century expansion of disciplinary and surveillance institutions in both Europe and North America. Michel Foucault outlines the prototypical version of the rise of disciplinary institutions in *Discipline and Punish*. More recent scholars have extended Foucault's notion of disciplinary power and governmentality to describe shifts in governance within the US. In the context of the early twentieth century, Miller and Rose identify 'new practices of government' meant to account for diverse economic agents spread across an international geographical and financial arena (58). As citizens became more widespread across geographical and political boundaries, Miller and Rose explain, the state looked to regulate individual activity by tying the ideology of individualism to the sphere of civil responsibility. For governments concerned with regulating the economic lives of their citizens, Miller and Rose contend, '[t]he individual was to be integrated into society in the form of a citizen with social needs, in a contract in which individual and society had mutual claims and obligations' (48). Flynt's vision of tramps as a group that can be governed anticipates these large-scale governmental changes inasmuch as it demands a larger regulatory system that would control this population.

The international comparison outlined above was especially critical to this last point, since Europe provided case studies that were ready for incorporation and modification domestically. If observers bemoaned the problem of tramping in America, they also understood that the global movements of tramps meant that one might learn about the effectiveness of different social policies by following the tramp's movement across borders. To observe the tramp's travels across Europe in many cases involved for American sources a glimpse of the future: by the time of McCook's 'Tramp Census', for instance, Germany and the UK were farther along in the industrialisation of their respective economies than was the US (Rodgers 46). The governmental policies in place there to address the consequences of industrialisation – such as the problem of tramping – were, in the eyes of reformers like Flynt and McCook, less relics of the Old World than signs of things to come for the US.

In depicting the mobility of tramps as an embodied form of labour, Flynt as well as Twain contribute to different degrees to the ongoing effort to construct vagrancy as a viable demographic category. As this transformation indicates, a variety of literary sources were invested in encoding a notion of work that would also shape the public welfare system later in the twentieth century. For these sources, the health of the nation state depends on productive citizens; to be productive entitled a citizen to both civil participation and assistance. The 'tramp scare' that played out in both newspapers and popular fiction during the last decades of the nineteenth century effectively set the stage for the major reforms that would occur later. In particular, the codification of travel as a form of labour serves to rationalise the state's ability to monitor even its most diffuse demographic. For as this transformative period makes clear, the brief legal vacuum that initially enshrouded tramps left these figures subject to arrest and, unofficially, to mob violence. But for Twain and Flynt, the tramp as a literary subject may move back and forth across national borders as he pleases – but he does so for the benefit of the American public in particular.

In making this form of movement the subject of popular literature, these writers underscored the indelible link between public representations of the productive nation state and the international world in which this conception is formed. Accordingly, the representation of travel, the defining feature of the tramp, as a type of labour removes vagrancy from the brink of vigilantism and into the jurisdiction of state authority. From the perspective of the juridical community, to rehabilitate the tramp – to do as Flynt suggests and make the tramp accountable to society – improves the health of the body politic as a whole. In this collection of sources, the tramp is always at work even as he travels abroad owing to (rather than in spite of) the figure's ability to cross social, political and literary lines. In constructing the vagrant as a figure always on the move, these writers placed travel even closer to the project of state construction. To different degrees, then, these tramping sources anticipate the debate surrounding the expansion of the public-welfare system later in the twentieth century insofar as they both equate productivity with moral responsibility.

Notes

1. For a thorough account of Twain's careful drafting and delivery of this speech – as well as his subsequent apology – see the 'Spirit of '76' in Justin Kaplan's *Mr. Clemens and Mark Twain*.
2. Bellesiles provides an overview of these sensationalised accounts. Specific headlines from 1880 alluded to here include 'A Girl Murdered by Tramps' in Trenton, New Jersey's *Daily State Gazette*, and 'A Tramp's Revenge. He Burns Up $10,000 Worth of Property Because He Was Refused a Meal' in West Virginia's *Wheeling Register*.
3. Michael Denning's *Mechanic Accents* helpfully identifies a wealth of popular texts in which this battle over the role of tramp played out. In particular, see chapter 8, 'Tramps, Outlaws . . .: Figures of the Great Strike'.
4. Twain's professed need to save money is clear in his correspondence with Howells. Another, less explicit factor in Twain's desire to flee the country may have to do with the backlash against his 1877 speech that compared Emerson, Holmes and Longfellow to tramps. Twain scholars note that the author was convinced the speech had damaged his image and that he needed extra privacy to continue his work (Twain, *Notebooks* 41). Messent likewise argues that the speech may have been a factor in Twain's flight to Europe, noting that widespread concerns about criminal tramps made the topic an especially sensitive one among American audiences at the time (140).
5. Another crucial aspect of Twain's tramp-like narrative scheme is the fact that he makes a concerted effort to avoid walking at all costs throughout the text (LeMaster and Wilson 743). Like his opening statement of purpose, this ironic presentation of tramping intentionally sells the reader short. Of course, in doing so he further inhabits on another level the role of the archetypal tramp huckster. Similarly, the tramps to which he looked for inspiration for his travel narrative were not limited to any single mode of transportation in their treks across national boundaries, preferring rail cars and steam ships to travelling on foot – the semantics of 'tramping' notwithstanding.
6. For more on James's critique of the American tourist abroad, see John Urry's 'The Consumption of Tourism' and Patricia McKee's 'Travel in *The Ambassadors*'.
7. Published in *Forum*, McCook's 'Tramp Census' provides an in-depth look at the lives of vagrants through a series of personal interviews conducted across not only the US but also England, Germany and France. The result of this research leads McCook to push for uniform laws across the country to contain and rehabilitate the worst aspects of the vagrant class (Bliss 1345). A scholar of municipal government, Kelly contends that 'vagabondage and all its attending evils would dis-

appear like magic from American soil – as it has already disappeared in Holland, Belgium, and Switzerland' (15).
8. In fact, Bellesiles points to a convention at Bryn Mawr College as the origin of the 'antitramp movement' in the US (122). The intersection of law, literature and education here further underscores the extent to which the tramp is a discursive construct.
9. Dorothy Ross provides an overview of how the social sciences contributed to Progressive Era reforms in *The Origins of American Social Science*.
10. Gavin Jones offers in *American Hungers* another important account of how the perception of poverty as an individual moral failure endured well into the state reforms enacted during the Progressive Era and, decades later, the New Deal.

Chapter 2

Vagrant Nationalism: Jack London and W. H. Davies on the Super-Tramp

On the subject of the tramp, British sources at the turn of the century were no less immune to international influence than their American counterparts. At the same time, one cannot speak of the tramp in Britain in the twentieth century without acknowledging the long history of vagabond literature there: tramp prototypes and adjacent groups – such as rambling men, tinkers and gypsies – abound in cultural sources from the British Isles since the early modern period. In the nineteenth century, representations of vagrant figures in literature shifted alongside wider transformations in British society as a result of industrialisation, expansion of the rail system and redoubled land enclosure (Robinson 28–9). Although this chapter will focus on authors in the early twentieth century – and the linkages between US and British authors in particular – it is useful to linger briefly on this earlier period in order to help distinguish the innovations I associate with the more modern version of the tramp-writer. Well before the American 'tramp scare' in the late nineteenth century, Britain's Romantic poets were making vagrants and vagabonds the subjects of their art. 'Romantic vagrancy', as Celeste Langan puts it, was concerned with vagrancy insofar as it is 'susceptible to analogy and subsequent idealization' (17). Vagrant figures appear everywhere in Romantic literature, in other words, but they appear primarily as abstractions removed from the social institutions that generate poverty. The turn from this abstract sense of vagrancy to embodied vagrancy is at the centre of this chapter.

William Wordsworth's 'Beggars' (1815) is illustrative of the abstract understanding of vagrancy that characterises Romantic writing on the subject.[1] The poem relates a brief encounter between the narrator and a pauper of 'Amazonian' appearance, who troubles the narrator's sense of time and place (11):

> Before me begging did she stand,
> Pouring out sorrows like a sea;
> Grief after grief: – on English Land
> Such woes I knew could never be;
> And yet a boon I gave her; for the Creature
> Was beautiful to see; a Weed of glorious feature! (13–18)

As these lines indicate, the beggar instigates the overflow of powerful feelings that is characteristic of Wordsworth's poetry. The focus therefore remains exclusively on the narrator's emotional response to the pauper – whose own story, so to speak, remains a mystery throughout the poem. The woman, whose skin is of 'Egyptian brown', is an enigma, one whose exotic features exist out of place in the poet's 'English land' (9, 15). If 'Beggars' foregrounds one version of the indigent poor at the time, it also reinforces the social gap between the sympathetic poet, on the one hand, and the silent vagabond, on the other. But as the preceding chapter argued, the appearance not only of tramps but of tramp-writers troubles precisely the distinction between poet and vagabond by suggesting that the vagrant – in the case of Mark Twain's cultural critic or Josiah Flynt's talented criminal – can be considered an exceptionally gifted artist in his own right. Following the proliferation of tramp writing in the closing years of the nineteenth century, the ground was set for a refreshed view of vagabond types in British popular culture as well. Long the object of art, vagabonds were ready to tell their own stories to a reading public eager to hear them.

The multiple points of contact between American and British sources on this mutual project of redefining the vagrant are the subject of the pages that follow. This transatlantic dialogue reveals the growing prominence of whiteness as a means for establishing the tramp's exceptional qualities among other populations of impoverished or homeless subjects. Although I return to the status of vagrancy in British Romanticism later in this chapter, the specific timeframe established here – focusing primarily on sources from the earliest years of the twentieth century – means that the greater backstory to British vagrancy is by necessity largely absent.[2] Instead, this chapter delimits a consequential moment of flux in the literary history of vagrancy, when specifically British conceptualisations of the vagrant come into contact with – and in turn are changed by – the transatlantic discourse surrounding the tramp figure in particular. As the previous case studies of Twain and Flynt have demonstrated, this discursive project crossed generic boundaries as well as literal state lines. But even if American authors looked to Europe for clarification on how to discipline this new vagrant population, it would be a mistake to view this dialogue from only one side of the Atlantic. The consensus that marks the tramp as a dangerous subject in need of rehabilitation can only be understood by way of an international comparison – in this case, via British sources contending with their own vagrant population. To examine the interplay between American and British tramp-writers is to disclose the other half of the transatlantic dialogue that the previous chapter established: spurred by the global scale of the tramp problem, legal codes and popular literatures alike travelled back and forth between the two countries.

Profound transformations become visible in the racial and national framing of tramps once we retrace the lines of this transatlantic dialogue. The works of several famous authors from this time showcase both how an archetypal version of the tramp proliferated at this time and, more importantly, how this archetype reinforced the sense that the tramp's exceptional qualities were an extension of his whiteness. A prominent example is in the work of American author Jack London. No literary figure was more associated with tramps in his own country or abroad than London, who became an international celebrity on the basis of his adventure novels such as *The Call of the Wild* (1903) as well as his own biography as a tramping adventurer. London's writing also provides a concrete point of connection between the American tramp archetype and the same figure in Britain. In his first-hand account of foreign poverty, *The People of the Abyss* (1903), London travels to England in the guise of a tramp to describe the poverty he finds there, which at the time afflicted nearly half a million Londoners. But even as he rails against poverty abroad, London is careful to draw distinctions between American and British forms of indigence. Throughout the text, he stresses the need to understand the exceptional tramp as a uniquely American phenomenon that could not exist in Britain's rigid class structure. The urban poverty he observes ultimately underscores the relative strength of the American liberalism that produced, if unintentionally, the tramp archetype: his own freedom of movement as a 'tramp royal' enables him to observe abroad the unremarkable 'gorillas' who can only thrash about in their cages (*People* 66, 151).

The American tramp is exceptional, London suggests, because his mental and physical acuity finds expression in a society that rewards individualism. The ease with which this language of national exceptionalism slides into the language of racial essentialism becomes clearer when we read London alongside Welsh poet W. H. Davies, who likewise explores the tramp's exceptional nature in his memoir, *The Autobiography of a Super-Tramp* (1908). Promoted by the likes of George Bernard Shaw, Davies exemplifies how the exceptionalism of the so-called super-tramp, coded as masculine and white, becomes naturalised in a distinctly British context. Set largely in the US and Britain, his autobiography uses the perspective of the wandering vagrant to elaborate on the cultural differences between the two countries and, more implicitly, the social institutions that operate there. In his telling, America is a land free from want, where tramps wander without having to fear repressive policing. Facile as it may appear, this image brings into focus Davies's larger criticism of a British social system that stifles autonomy and innovation, both of which are features embodied in the person of the artistic tramp figure. Like London and the writers before him, Davies speaks from the perspective of the tramp – who travels extensively back and forth across the Atlantic – to critique the poor laws and nascent welfare policies of his homeland. At the same time, Davies marks a turning point in this literary history to the extent that he disentangles the exceptionalism of the tramp from the Americanisms underlying the works of Twain, London and Flynt. As the pages below will elaborate, this innovation is essential for imagining the social problem of tramping as something that is at once distributed globally while also subject to the laws and practices of a given country. In other words, these exceptional vagrant figures – these super-tramps, to adapt Davies's coinage – appear more amenable to the nation state than observers during the nineteenth-century 'tramp scare' could have predicted.

The idea that vagrants can put their talents to work for the good of the country is the culmination of the legal-literary timeline established in this book's preceding chapter. The super-tramps that appear in both London and Davies are not exceptional in the same sense encountered in the pages of Twain and Flynt; they are exceptional because they represent the very best of their respective nation states. This emphasis is significant not only for tramping literature but for the larger social project of rehabilitating white vagrancy and, consequently, the social politics of the early welfare state. While Davies's writings engage with and rebut London, he leaves untroubled the essentialist logic that contrasts the highly mobile, invariably white tramp figure against subjects whose lack of mobility appears to be encoded into their very biology. To fully elaborate on the extent to which literary sources at nearly the same time equate the vagrant's exceptional talents with whiteness, this chapter also turns to a final case: Rudyard Kipling's novel *Kim*, which was published in 1901 to immediate fame. Kipling's vagabond protagonist is a white orphan who thrives in the dynamic cultural context of India but struggles to internalise the cultural identities that are imposed upon him. Throughout, Kipling characterises his vagrant hero by his exceptional mobility, which enables him to relay information to the colonial state about the inner workings of foreign places. As this last point suggests, Kipling's vagabond begins to resemble more an asset than a problem to the government. Read together, these contemporaneous sources all stress an image of white vagabondage that is both highly mobile across borders and, to different degrees, valuable for the workings of the state.

Ultimately, what emerges from these accounts is an image of the tramp-citizen, both exceptional in habits and wholly contained within the national fabric. Unlike Wordsworth's beggar, who remains ever outside the observer's comprehension, Davies's tramps are ready for incorporation into British social life. As this provocative phrasing suggests, the tramping model that circulates among London, Davies and Kipling easily adapts itself into the parlance of governance in the context of the social reforms occurring at the turn of the century. As is the case with *The American Vagrant in Literature* as a whole, this chapter in particular approaches this literary-historical timeline through the lens of Michel Foucault's work on the amplification of state power in the early twentieth century, especially in regard to the discourse of scientific racism he associates with the early twentieth century (*Society* 82). As I argue below, the fixation on racial and national distinctions that spans Davies, London and Kipling represents an emerging consensus regarding the superlative quality of the white vagrant type.

The language of demographic ordering and racial distinction that ties these sources together does not appear in isolation, but rather brings into view the ideological foundation upon which political actors would consolidate the state's regulatory power in both the US and the UK. In view of this intersection, the final pages of this chapter analyse the tramp-citizen template alongside the British government's welfare reforms of 1906, which included efforts to modernise state tools for rehabilitating vagrants. If Davies suggests that the status of tramps reflects on the environment that surrounds them, we should see the government's attempts at singling out vagrancy for reform as a signal of the state's interest in shaping the national health. To consider the discourse of tramping that travels from the US to Britain, then, by necessity broaches the question of where the line between culture and the state is drawn.

London and Davies: Making the Super-Tramp

By the time he arrived in the East End, Jack London was no stranger to poverty and homelessness. London wrote extensively in his lifetime of his own experiences tramping in the wake of the financial crises of the 1890s. When he again donned the guise of the tramp to conduct his observations for what would become *The People of the Abyss*, the conventions of tramp writing had already come into being. Most immediately, London's performance of the amateur tramp-ethnographer rehearses the role Flynt had established in the decade before. London himself makes clear this direct line of influence in *The Road*, his collection of tramping essays, which he dedicates to 'Josiah Flynt: The Real Thing, Blowed in the Glass'. The ethnographer's influence is elsewhere apparent in *The People of the Abyss*, which approaches tramping as a means for accessing the inner circles of social groups otherwise invisible to the more comfortable classes in society. London's vagabondage text stresses again the sense that the tramp-writer is uniquely or acutely empowered to connect the local, lived conditions of homelessness to the international materials that produce it. As these pages will demonstrate, London and contemporary tramp-writers pose the argument that to understand the social politics of poverty at home one must look to neighbouring examples. In this manner, these sources turn the tramp's exceptional mobility into less an enigma than a vehicle for revealing what they see as the bare facts of society, its people and its governing institutions.

The tramping narrative as described here generates social commentary by way of stressing differences and potential continuities between states vis-à-vis their treatment of vagrant groups. To be sure, London (unlike Flynt) is concerned in his writings with decrying all manner of social ills, not just those related to the criminality (and criminal laws) associated with vagrants. London himself identified as a socialist, and writings like *The People of the Abyss* were taken up by social reformers during his lifetime.[3] But as the reference to Flynt should also suggest, London's tramp abroad is concerned not only with the population he sees there, but but – in line with the emergent tramp subject outlined in the previous pages – the country he has left behind. Set against the backdrop of Edward VII's coronation, London observes the dramatic economic gap between the imperial nation's richest subjects and the squalor he sees everywhere apparent in communities in and around notoriously impoverished areas such as Whitechapel. At the same time, *The People of the Abyss* is interested as much in charting the author's subjectivity as it is in providing empirical accounts of poverty in the British slum. Most immediately, this dynamic is evident in the estranging language he uses to describe the urban poor he observes in London. In this setting, a 'new race has sprung up', he declares, 'a street people' (*People* 122). Elsewhere in the narrative he expands on the characteristics of this new race: 'At the bottom of the Abyss they are feeble, besotted, and imbecile', he notes. 'The work of the world goes on above them, and they do not care to take part in it, nor are they able' (*People* 20).

The setting of the British slum, complete with descriptions of its inhabitants, provides a crucial point of distinction for London's estimation of his home country. In his telling, the enfeebled underclass of Britain stands in contrast to the hearty people of the US – the nation 'out West' where exceptional subjects like him thrive. 'I thought of my own spacious West', he declares, 'with room under its sky and unlimited air for a thousand Londons' (*People* 16). Here, the vast spaces of the US connote a freedom of movement that contrasts with the tight spaces hemming in London's urban squalor. This contrast is especially clear in his description of the spike, the workhouse casual wards that housed the country's vagrant population on a per diem basis. 'Several men in the line had been to the United States, and were wishing that they had remained there', London explains. 'England had become a prison to them, a prison from which there was no hope of escape. It was impossible to escape . . . The country was too overrun by poor devils on the "lay"' (*People* 48). As before, London is careful to delineate a specific breed of 'English hardship', one born of a mix of institutional oppression and social degeneracy (*People* 48). As these cases already suggest, the American scene of boundlessness and mobility provides for London the standard against which British society is to be judged.

The abiding contrasts London poses in his text – between the US and the UK as well as between himself and the foreign poor he observes – underscores the extent to which the American tramp is, in this text, synonymous with the kind of normalising subjectivity that belies the figure's embodiment of exceptional poverty. For London, the British poor 'reminded me of gorillas . . . The slum is their jungle, and they live and prey in the jungle' (*People* 151). As noted above, the essential difference already so vividly on display here assumes a more explicitly racialised form elsewhere in the text. 'The streets were filled with a new and different race of people', he continues, 'short of stature, and of wretched or beer-sodden appearance' (*People* 3). In these instances, London comes across less as a tramp among the downtrodden than a settler in colonial territories. Mark Pittenger's account of undercover narratives – a genre which London's text exemplifies – finds parallels between this passage and other investigative writers of the time, who frequently presented the poor in terms that invoked tropes of primitivism. Even authors nominally sympathetic with the poor, Pittenger points out, tended to assert the fundamental distance between themselves and the people they observed (32). By conflating race and class, even implicitly, such literature posed 'a perception of unbridgeable difference' between a white middle class and the racially ambiguous underclasses (Pittenger 34). The mixed messaging here also extends across London's work as a whole, which tends to disdain elitism while also advocating for the racial superiority of whites (Paul 27). At the same time, it is worth elaborating on how London's performance of tramping in *The People of the Abyss* extends beyond his own vexed politics to a larger turn in tramp writing towards a logic of demographic sorting based on race. In other words, it is not the case that London looks down on the British poor *despite* his own connection to tramping but rather *because* of it.

The dehumanising terms that appear in London's text extend from his own sense of the American tramp's inherent superiority, a position he embodies in his narrative. When he dons the costume of the tramp early in his travels, for example, London notes how he is immediately accepted by the slum's population as a fellow resident, albeit an exceptional one, of their community:

> No sooner was I out on the streets than I was impressed by the difference in status effected by my clothes. All servility vanished from the demeanour of the common people with whom I came in contact. Presto! In the twinkling of an eye, so to say, I had become one of them. (*People* 6)

London's seamless transformation stresses his own mobility from the centre to the margins of society as well of the versatility of the tramp character. In spite of the initial distance between himself and his strange subjects, he is confident in his ability to move in and among this foreign population. For his part, London sees this transformation as a liberating gesture in more ways than one. Most immediately, he explains, it affords him a way of travel through Britain that is not open to 'the average American abroad' (*People* 7). The panhandlers who otherwise treat the American tourist as a hapless mark now treat him as one of their own. This fraternal form of association allows London further benefits as an author as well. 'For the first time I met the English lower classes face to face', he writes, 'and knew them for what they were' (*People* 7). By adopting the specific guise of the tramp, London not only details the conditions of poverty in Britain but, in his telling, gains insight into the essential character of the people who reside there.

Given the chronology around tramping developed thus far in *The American Vagrant in Literature*, London's specific presentation of the American tramp should appear in many respects to extend the tramping discourse from previous cases. He is a keen social observer, remarking on the lives of others from society's margins. The tramp is also a restless traveller, moving across continents and overseas without apparent difficulty. This skillset, as displayed in sources from Twain and Flynt to London, makes tramps appear less a threat to society than a potential asset – insofar as they evaluate social problems in one context against a larger, international backdrop of states and communities dealing with the same problem. At the same time, London expands on this exceptional framing of the tramp figure in a manner that exceeds what appears in the work of predecessors such as Flynt. In *The People of the Abyss*, the tramp embodies something like the very best of the entire nation. Along these lines, London holds up the few Americans he encounters in the foreign slum as paradigms of virtue in comparison with their British counterparts. Indeed, London refers to these American 'tramps royal' as the archetypes for vagabonds 'whose mate is the wind that tramps the world' (*People* 66). London's valorisation of these Americans is palpable in his narrative: 'They were all cheerful, facing things with the pluck which is their chief characteristic', he observes, 'withal they were cursing the country with lurid metaphors quite refreshing after a month of unimaginative, monotonous Cockney swearing' (*People* 66). In this instance, London presents what he stresses is an uniquely American form of vagabondage that rearticulates from the margins a version of American exceptionalism. While his text expresses concern for the plight of the poor in Britain, it nonetheless implies that their suffering is, to a certain extent, the result of deficient characteristics that map onto physical or biological differences.

Implicit in London's depiction of the tramps royal is the sense that vagrants' superlative abilities are nurtured by – and reflected in – specific social systems. London thus valorises both his tramping and the Americans tramps he encounters abroad in terms that stress their staunch individualism. Their quick wits and 'pluck', he argues, are especially evident in contrast to the 'unimaginative' British vagrant. From this basis of comparison, London expounds on the political system that these vagrants represent:

> In the United States the tramp is almost invariably a discouraged worker. He finds tramping a softer mode of life than working. But this is not true in England. Here the powers that be do their utmost to discourage the tramp and vagabond, and he is, in all truth, a mightily discouraged creature. (*People* 104)

In London's telling, the divergent incarnations of the tramp between the US and UK bring into focus the governing institutions in each respective society. According to London, the lack of tramps royal in England points to a larger problem in the way 'the powers that be' govern their subjects. In this formulation, tramps signify a basic rejection of oppressive governing practices on behalf of the country's poor. No surprise, then, that London sees the British street people – no tramps royal among them – as 'mental, physical, and moral wrecks' (*People* 104). While he takes pains in the preceding passage to identify 'the powers that be' as the engine of this degeneracy, he nonetheless represents these paupers in thoroughly demeaning terms.

As the reference to 'moral wrecks' further underscores, London relates the relative integrity of the white vagrant subject to the overall 'moral' health of the society that produced him. While London applies this metric to extol the American tramp in relation to his British equivalent, his contemporary, W. H. Davies, reimagines a version of it in his tramping memoir from a distinctly British perspective. An archetype of the literary success of vagabond writers in Britain, Davies made the transition from real-life tramp to literary sensation after the publication of *The Autobiography of a Super-Tramp* in 1908 (Howarth, *British Poetry* 141). In its form, Davies's narrative stays close to the conventional structure of the autobiography: he relates in detail his place of birth, his family and his early years before recollecting his first tramping expedition. His use of the autobiographical form, in particular, highlights the extent to which the literary roots of the vagrant figure have become reified in non-fiction prose: his memoir presents even the most stereotypical aspects of the tramp as a matter of fact, even as it participates in the literary discourse that romanticises tramping. Along these lines, the hobo memoir – while ostensibly celebrating the autonomy of the tramping subject – places vagrancy closer to hegemonic social discourse. In this case, Davies uses the generic conventions of autobiography, whose celebration of self-actualising individualism reflects the governing discourse of Western liberal states.[4] On this basis, Davies stresses the aspects of vagrancy that nurture self-actualising subjects under the aegis of the civil sphere. At once, he propagates an idealised picture of the tramp while also providing a sociological depiction of sorts of the way vagrants as a population live.[5]

Presenting himself as the definitive (British) tramp in America, Davies reiterates the comparative logic encoded in vagrancy narratives while also reversing the trajectory of previous vagrancy writers such as Flynt and, most prominently for Davies, London. The presentation of the US as a setting where the characteristics associated with tramping thrive – expressions of autonomy, masculinity and individualism – establishes the discursive points that connect these sources. In all the vagrancy writers considered thus far in *The American Vagrant in Literature*, the tramp is an adept reader of national types. Implicit in cases from the nineteenth century, this convention comes to the foreground of Davies's work. In his autobiography, tramping's insight into cultural norms is always apparent; tramping abroad is important not only because it allows him to escape from the confines of wage labour, but also because it gives him the chance to test his social upbringing against foreign examples, most notably in the context of the US.

Before elaborating on the racial subtext to the vagrancy discourse linking Davies to London, it is necessary first to situate Davies's writing among the American tradition of tramp-writers. Early in his memoir, Davies hears tales of life in the US from a traveller in Liverpool. The traveller's retelling immediately draws on conventional images of the boundless opportunities associated with American society and the imagined American landscape:

> In him I placed implicit confidence, and received such an extraordinary description of that country, the number of stories of some of its highest buildings which were called skyscrapers; the houses of wood which could be moved from one street to another without in any way interfering with the comfort of the people within, cooking, sweeping and washing going on without hindrance; the loneliness of its prairies and deserts; engineering triumphs over high mountains; and how the glorious South was flushed with roses what time the North could not

save a blade of green from the snow; all this happening under the one wide spreading flag. (*Autobiography* 20)

On one level, the description of the US that Davies offers here rehashes the fantasy a traveller abroad might associate with the American frontier at the turn of the century – namely, an expansive geography populated with a people 'naturally proud of their country' (*Autobiography* 22).[6] An outside observer of American culture, Davies retreads familiar ground. For instance, he revisits the cultural insights that Alexis de Tocqueville had offered in *Democracy in America*, published in the first half of the nineteenth century. But unlike Tocqueville's voluminous first-hand account, Davies's representation of American exceptionalism derives tenuously from hearsay and rumour – a fact that he makes clear. From the earliest pages of the memoir, Davies already undergirds the image of the exceptional tramp with the type of conventional imagery that the 'extraordinary description' of America represents. The intersection suggests that Davies is interested in delineating his tramp persona in terms that, while stressing his exceptional abilities, are thoroughly familiar to his readers.

As this last point suggests, Davies's 'Super-Tramp' persona intersects the extraordinary with the commonplace. As was the case with the narrator in Twain's *A Tramp Abroad*, Davies's text traffics in conventional wisdom. At the same time, Davies carefully highlights his own creative agency in the proliferation of these cultural norms. In the role of the author, he reproduces in his autobiography the same kind of persuasive storytelling that initially captured his imagination back in Liverpool. In view of this authorial position, one begins to see the extent to which his figuration of the North American landscape reflects primarily his own craft as a storyteller. Davies makes this notion of artistry especially clear in his frequent descriptions of his natural surroundings:

> What a glorious time of year is this! With the warm sun travelling through serene skies, the air clear and fresh above you, which instils new blood in the body, making one defiantly tramp the earth, kicking the snows aside in the scorn of action. The cheeks glow with health, the lips smile, and there is no careworn face seen, save they come out of the house of sickness of death. And that lean spectre, called Hunger, has never been known to appear in these parts. (*Autobiography* 152)

Recalling the initial tale of American abundance, this scene celebrates both open expanses and the individualism these landscapes seemingly engender. But even as Davies celebrates his freedom to 'tramp the earth', the narrative structure of his memoir indicates that this lifestyle is far from self-sustaining (*Autobiography* 152). Rather, Davies must riff on the well-worn conjectures regarding opportunities in North America not only to praise tramping but in order to talk about poverty in Britain as well.

In other words, the rhetorical viability of the US as the primary setting for vagabondage depends on the juxtaposition of these scenes to life back home. The 'spectre' of hunger, Davies goes on to explain, is absent in America but is 'often seen in the overcrowded cities of Europe' – and especially in 'the Thames Embankment, in front of the fine hotels where ambassadors and millionaires dine sumptuously' (*Autobiography* 152). The social critique in Davies's writing is most apparent in scenes such this one, where his presentation of an idyllic US ultimately brings into focus a picture of a dysfunctional British social system. As this passage also makes clear, the generalised description of his travels abroad – 'warm sun', 'serene skies' – stands in direct contrast to the specificity of his allusion to the social inequality of the Thames Embankment and the specific order of people who populate that space. In both cases, Davies and London refer to the land 'out West' (London, *People* 16) in order to discern the specific injustices that attend poverty in England.

More than a simple reverence, the shared allusion to the US in the works of London and Davies creates in each case a metric for evaluating the societies through which tramps travel. While Davies has not typically been read alongside the naturalist movement so closely associated with Jack London, his depiction of a crowded and malnourished European urban space evinces a similar frame of reference about the poor.[7] On the one hand, abysmal working conditions and unclean slums generate an enfeebling despair that is difficult to escape. On the other hand, the exceptional figure of the white vagabond – who escapes from this misery by means of his so-called natural talents – stands in contrast to the multitude of people who remain seemingly fixed in place.[8]

By replicating this tension, Davies's narrative also intersects with debates at the time over the role of governance in dealing with the problem of the urban poor. Gavin Jones's overview of poverty in American literature explains that even sympathetic accounts of the poor near the turn of the century suspected members of this social group of an 'inborn pauperism' (83). According to this reasoning, those who toil in the underclasses are unequipped to climb the social ladder, owing not only to systemic inequality but to their own physical or biological deficiencies. On the surface, Davies does not contend with the underlying assumption that links social undesirables to physical weakness; rather, he makes full use of this reasoning to present the tramp as a healthy and therefore socially productive figure. In this case, Davies characterises the US in terms of what it lacks: its unpopulated vistas and uncrowded cities ensure, in his telling, that able-bodied subjects can sustain themselves. Even as he compares this situation unfavourably with what exists in Britain, he makes the case for seeing environmental factors as a determinant of social character. At the same time, his defiant tramp can remove himself from his deleterious environment and, in doing so, can report on what he finds abroad back to an audience of curious readers. In short, Davies's concern for the plight of the poor back home rests alongside his superlative rendering of the tramp as a singular figure distinct from this mass of impoverished people.

This narrative framework, which intersects a staunch individualism with a concern for social types, generates further insight into matters of state administration as well. On the subject of begging in the US, for example, Davies quickly takes his England to task for its ineffective welfare policies. In an address to 'Brum', his American tramping companion, Davies exhorts the generosity of his adopted social sphere with an eye to his British audience:

> 'Ah,' I said to Brum, as we sat in a shady place, eating a large custard pudding from a boarding house, using for the purpose two self-made spoons of wood – 'Ah, we would not be so pleasantly occupied as tramps in England. We would there receive tickets for soup; soup that could be taken without spoons; no sign of a pea, onion, or carrot; no sign of anything, except flies.' (*Autobiography* 30)

Here and elsewhere in the text, Davies offers an explicit critique of British policy in regard to its homeless population in particular and its class structure in general.[9] In this light, his observation subtly conflates England as a nation with the more material aspects of the British state's regulatory institutions. In contrast to the expansive US, British society operates according to the metonymic image of the meal ticket, as well as the 'blind alleys' and 'quiet courts' that Davies describes elsewhere in the book (*Autobiography* 32). In addition, Davies uses this instance of charity to stake out an ethical position in relation to institutionalised welfare in Britain. The direct object of Davies's ire in the scene above is less the lamentable soup and more the British system of exchange – embodied by the ticket – that regulates the tramp's labour. If begging constitutes a 'fine art' in Davies's eyes, then the substitution of the ticket for the meal reflects an undue mediation of the artist's craft (*Autobiography* 24). Through a sustained contrast with an idealised US, the narrative presents an idea of British society whose regulatory power imposes an undue burden on the vagrant subject. If Davies exhorts the powers of the tramp, he further suggests that these powers work for the common good – both in the sense that his text informs a readership eager to learn more about tramps in general as well as in his specific critique of British poverty. His scrutiny of social politics in the latter case appeals to the individualism of the tramp and, more implicitly, the tramp's ability to participate in the social and economic exchanges at the centre of the polity. Along these lines, Davies's text begins to bridge the gap between the tramp as a subject of policy and the tramp as an enabler of reform.

Kipling on Whiteness and Exceptional Vagrancy

For both London and Davies, the other side of the Atlantic provided an estranging lens for viewing their respective countries' own social fringes. Their individual texts aimed to rouse their readers from their complacent acceptance of widespread poverty at home by identifying the institutions (such as counterproductive legal codes and social practices) that allowed poverty to persist. In spite of the humanistic appeal of these texts, however, their comparative frameworks have the effect of reinforcing an ultimately nationalist perspective in which the mores of home become the standard against which foreign societies are measured. This embedded nationalism should come as little surprise given the imperialist imagination that characterised much of anglophone travel writing during the nineteenth and early twentieth centuries.[10] Inasmuch as their overseas tramping narratives borrow from and intersect with the genre of travel writing, London and Davies extend the form's underlying hegemonic imagination. As the previous pages have argued, this process is evident in the prolific use of regional stereotypes in these narratives. The representation of each country – along with its respective class of vagrants and homeless – is in part a construction born of each author's preconceived notions about how their overseas counterparts live. Both authors thus contribute to a long-standing discourse concerning national differences, even as they traverse national boundaries.

At the same time, to view the comparative framework in these texts primarily as expressions of the nationalism often latent in travel writing overlooks the more complex social politics associated with white vagabondage, a discourse to which both London and Davies contribute. The tramp's international mobility brings into focus in both cases the relative strengths (as they perceive them) of certain social practices (as mapped onto national or racial distinctions) in comparison with foreign examples. The apparent and growing disconnect between the transatlantic circulation of ideas regarding homelessness and social politics and the entrenched nationalism that already registers in the implicit dialogue between the two authors will become more apparent in the chapters that follow. In the meantime, it is worth stressing the extent to which London and Davies draw from, and further develop, the concept of social value that is interconnected with the tramp's expression of racial and national characteristics in the narratives of both authors.

In order to best scrutinise the specific figuration of white vagrancy that appears in these latter presentations of the superlative tramp, one needs to look beyond authors working explicitly on the figure of the tramp to other, familiar British literary sources. These influences are especially apparent in *The People of the Abyss*, wherein London invokes Charles Dickens when he self-consciously imagines himself playing the role of 'Oliver Twist when he asked for more' (*People* 12). The most prevalent literary presence in London's text is, however, Rudyard Kipling, whose writing colours London's presentation of both the urban poor and his exceptional tramps royal. For instance, in describing a workhouse labourer, London refers explicitly to an 1890 poem by Kipling, noting, 'his was the unmistakable sea face and eyes; and at once there came to me a bit of Kipling's "Galley-Slave"' (*People* 33). This allusion to Kipling is far from anomalous in London's work. Indeed, the press at the time marketed London as the 'Kipling of the Klondike' – a recognition of Kipling's status as the paradigmatic journalist-cum-novelist at the turn of the century (Glass 86).[11]

Kipling's prominent place in London's imagination also touches on issues of whiteness and masculinity – two features inseparable from the popular figuration of tramping. London elsewhere makes his interest in Kipling's depiction of whiteness explicit in 'These Bones Shall Rise Again', his essay vigorously praising Kipling's work. Written as a eulogy of the older British author – who would in fact outlive London by many years – the essay celebrates the triumph of the 'Anglo-Saxon' and names Kipling as the chronicler of 'the war march of the white man round the world' ('These' 72). Subsequent criticism is adamant that London in fact misreads Kipling, making him 'the mouthpiece of his own Anglo-Saxon racism' (Sinclair 74). Nevertheless, London's essay is useful for highlighting how the author understood Kipling and, more to the point, how this form of literary appropriation resonates across London's influential imagination of tramping. According to London, the so-called Anglo-Saxon race is defined by a competing impulse between acts of violence and domination, on the one hand, and an inclination to labour and organisation, on the other. According to London, Kipling's writings prove that the 'Anglo-Saxon' is 'a pirate, a land robber and a sea robber' and also 'a master of matter' and 'an administrator of justice' ('These' 68, 69). What emerges from London's account of Kipling is a specific concept of ethnic exceptionalism that is at once rugged, defiant and committed to succeeding at work – in whatever form work takes. As this last point implies, Kipling already contributes to the discourse of tramping at least by way of London, who makes him a frequent touchstone in his own vagabondage narratives.

Yet Kipling himself elaborates the subject of white vagabondage directly. To consider Kipling's own work alongside that of London and Davies reveals a substantial overlap in all three authors' presentation of white vagabondage at the turn of the century. The extraordinary adaptability that London and Davies associate with tramping finds a particularly strong parallel in Kipling's popular novel *Kim*. Published serially before appearing in novelised form in 1901, Kipling's text elaborates on the larger discursive construction of white vagrancy among anglophone sources at the turn of the century. The novel's titular protagonist is an Irish orphan whose adventures in British India make apparent his extraordinary ability to adapt to his surroundings. Kim's adept movement within and among the diverse populations of India makes him a useful companion and agent for various social actors in the novel, from a local horse trader to a Tibetan lama – and eventually, the British colonial government. In this last role, Kim trains as a spy to protect British interests against Russian incursions on the subcontinent, turning the adaptability he first honed as a vagabond into a governmental asset.

Kipling's last and most famous novel, *Kim* is a prominent example of literary fiction picking up the discursive threads of vagabondage once observed, as the previous chapter demonstrated, in the fields of ethnography and autobiography. In each case, the vagabond's fluid mobility is an expression of liberal autonomy most at home in democratic societies. As noted above, the US plays this role for Davies and London alike. For Kipling, this mobility is found among India's diverse social and racial groupings, a setting the narrative describes as 'the only democratic land in the world' (3). Against this idealised picture of British India, Kipling's novel renders its protagonist's vagabondage in terms of autonomy and fluidity. For many critics, Kim's exceptional mobility is the clearest reflection of the novel's thoroughly colonialist ideology. Edward Said, to name the most prominent example, calls the very scenario at the centre of the novel – a white character effectively passing among non-white subjects in India – a 'fantasy' inseparable from British imperialism (161).

Although the imperialist framing of *Kim* has been the subject of extensive criticism, the novel's contributions to the discourse of white vagrancy warrant further elaboration.[12] As noted above, Kim's exceptional mobility equips him to observe (and in effect, spy on) the people of the subcontinent and relay the information he gathers back to the British government. Moreover, Kim thrives in spite of his poverty, owing to his racial, ethnic and social flexibility: he 'was white', the narrative tells us, but he is nonetheless 'burned black as any native' (1). Kim's whiteness is the engine for his dramatic displays of intrigue and espionage. As Judith Plotz points out, '[s]o flexible are the boundaries of Kim's identity . . . that he seems to don a new consciousness with each set of new clothes' (113). By reframing *Kim* as a novel about white vagabondage in addition to British imperialism, I am stressing the text's reproducible imagination: Kim is both a singular hero and, as Said argues, an expression of a much larger collective fantasy. In other words, the intersection of ethnic exceptionalism, mobility and nationalism is not unique to Kim but characteristic, the novel suggests, of an entire demographic. As a British mentor in the novel puts it, Kim is but one of a breed of men 'who have a lust to go abroad at the risk of their lives and discover news' (129). In this role, Kim directly contributes to British efforts to disrupt Russian encroachment upon their colonial sphere of influence, 'The Great Game' that provides the novel's backdrop. In this context, Kim's tramping sensibilities – chief among them, his ability to surveil and mimic local customs – make him a valuable resource for the colonial state.

This elaboration on the specific understanding of white vagabondage in Kipling's novel gestures to the wider literary and cultural contributions to the shifting discourse on vagabondage at the turn of the century.[13] By reading *Kim* alongside non-fictional and autobiographical texts by London and Davies, I mean not to elide the formal differences between these works but to stress their shared consensus regarding the racial features of exceptional forms of tramp mobility. At the same time, the transition from the novel to nominally non-fictional texts involves a less dramatic shift than one might otherwise suppose.¹⁴ Rather, the tramping memoir is emblematic of the intersecting lines of influence between these genres by the time Davies and London are writing. London himself is a high-profile example of the push to incorporate features associated with literary realism into journalistic reporting as well. Indeed, London and like-minded authors worked to broaden the scope of literature by blurring the lines between the artist and the journalist (Roggenkamp 23).

In view of Kipling's novel, the wider cultural discourse informing London's presentation of vagrancy comes into focus. Like Kipling's young protagonist, London stresses adaptability as the defining feature of the tramp's exceptional vagrancy. The notion of creativity implicit in this identity informs his idea of authorship as well. At once, he moves among the British poor while also reporting the news (as the novel puts it) that he finds there. If Kipling's novel looks for common ground between the cultures it depicts, London's text reinforces the cultural divide between the observer and his surroundings. London's presentation of Kipling-esque tramps royal as uniquely American in *The People of the Abyss* is the most obvious reflection of this division. But while much of this chapter has focused on London's apparent debt to Kipling, the concept of the white vagrant's exceptional mobility, as well its potential usefulness for the nation state, is best articulated by Davies. After all, Davies acknowledges in his writings that he is not interested in identifying which tramps are the absolute best, as it were, at tramping. Instead, he is interested in how different national types of tramps fare on the road, an observation he argues provides insight into the overall national character of their respective homelands. In this sense, Davies articulates a demographic ordering of vagrants that, while paying homage to the exceptional qualities one observes in vagrancy texts by Kipling and London, anticipates more directly one of the questions that early welfare governments would consider – namely, how can we make the claims and responsibilities of a given nation state become incumbent upon highly mobile and autonomous subjects?

Distinguishing Modern Vagrancy: Literature and British Welfare

The preceding pages have argued that the archetype of the white vagabond that appears across fiction and non-fiction texts in the first decade of the twentieth century derives from a geopolitical context that spans both the United States and the United Kingdom, along with other countries in the industrialised West. But to read these sources together is not meant to elide the different political exigencies between these states. By the end of the nineteenth century, the American rail system provided the means for tramps to move across the continent and between industrial urban centres (Monteiro 61). For American readers in particular, literary accounts of tramping connected the particular economic hardships in the US at the time to the genre of the American 'road' narrative (Tichi 21). In the context of Britain, tramps spoke to a similarly industrialised landscape but to a distinct history of literary tradition and economic development. Since the Industrial Revolution in the eighteenth century, a significant portion of Britain's population had migrated from rural to urban areas. This trend only intensified in the last decades of the nineteenth century, which expanded the industrial economy and urban centres at the cost of a dwindling agrarian population (B. Harris 115). Moreover, the prolonged economic crises of the 1870s and 1880s had lasting effects in Britain as well as in the US. By the first years of the twentieth century, the combination of rural influx followed by decades of boom-and-bust markets had left urban centres like London with a sizeable population of people unemployed, impoverished or homeless (Englander 27).

It is important to reiterate this economic context to distinguish the cultural or literary discourse around the white tramp from the anti-tramp sentiment prevailing on both sides of the Atlantic. As these pages have argued, the emphasis on distinction in these narratives – on this vagrant figure's exceptional embodiment of whiteness, mobility and adaptability – parallels the growing consensus across industrialised states on the need to distinguish the so-called deserving from undeserving poor for the purposes of providing welfare relief. For legislators during the reform years of the early twentieth century, the tramp was the limit case for imagining how such demographic sorting might work.

The British government, for example, endeavoured to separate vagrants from the general unemployed population as part of its efforts to create manageable categories for welfare assistance. Parliamentary committees at the beginning of the century understood vagrancy as an 'elastic' category, in which the unemployed but otherwise 'bona fide working man' coexisted with the 'habitual vagrant, the man who professes to be in search of work but . . . has no desire to find it' (Departmental Committee on Vagrancy 24).[15] In spite of this demographic category's potential breadth, the defining feature of the vagrant in the public eye hinged on his refusal to engage in productive labour at all costs. This understanding of the tramp is key to the popular reaction against this underclass at large in Britain: vagrants who had no settled domicile and subsisted on workhouse relief were 'the lowest of the low' and 'beyond redemption', existing in 'a borderland between indigence and criminality' (Englander 33). If the economically secure classes balked at supporting the urban homeless in general, vagrants in particular were associated with the most abject and incorrigible of all who received poverty relief. As a result, vagrants faced much more repressive conditions within state-sponsored workhouses than any other demographic group from within the large population of the urban poor (Englander 32). But even while Britons associated this group with the worst of human behaviour, the demographic continued to grow. After a century of rapid industrial expansion, the extant laws meant to govern the distribution of relief to the country's unemployed could no longer address the needs of the poor without considerable reform (Englander 2–3).

Against the backdrop of the tramp's vilification in the public eye, governing institutions began in earnest to consolidate their regulatory powers on a national scale. In general terms, the turn of the century was marked by the transition from the laissez-faire economic policy of the industrial era to a period of greater state intervention and social collectivism (B. Harris 150). While this economic turn influenced states on both sides of the Atlantic, the British system looked for methods of nurturing its distinct system of social welfare. With the election of the Liberal Party to government in 1906, reforms targeting poverty, healthcare and education began in earnest to supplement alms-giving laws in effect since the Tudor era. The legislation most subject to revision over this time, the English Poor Laws, had for centuries placed the onus of welfare relief on local communities. In particular, the 1834 Poor Law Amendment Act produced the most visible aspects of welfare relief in Britain prior to the rise of the welfare state in the twentieth century. According to this piece of legislation, paupers were by definition a local problem; in response, the legislation mandated that each parish maintain workhouses staffed with permanent employees and governed by a regulatory board of guardians (Englander 13). By the twentieth century, the workhouse had therefore become the most visible sign of the British government's efforts to control unemployment in general and vagrancy in particular. However, these workhouses were governed on the assumption that vagrants would continue to reside in a given local community. Instead, the modern tramp – highly mobile, yet bereft of the resources valuable to an industrialised economy – posed a problem that legislation after centuries of precedent was ill-equipped to resolve.

If regulatory institutions struggled to identify and track the movements of vagrants as they traversed state lines, tramp narratives like those of Davies and London provided for a way of thinking about vagabondage and nationalism as mutually compatible. London's account of the exceptional American tramp as a figure that shines even among the perceived gloom of the British slum provides the most immediate point of departure for Davies's own celebration of British vagabondage. Davies presents a distinctly British breed of tramps that nonetheless internalise the autonomy that London's account had denied them. Davies therefore takes up the notion, present in London's work, that successful tramps are a measure of a nation's social strength. On this note, Davies opens *Beggars*, the sequel to his popular memoir, with an explicit meditation on the subject:

> There is no question but that the American beggar is the finest in his country; but in that land of many nationalities he has a number of old-country beggars to contend with. Perhaps it would interest – it certainly should – a number of people to know how well or ill their own nation is represented by beggars in that most important country. (1)

While continuing to pay homage to the convention of US exceptionalism, Davies provides room for Britons to assert their individualism through vagabondage. As is the case in his autobiography, here Davies uses an idealised US as a means for considering the strength of British subjects. In the face of the example set by Americans, Davies concludes, the English 'easily come next ... especially when England is represented by the Cockney' (*Beggars* 6). The strengths of this vagrant form, he goes on to explain, derive from his command over forms of expression:

> He will often attain his ends after failing in a cross-examination and discovered in a lie; for his witty excuses and peculiar manner of expression are not to be resisted by Americans ... The Cockney – and he alone – is admired by those extraordinary beggars who are born Americans, and who are conceited enough to think that they could by their energies live as well as beggars in the poorest slums in the cities of Europe. (*Beggars* 6–7)

As the passage makes especially clear, Davies sees the cockney's imaginative form of vagabondage as a point of pride for English society at large. Like London, Davies points to the tramp's ability to express himself as the key indicator of his individual agency. Where London sees 'unimaginative, monotonous' speech, Davies describes 'witty excuses' and a 'peculiar manner of expression' that confound Americans with ease (*Beggars* 6). The gulf between the authors on this point further underscores the subjective form of description that appears in both sources. The tramp is a potent representation of his native country for Davies as well as for London. Furthermore, both authors see the distinctions between American and British forms of tramping as particularly useful in delineating the differences between these societies writ large. But the two authors nonetheless differ dramatically in their description of the British tramp's agency in this context, even as both appeal to first-hand accounts in their narratives.

In this light, Davies's memoir substantiates and defends the figure of the British tramp within a political system that suffered from an inability to control this population. For many, vagrancy posed a threat that could only be addressed by reforming and strengthening police and welfare institutions. In London, swelling populations of 'loafers', a catch-all term describing petty criminals and idlers, meant that even affluent residents of the city could not ignore the underclasses, who were associated with the threat of wanton violence (Robinson 134). For social observers at the time, such threats warranted extreme measures. In 1904, for example, a departmental committee recommended that the entire population of vagrants be rounded up and transferred to police control (Englander 33). Along similar lines, British author William Harbutt Dawson proposed in his 1910 text *The Vagrancy Problem* to use all levers of government to eliminate the vagrant population altogether. Dawson writes, 'The leading contention here advanced is that society is justified, in its own interest, in legislating the loafer out of existence, if legislation can be shown to be equal to the task' (ix). Acknowledging the limitations of the workhouse system up to this point, Dawson advocates for a more repressive state that would target the few for the benefit of society as a whole. Dawson's allusion to a society 'justified' in taking violent action foregrounds the central anxiety within the British polity concerning not only vagrancy but also population control. Vagrants served along these lines as a poignant reminder to state authorities of the existing limitations to any attempt to manage the lives of all British citizens.

In response, regulatory bodies in the wake of the Liberal election promised to turn the tide in the state's fight against vagrancy. Most immediately, these new officials proposed a systematic overhaul of the workhouse system. A Departmental Committee commissioned by Parliament in 1906 promised to offer – in the words of member William Chance – a 'thoroughly scientific manner' of addressing the country's vagrancy problem (Chance 1). First and foremost, the committee's report recognised vagrancy as a national issue in need of a truly nationalised framework of state-run institutions. Chance explains in his review of the committee's findings that the failure of the old system was a result of the 'most extraordinary variety of practice' among the local parish workhouses (6). The British state must take a more active role in the administration of these institutions, the committee reasoned, rather than leaving this power to a patchwork of small governing bodies. The reforms the committee proposed therefore focused on bringing state disciplinary powers into closer proximity to the movements of the vagrant class: placing labour colonies under the direction of the police as well as introducing a documentation system consisting of a 'way-ticket' (issued by the police) that contained the identity and itinerary of each person who passed through the casual wards (Departmental Committee on Vagrancy 44).[16] The Departmental Committee's findings emphatically forecast the direction that the British state would take in dealing with vagrants, the population that up to this point had overwhelmed its patchwork welfare system. Rather than cast these citizens out of civil life, the state would take measures to put vagrants into full view of British authorities. Long the bane of local welfare institutions, the vagrant illustrated to the state at large the need to consolidate its regulatory power.

Given these governmental efforts to eliminate vagrancy, the claim that tramp-writers like Davies articulated a rationale for the expansion of state power may seem surprising. The fixation on demographic categories, national archetypes and, to different degrees, racial superiority that extends across these writers nonetheless underscores how their narratives intersect with this governing discourse. Furthermore, Foucault's relation of race theory to state power in the twentieth century provides another large-scale view of these historical developments. According to Foucault, racist discourse prior to the nineteenth century largely revolved around political or dynastic conflicts that were then superimposed onto pre-existing geographical, linguistic or religious differences. By the end of the nineteenth century, however, the preponderance of biological arguments after Darwin as a means for explaining social difference changes this dynamic. Rather than antagonism between two warring groups, the discourse of 'race struggle' is preoccupied with the danger of racial contamination and looks to the state to uphold racial purity (Foucault, *Society* 81). The intersection between scientific racism and reform movements of the nineteenth century – as evident in the Progressive Era in the US, as the previous chapter explained – encouraged the public to defend itself from domestic threats that imperilled the country's biological or ethno-national integrity. As Thomas Lemke points out, this configuration of race meant that social distinctions were 'matters of accident more than substance', bringing forward the underbelly of a society (such as foreigners and social deviants) as the pre-eminent threat to society itself (230).

The emergence of race-struggle discourse not only unfolds alongside the appearance of the tramp, it helps clarify how examples of tramping literature – a genre that nominally celebrates freedom from social conventions and national borders – nonetheless reiterate distinctions based on racial and national differences. In cases such as London and Davies, tramping and vagabondage provides one with an ideal view to evaluate nations based on how well their respective tramp types thrive. Moreover, the social Darwinism that Foucault alludes to in his account of state racism is especially evident in London's comparative reading of the American and British underclasses. The fact that, in London's eyes, individual American tramps innovate while the British poor waste away signals not only a social difference but a biological one as well – hence the language of dullness in London's description of the latter. To be sure, London wrote *The People of the Abyss* to bring attention to the plight of the poor and bring shame on the powers that generate poverty in the UK. By reading London alongside Davies and Kipling, however, we not only see an emerging literary consensus regarding the superlative quality of the white male tramp; we also see how this consensus facilitates the process of demographic ordering or distinction-making that is central to the operation of the modern state as it enters the twentieth century.

Anticipating Modern Vagrancy in the Twentieth Century

To return to the point that opened this chapter, neither Davies nor his contemporaries were the first to depict vagabond types as worthy of greater public interest. But although Romantic poets such as Wordsworth celebrated the freedom that vagabondage symbolises, they were less inclined to represent vagrants as more than the objects of art. Given this literary history, the appearance of the tramp-writer near the turn of the century indicates at a minimum a literary transition from the abstract vagrants who had decades earlier populated Romantic poetry. For unlike his Romantic predecessors, Davies literally embodies the kind of vagrancy that writers like Wordsworth had wished only to internalise. In texts such as *The Autobiography of a Super-Tramp* and London's *People of the Abyss* the vagrant is more than the figurative representative of the artist. Here the artist and the tramp are not analogous but are one and the same.

This chapter has elucidated a moment of transition in the literary history of tramping and, more broadly, the politico-legal history of vagrancy. This transition involved an international network of sources that, while not working in official collaboration, nonetheless modernised the discourse of vagrancy. As I have argued above, the circulation and emulation of American tramping narratives within the UK helped familiarise readers across the Atlantic with the features of the modern tramp figure. These features, moreover, appear in the writings of London, Davies and even Kipling to be less antagonistic and more beneficial to the nation state – a strong contrast to the anti-tramp writings of criminal reformers of the time. By making the tramp something of a national hero – from London's American tramps royal to Davies's cockney tramps – these authors do more than defend vagrancy from criticism; they make the case for incorporating the tramp into the fabric of society in a manner that is ultimately amenable to more robust state systems of power. In other words, these texts all contribute to the sense that white vagabondage, long associated with an anti-modern subjectivity, has transformed into something new by the twentieth century. The exceptional tramps that populate these pages thus brush up against a larger question important for both writers and legislators of the day: to what extent are vagabonds, tramps and hobos the products of the modern world rather than outcasts from it? To recognise the tramp as part and parcel of modernity would – to paraphrase Foucault's axiom in *Discipline and Punish* – provide the framework for controlling and surveilling this population rather than exterminating it.

As I have argued, writers such as Davies assist with this project inasmuch as they refigure the internationalism associated with wandering tramps into expressions of national character. Indeed, Davies's overarching impulse, as he first makes clear in his memoir and then develops in *Beggars*, is to represent the English tramp as a wholly coherent subject position within the civil sphere. To reiterate the points raised above, this involves an appropriation of the tramping motif that writers such as London – himself retooling material from Kipling – would otherwise argue is unique to the American context. At this point, Davies effectively naturalises the archetypal tramp within a British context. Residing on the margins of society, he reasons, the tramp nonetheless demarcates local forms of identity that are otherwise invisible to the population at large. Accordingly, the tramp is a subject-citizen who participates fully in the polity, in spite of – and, indeed, owing to – his estranged relation to cultural norms.

By stressing a model of adaptability, the figuration of the tramp-writer in Davies and London effectively moves vagrancy into the orbit of the nascent welfare state. As the 1906 Departmental Committee promising 'scientific' reform argued, the state cannot hope to produce more effective measures of controlling the vagrant population so long as it fails to recognise vagrancy in its modern forms. Davies's works in particular further gesture to the historical dimensions of even the most archetypal examples of tramping in the British context. Indeed, his tramp takes shape in view of not only extant British sources but also emerging sources (such as Jack London) in the US as well. For a variety of sources, then, regulating vagrancy involved an extensive mediation of the figure's interdisciplinary and international roots. In the era of Davies's 'Super-Tramp' persona, governing institutions were beginning to recognise the vagrant's relevance to the modern sphere.

In the period surrounding the publication of Davies's memoir, the discourse shaping citizenship and civil responsibility shifts. In this light, one sees in the vagabond's adaptability something more akin to the type of citizenry that the liberal welfare state wishes to create. Vocal proponents in the British context of a more versatile understanding of civil roles included David Lloyd George and Winston Churchill, both of whom would to different degrees shape governmental policy in the interwar period. Churchill himself outlined this approach to governance at this time, declaring, 'No man can be a collectivist alone or an individualist alone. He must be both an individualist and collectivist. The nature of man is a dual nature' (qtd in B. Harris 157). According to this reasoning, the early stages of welfare reform in Britain depended not only on the expansion of the regulatory power of the state but also on the governed subject embracing his or her place within an appropriate social demographic. In essence, this ideology takes the first steps towards what Peter Miller and Nikolas Rose term 'new practices of government' meant to account for diverse economic agents spread across vast geographical expanses and global networks of finance and exchange (58). The logic of citizenship in this context embeds itself in Davies's vagabond narrative, in which the tramp adopts the discourse of civil responsibility while also presenting himself as the representative of a specific demographic.

Advancing this claim, Davies's text bridges the gulf between literary figurations of the vagrant and the figure's codification in official sources. Most immediately, Davies himself constructs a narrative that alternates between sociological description and Romantic revelry. Furthermore, Davies's work provides his readers with a means for thinking about vagrancy in a properly national context: his tramps are reflections of a larger national identity, and as a result, their success or failure on the road speak to both their national affiliations and the governing system within their respective nation state. Davies's work outlining the archetypal form of the British tramp contributes, along with the reforms occurring in government during this time, to helping the public visualise the tramp.

Ultimately, Davies's autobiography is a useful case study in how this concern about the tramp's place in modern society is evident even in the contemporary reception of tramping texts. For example, Davies's text – while little known to readers today outside the UK – received critical attention from the pioneers of high modernism, such as T. S. Eliot (who found fault in the author's lack of philosophical introspection) and Ezra Pound (who compared Davies favourably to Wordsworth).[17] While Davies shares little aesthetically with modernists of the time, the scenes of industrial decay and human abjection at the core of the tramping memoir cover much of the same thematic ground as this literary movement (Harding 181–2).

Literary critics elsewhere have made more explicit evaluations of the subject of modernity in Davies's writings. Among the most famous literary authors of his time, George Bernard Shaw was a champion of Davies's work on the grounds of the tramp-writer's idealised presentation of vagabondage. In a prefatory essay to *The Autobiography of a Super-Tramp*, Shaw presents Davies as a thoroughly atemporal writer whose artistry is out of step with the popular conventions of the modern moment. Davies's account of vagrancy, Shaw argues, shows the author to be nothing less than a 'real poet', a 'genuine innocent . . . living quite out of the world' in which the comfortable classes reside ('Preface' ix). For Shaw,

Davies's callowness provides the more perceptible onlooker with an opportunity to better appreciate the modern condition. Further, he concludes that Davies's account of his life as a 'poor man' puts the tramp at odds with the modern world and its corresponding 'literary vulgarity' (ix). The claim that literary authenticity derives from one's connection to nature – to what Shaw defines as 'natural liberty' (xii) – was far from new at the time of the autobiography's publication. According to this logic, the literary merit of Davies's memoir rests precisely in its untimeliness; it paints a critical picture of modernity by failing to conform to modern literary standards. Although Shaw honours Davies as a 'real poet', he nonetheless places the tramp outside the bounds of modern art.

While Shaw is concerned specifically with Davies's literary talents, his consideration of the modernity or non-modernity of the vagrant subject intersects with contemporary governing concerns as well. In particular, he mirrors the language of those official sources searching for new tools with which to bring the tramp into the fold of industrial society and civil responsibility. Davies himself provides a crucial component of this process, inasmuch as he identifies the international and local governing forces that shape examples of tramping. In addition, Davies makes it especially clear that his version of vagrancy delineates an embodied way of life in a way that previous Romantic forms did not. In other words, he acknowledges the literary history of tramping while still accounting for the demographic realities of tramps in Britain. Shaw sees Davies's narrative versatility – shifting between scenes of curt description, idealised revelry and social critique – as the essential expression of the tramp's atavistic naivety. While Shaw may praise this outlook, he nonetheless doubts the tramp-writer's integrity as a member of the public sphere. If literary circles express ambivalence towards the vagabond's social relevance, state institutions will clarify this social role in the years following the publication of Davies's memoir. The reverberation of the welfare state in the vagabond narrative during this later era is at the centre of the next chapter.

The presentation of the tramp as an exceptional expression of national – and more implicitly, racialised and gendered – characteristics links the vagabondage authors considered in this chapter to a larger Anglo-American governmental discourse. For sources from Kipling to Lloyd George, subjects must both proclaim their individuality while also contributing to the collective good. Davies's sense of the British tramp as a subject informed by his (natural as well as cultural) environment therefore is encoded in the policy reforms that expanded the welfare state in the years after the publication of *The Autobiography of a Super-Tramp*. But the cultural currency of the tramp persisted in Britain well after this transitional period in government. The following chapter picks up this thread in the context of the interwar period in Britain. By this time, the social viability of the tramp-writer that London exemplified, and Davies celebrated, will have changed in the face of further governmental oversight of vagrancy. If Davies pointed the way for the government to shape culture, British authors such as George Orwell must negotiate the refigured status of vagrancy in this new social system. In doing so, these authors will question the usefulness of American sources such as London for writing about this new, penalised version of vagrant life.

Notes

1. Wordsworth looms large in studies of Romantic poetry's abiding fixation on vagrant figures. Studies on how Wordsworth's poetry engages with policy regarding the poor include, in addition to Langan's work previously mentioned, Quentin Bailey's *Wordsworth's Vagrants*, Gary Lee Harrison's *Wordsworth's Vagrant Muse* and David Simpson's *Wordsworth's Historical Imagination*.
2. Fortunately, many worthy studies have elaborated upon this specific national history and the literary contributions to it, which range from the work of early modern playwrights to nineteenth-century poetry. Thorough investigations that consider how vagrancy factored into English culture and law before the twentieth century include Alistair Robinson's *Vagrancy in the Victorian Age*, David Hitchcock's *Vagrancy in English Culture and Society, 1650–1750*, Linda Woodbridge's *Vagrancy, Homelessness, and English Renaissance Literature* and Celeste Langan's *Romantic Vagrancy*.
3. For more on London's particular brand of socialism, which nonetheless circulated racist stereotypes regarding the superiority of whites, see Jonathan Berliner's 'Jack London's Socialistic Social Darwinism' and Jonathan Auerbach's *Male Call: Becoming Jack London*.
4. Sidonie Smith and Julia Watson point to the autobiography's embedded celebration of Western forms of subjectivity in their recent overview of the genre, *Reading Autobiography*.
5. Indeed, Davies's narrative style lends itself considerably to this task of sociological description. In the text, all of the events that the author describes – whether the loss of his leg or a visit to a particularly nice Salvation Army – appear in flattened, dispassionate prose. For critics like Peter Howarth, the simplicity of the narrative further separates

Davies from his immediate peers (such as Jack London) and their propensity to shock their readers with lurid description ('Simplicity' 161).
6. Like Tocqueville, Davies views the US through the lens of comparison, drawing lines of distinction between Americans and their English counterparts. Specifically, see Tocqueville's discussion of what he terms American vanity in the second volume of *Democracy in America*.
7. Jennifer Fleissner touches on Jack London's central place in conventional critical appraisals of naturalism in *Women, Compulsion, Modernity*. According to Fleissner, London's emphatic fixation on masculinity and 'Anglo-Saxon glory' has tempted scholars up until the end of the twentieth century to associate these tendencies with all naturalist writers (18–19).
8. Jude Davies provides an overview of this tension in naturalist fiction, noting how the genre sympathetically foregrounds scenes of abject poverty while also distancing its middle-class readership from the impoverished figures in these texts.
9. A mentor of sorts to Davies, Brum further adds to this implicit indictment of the British class system based on his own time spent tramping abroad. On the subject of begging in England, Brum explains that one must lower one's expectations in a country 'where even the rich live poorer, with regards to diet, than the labouring classes of this country' (*Autobiography* 32).
10. For an overview of travel writing during its peak in the nineteenth century – along with the ideologies embedded in the form – see Tim Youngs's *Travel Writing in the Nineteenth Century*.
11. See Loren Glass's *Celebrity Inc.* for more on London's literary influences and the plagiarism charges that dogged him during his career.
12. In addition to Said's appraisal of the novel in *Culture and Imperialism*, Sara Suleri stresses its colonial imaginary in *The Rhetoric of English India*. Jed Esty offers another view of the text in *Unseasonable Youth*, which links the narrative to a larger literary trend of stalled coming-of-age narratives in British fiction. See also Tim Christensen's 'The Unbearable Whiteness of Being' for an example of an argument that, while offering sharp criticism of Kipling's work along these lines, recognises his comparatively lucid understanding of the colonial situation.
13. Although not the focus of this chapter, British imperialism undoubtedly played a role in the proliferation as well as creation of new vagabond types during the turn of the century, as the example of *Kim* already indicates. In his study, Robinson explains that the expansion of British imperialism in the Victorian era into diverse parts of the globe created in turn new types of vagrant figures, such as the 'beachcombers' who roamed the shores of the South Seas and appeared in adventure novels in the late nineteenth century (196).
14. Of course, the temporal dimensions to journalism and print media have been the subject of considerable scholarship. The most axiomatic

source for this debate is Benedict Anderson, whose argument in regard to 'homogenous, empty time' engendered by both the novel and print journalism has become the point of departure for subsequent scholarship on the subject (24).
15. I examine the 1906 Departmental Committee report that produced this language below. The relevant section of this legislative document is chapter 3, 'Description of Vagrants'.
16. Chance provides a brief outline of these recommendations in his *Vagrancy* text, especially in section 3. The labour-colony system is the subject of section 7 of the Departmental Committee Report.
17. T. S. Eliot in *The Varieties of Metaphysical Poetry* faults Davies in particular for writing without sufficient philosophical direction (211). Howarth's *British Poetry* makes note of Pound's admiration for Davies's poetry (see 157). In a letter to the editor Harriet Monroe, Pound explained that Davies's strength resides less in his verse than in his presentation of it 'in his own voice' (81).

Chapter 3

Tramps in the Machine: Interwar British Vagrancy

Charlie Chaplin's 1936 film *Modern Times* presents a provocative image of its tramping hero in a moment of extreme duress. The film follows Chaplin's Little Tramp – whose vagabond garb, consisting of baggy pants, bowler hat and toothbrush moustache, remains iconic to this day – as he works a variety of jobs against the backdrop of the Great Depression. One of the most memorable scenes occurs on the factory floor, where the Little Tramp struggles to keep pace with the frenetic activity of the assembly line. After throwing himself on the conveyer belt, he is quickly swallowed by the gargantuan machine and finds himself trapped among its cogs. As this brief description already implies, the scene is heavy with symbolism in a film that, alongside its slapstick comedy, casts into relief the hardships faced by a significant portion of the population around the world during the interwar period. The social context of the factory scene becomes especially clear in the moments immediately following the Little Tramp's journey into the machine. Sent into a work-induced frenzy, the Little Tramp continually turns knobs, pulls levers and wrenches bolts until he is whisked away from the factory first by a policeman and then by a medical doctor who believes he has suffered a nervous breakdown. Soon after, he runs afoul of the law again and, this time, is thrown into jail. Chaplin's tramp character traverses the factory floor and the jailhouse; he is treated medically so that he can continue working and then arrested when he proves he cannot. In short, *Modern Times* locates its famous tramp character in a setting where police power and medical oversight combine to regulate public health – and rid society of harmful influences. If the archetypal tramp figure once connoted exceptionally mobile characters, as the previous chapters have attested, then Chaplin asks audiences to reckon with a profound transformation in the tramp's relationship to the state. Rather than being on the outside looking in, the Little Tramp is – quite literally – at the centre of this industrialised society.

The transformed conditions attending vagrancy both in popular culture (as in Chaplin's case) and in law are at the forefront of this chapter. *Modern Times* is a transitional film in a number of ways. Much of the commentary surrounding it has to do with the film industry itself and Chaplin's role in it. The film marks the final appearance of Chaplin's Little Tramp character, and it is a late example of silent filmmaking during a time when the industry had largely moved on to sound films.[1] The film also takes stock of a transitional period in British welfare governance in the years prior to World War II. After all, the machinery that confines the Little Tramp includes more than just the assembly line on the factory floor; there is also the hospital bed and the jail cell, both of which work in tandem not so much to punish but to ensure the production line continues unimpeded. Finally, the film sheds light on another transitional moment, the development of the tramp character in the wake of the 1929 Great Depression. To decode this provocative image – the tramp in the machine – this chapter turns to George Orwell's 1933 tramp narrative *Down and Out in Paris and London*. As this chapter will demonstrate, Orwell's well-known text extends the tramp-writing tradition associated most immediately with the American author Jack London. But if Orwell picks up a literary thread from the early twentieth century and extends it to interwar Britain, he confronts a socio-economic reality in which vagrants are subject to constant policing and medical oversight. As is the case with Chaplin's Tramp, Orwell's vagrants find themselves trapped in the machinery of the state: the workhouse system collects them, subjects them to humiliating medical examinations and documents their movements. Both cases therefore bring into focus the point at which tramps as literary figures cease to reflect a dangerous exceptionalism and begin to resemble something else entirely: an institutionalised population.

As this last point suggests, to study the development of the tramping archetype in Orwell's work is to shed light on the legal codes that subtended vagrancy in British society. His first-hand account calls attention to the state's oversight of public health in the years prior to the de jure creation of the British welfare state, which scholars conventionally associate with the publication of the Beveridge Report in 1942 and the creation of the National Health Service (NHS) in 1946.[2] As is the case with *The American Vagrant in Literature* as a whole, this chapter pushes back against any reductive chronology for the development of the welfare state in either the US or Britain. By focusing on the treatment of vagrants, Orwell certainly portrays the scaffolding of the welfare state in place even if it had yet to reach its institutional apex. This chapter stresses Orwell's adept dramatisation, like Chaplin's, of the otherwise large-scale transformations unfolding at the time of his writing. In terms of social policy, Britain in the 1930s witnessed something of a consensus turn towards more collectivist governance. In 1936, for instance, *Modern Times* was released around the same time as John Maynard Keynes's *General Theory of Employment, Interest and Money*, whose emphasis on state measures to create a robust labour force would dominate Anglo-American policy for decades.

Orwell's text does more than describe the social conditions attending to this shift in policy, however; it actively intervenes in the development of the tramp archetype in response to these changing social conditions. In the preceding chapters, the features of the tramp narrative – and the characteristics of the tramp-writer – came into clear view. Associated with Jack London in particular, the tramping memoir by the time Orwell wrote stressed the exceptional qualities of the vagabond in ways that easily map onto pre-existing social hierarchies of race, gender and nationality. The previous chapter argued that London's *People of the Abyss* imagined the tramping subject position as ideal for evaluating the relative strengths and weaknesses of a given society. In his telling, the exceptional wit and cunning of the white, masculine, American tramp brings into focus, by way of contrast, what he sees as the dull, debased nature of the British urban poor (*People* 151). The first half of the present chapter builds on the continuities that connect Orwell to his literary forebears in tramp writing and elaborates on the differences that distinguish his text. The comparative imagination is likewise encoded in *Down and Out in Paris and London*, which is explicitly modelled on London's text (as the pages below will demonstrate) and stresses the distinguishing features that separate France from Britain. At the same time, the sense of the tramp's exceptionalism is markedly missing from Orwell's account, which presents British vagabondage as completely subject to state power. Unlike formative writers in the development of the tramp narrative, who envisioned the vagabond as a social critic moving along the social margins, popular British authors such as Orwell, Chaplin and J. B. Priestley argue that tramps no longer exist anywhere but inside the structures that regulate public health.

In both Chaplin's film and Orwell's text, tramps suffer acutely from their institutionalisation, but this harm is not limited to them.

Rather, their bodies bear the brunt of the violence, both sources imply, that is meted out against the poor and vulnerable classes more generally. The discourse of population control and demographic attenuation that informs these works is at the centre of the second half of this chapter, which adds further nuance to the historical timeline conventionally associated with social welfare, its development and its dismantling. Orwell's text offers a precursor in the early twentieth century to more contemporary critical approaches to structural violence along the lines of what social theorist Lauren Berlant describes as slow death: 'the physical wearing out of a population' in a manner that comes to define this group's very existence (95). Slow death, like other theorisations of precarity, is typically seen as a direct consequence of neoliberalism or else located historically among the neoliberal turn of the 1970s.[3] In contrast, Orwell's narrative – which foregrounds the harm that tramps suffer from their treatment by the state – calls attention to an earlier model of slow death operating during the interwar years, when the building blocks of the British welfare state were firmly in place. By reading this narrative beyond its immediate socio-historical context – a practice made possible by the literary history of vagrancy writing – this chapter extends the critique of neoliberal-era state power in Berlant's account to the early twentieth century.

As presented here, Orwell offers a fully-fledged account of how vagrant bodies literally change as a result of state intervention. The sense of what has changed would be lost, however, without reading *Down and Out in Paris and London* in dialogue with previous tramping texts that established the archetype that, in Orwell's work, no longer seems to function as it once did. Although Orwell eagerly assumes the mantle of the tramp, he expresses profound shock at the enfeebled vagrants he encounters on his travels. The gap between his romantic vision of tramping and the cold reality he faces is crucial in my account because it is here that Orwell registers his awareness of social policies having, in fact, altered the tramp population. In other words, he does more than take a snapshot of the state of vagrancy at the time; he contemplates the social conditions that transformed vagrancy and considers where these policies might lead.

The final pages of this chapter expound on this last point by focusing on the governmental imagination that informs Orwell's critique of state policy after the tramp's disappearance, so to speak, into the machinery of the state. In *The Road to Wigan Pier* (1937), Orwell hammers the final nail into the coffin of the tramp narrative's viability as a form of social-activist writing: 'you do not solve the class problem by making friends with tramps', he writes (154). By the time he writes this book, he is no longer concerned with formerly 'exceptional' figures like tramps but with more typical embodiments of the working class – in other words, entire families – and the social policies that affect this demographic (*Wigan* 155). Taken together, the sequence of these two texts evokes a critical development in tramp writing: once this category of vagabond is institutionalised, what comes next? Orwell's move from singular tramps to working-class families as the subject of his social criticism reflects not only the decline of the tramp as a popular figure in culture but also, as these pages will argue, the deployment of state power to monitor the productivity of larger swathes of the population. If Orwell launches a clear attack on the state's treatment of vagrants, he nonetheless recognises and affirms its power to produce a healthy, robust population. The ease with which this notion of population control assumes racialised and heavily gendered connotations is not incidental, but rather an expression of the racialised imagination that is encoded in the tramp-writing template that Orwell adopts.

The Normalisation of Tramping

In *English Journey*, the British author J. B. Priestley observes a single tramp outside Boston, England. Published the year after Orwell's *Down and Out in Paris and London*, Priestley's text shares a broadly similar concern: to travel across the country and assess the state of England during a time of economic depression and social unrest. Like Orwell's work, *English Journey* met with popular acclaim and helped raise public awareness about the plight of the working classes in the interwar years.[4] The country's economic troubles also meant that Priestley would frequently observe vagrants on the move. The sight of the tramp in turn set Priestley thinking about the social forces that might shape the vagabond's travels: 'The distribution of tramps about the country is a subject I should like to see handled by a competent authority', he writes. 'What determines their migrations?' (375). Unlike Orwell, Priestley is less interested in taking up the role of the vagrant; his travels are more akin to a tourist crisscrossing the country than the movements of an unemployed labourer looking for work or a vagrant looking for shelter. Still, his question raises the point that tramps are not quite free in their movements, notwithstanding the popular connotation of this population as uncontrollable. Instead, their travels suggest for Priestley something systematic – even if he struggles to identify exactly what this system is.

If Priestley is unsure what determines the movements of tramps, he nonetheless recognises that they follow a distinct pattern devoid of individual expression. He continues:

> At one time, I lived in the country just north of Oxford, and there ... I saw more tramps than I have ever seen before or since. Winter and summer, in all weathers, there were dozens of them lining that road. I cannot understand why there were more there than anywhere else. (375)

Priestley thus raises a question – what forces determine the migrations of tramps? – that, while unanswered in his narrative, Orwell's vagabond narrative directly considers. The rules, policies and institutions that regulate vagrancy in Britain are front and centre throughout *Down and Out in Paris and London*. The text relates Orwell's experience living among the poor and compares the day-to-day struggles facing this class in each city. I return later to the French portion of his narrative and its relation to the comparative imagination that, I have argued, characterises much of tramp writing up to this point. In the meantime, I focus here on the book's specific presentation of British social policy. Orwell explicitly highlights – and frequently criticises – the 'absurd English laws about begging' that determine how and where vagrants move about the country (*Down and Out* 172).

This governmental power is nowhere more apparent than in the casual wards of the workhouses, or 'spikes', where people without fixed addresses were temporarily detained in exchange for food and shelter. For the inhabitants of the spike, the conversation tended to focus not on how to escape the workhouse altogether but how to navigate between institutions in the least harmful way:

> It appeared from what they said that all spikes are different, each with its peculiar merits and demerits, and it is important to know these when you are on the road. An old hand will tell you the peculiarities of every spike in England; as: at A you are allowed to smoke but there are bugs in the cells; at B the beds are comfortable but the porter is a bully; at C they let you out early in the morning but the tea is undrinkable; at D the officials steal your money if you have any – and so on interminably. There are regular beaten tracks where the spikes are within a day's march of one another. (*Down and Out* 142)

The image of institutionalisation in this scene parallels and expands on the mise-en-scène from *Modern Times* that opened this chapter.

In Chaplin's film, the Little Tramp is not so much devoured by the machine as he dives headfirst inside it in a work-induced frenzy; he subjects himself to poking and prodding because, the viewer knows, there is no viable recourse to surviving without a job outside the factory. The tramps in Orwell's case move within an abusive system in a similar acknowledgement of what few alternative options appear viable to them. Moreover, the tramps here become in effect appendages of the sprawling workhouse institutions. They move between sites in large part because the system forces them to, since casual wards could only shelter residents for a single night. In addition, managers of several wards implemented a 'way-ticket' scheme that directed foot traffic to other areas and spikes along the way (Vorspan 70). In Orwell's telling, the tramp's 'beaten tracks' literally create a map of the spikes and, in doing so, connect these various sites together. Tramps thus call attention to the most minute effects of welfare policy – not only the laws regarding vagrancy but also the beds, teacups and insects that occupy and constitute the spikes – even as they are the subjects of this system. While far from the only population to pass through the doors of the workhouse, tramps are the most highly visible markers of social policy at work.[5]

The provocative presentation of tramps in this passage should immediately signal a point of transition between Orwell's vagrancy text and those that came before it. His vagabonds are no longer expressive of dangerous mobility but are instead inmates of the workhouse system. As this last point makes clear, the full account of vagrancy in this work – including not only vagrancy laws but also the popular perception of tramps and vagabonds – is lost if read in isolation from the larger tradition of tramp writing from which Orwell draws. *Down and Out in Paris and London* describes the lived experiences of tramps, but it also registers Orwell's own sense of nostalgia for the tramping archetype – and his consequent mourning of its passing. The text, as this point implies, blurs the line between fiction and non-fiction. On the one hand, Orwell explains in *The Road to Wigan Pier* that 'nearly all' the events in *Down and Out in Paris and London* 'actually happened, though they have been rearranged' (152).[6] On the other hand, he is particularly mindful of previous tramping accounts and modelled his narrative structure, and his personal performance of vagabondage, on these earlier works. Biographers acknowledge that W. H. Davies's *Autobiography of a Super-Tramp*, London's *People of the Abyss* and Mark Twain's *Roughing It* were the primary influences on Orwell's narrative (Gordon 58). Orwell himself writes in *The Road to Wigan Pier* that

London's text in particular informed his understanding of the British working classes (140). Orwell's self-conscious reverence for these texts reiterates the influence of the tramp-writing tradition that has been at the forefront of this book as well as its enduring relevance in the world of social-policy debates (as exemplified in Orwell's text) into at least the 1930s.

In addition, Orwell's decision to model his work on these precedents means that his own emotional attachment to the tramping archetype is front and centre in the book. Orwell is, to be sure, resorting to tramping not out of any pressing need but as an aspect of his investigative journalism. In fact, he was but one of many British 'bourgeois intellectuals' who sought more direct encounters with the working class during the 1930s (Seaber 62). But owing to his encounter with the tramp literature genre, Orwell structures his cross-class voyage with a keen sense of what this tramping performance should entail. His text registers by turns the thrills, surprises and disappointments he experiences on his travels. Orwell reflects on these feelings in *The Road to Wigan Pier*: 'In the sub-world of the tramp', he writes, 'I had a feeling of release, of adventure, which seems absurd when I look back, but was sufficiently vivid at the time' (152). Orwell's claim that he was 'very happy' to take on the role of the tramp undoubtedly reflects something of the fictive elements that creep into his writing (*Wigan* 152). As Carolyn Betensky points out, the urban slum for Orwell is as much an imagined site as a real place of hardship, an invention that comes across via his own romanticisation of vagabondage (134).

Although one might not turn to *Down and Out in Paris and London* for a fully 'authentic' account of tramping (Betensky 134), the text does provide an acute sense of how the lingering tramp archetype has come into conflict with the social reality shaping vagabondage by the time Orwell writes. Recalling the first time he assumed the role of the tramp in England, Orwell notes, 'Dressed in a tramp's clothes is very difficult, at any rate for the first day, not to feel that you are genuinely degraded. You might feel the same shame, irrational but very real, your first night in prison' (*Down and Out* 129). The shame that carries into Orwell's personal performance as the tramp demarcates a stark point of divergence from tramping as presented by London and Davies writing two decades earlier. Whereas these earlier authors had represented tramping as a way to mark the vagabond's exceptional qualities, Orwell's account stresses a sense of guilt or self-judgement. Indeed, by referring to the tramp's 'shame', he brings into focus the powerful sense of recrimination that comes with straying too far from the norm. In short, he acknowledges his own internalisation of stereotypes regarding criminality and moral behaviour – which moves him to equate tramping with the sensation of being in prison – even before he spends his first night in a casual ward.

The sense of shame that Orwell associates with tramping is not unique to all vagabonds per se, however, but expressive of what he understands to be a specifically English identity. On this point, Orwell again picks up a thread that runs through tramp literature – namely, that tramping facilitates the comparison of one culture or community with another and, in doing so, brings into focus some essential differences between these groups. W. H. Davies, the subject of the preceding chapter, made this aspect of tramp writing especially clear both in his *Autobiography of a Super-Tramp* and in *Beggars*, the latter of which presents tramps as the embodied essence of their respective nations. Like Davies, Orwell's own sense of English identity comes into focus through a comparison with foreign figurations of vagrancy:

> Deliberate, cynical parasitism, such as one reads of in Jack London's books on American tramping, is not in the English character. The English are a conscience-ridden race, with a strong sense of the sinfulness of poverty. One cannot imagine the average Englishman deliberately turning parasite, and this national character does not necessarily change because a man is thrown out of work. (*Down and Out* 202)

Orwell makes the point that poverty, even in its most extreme cases, does not turn people into debased versions of themselves. While this claim is easily given, it operates in tandem with another, more provocative claim. For Orwell, to study tramping is to gain insight into nothing less than the 'national character' of any number of countries. London's popular tramping writings thus clarify for Orwell not only what it means to be a tramp but what it means to be an American and, in contrast, what it means to be British. This assertion reiterates the role that prominent tramp texts such as London's played in consolidating the perception of national – and, as the last chapters of this book will argue, racial – differences. In these earlier cases, tramps embodied the best of their respective countries. In Orwell's case, however, British tramps are not superlative representatives of their nation. Instead, they are no different than 'the average Englishman' (*Down and Out* 202). No longer the exceptional super-criminals depicted in sensationalised accounts from the turn of the century, the tramps in *Down and Out in Paris and London* appear alongside other iterations of working-class poverty.

To return to the point raised above, Orwell stands out among tramp-writers inasmuch as he elaborates upon this moment of rupture. He still valorises the tramp archetype, even as this lingering admiration runs up against the reality of vagabond life as he experiences it. As the previous reference to London's *People of the Abyss* should indicate, Orwell followed a well-known blueprint for performing the role of the tramp-writer. Soon after arriving in England from France, for example, he enters into a clothing shop and emerges with the distinctive accoutrement of the tramp:

> The clothes were a coat, once dark brown, a pair of black dungaree trousers, a scarf and a cloth cap ... It gives one a very strange feeling to be wearing such clothes. I had worn bad enough things before, but nothing at all like these; they were not merely dirty and shapeless, they had – how is one to express it? – a gracelessness, a patina of antique filth, quite different from mere shabbiness. (*Down and Out* 128)

At first glance, this division between the 'mere shabbiness' of the poor and the tramp's own 'antique filth' appears to contradict Orwell's appeals to the tramp's averageness. Rather than an outright contradiction, this gap is another manifestation of the lag that I argue runs throughout the text: Orwell still acknowledges the hypervisibility of the singular tramp figure while also beginning to locate tramps alongside, rather than in opposition to, members of the working class. In short, the lingering familiarity of the tramp – and his associated characteristics – has yet to catch up to the changing nature of poverty. Orwell elsewhere registers this delayed recognition in more literal terms. He writes, 'I saw a hang-dog man, obviously a tramp, coming towards me, and when I looked again it was myself, reflected in a shop window' (*Down and Out* 129). The tramp's excessively familiar image means that Orwell can recognise this figure even before he recognises himself.

The prominence of the tramp archetype here is clear; the sense of what is distinct in this portrayal becomes apparent only in view of the literary history that informs Orwell's text. Michael Shelden's biography of Orwell identifies London's *People of the Abyss* as a 'definite source of inspiration' for the author, who 'was following its example when he chose to assume a disguise before entering the unfamiliar world of the slums' (121). In London's case, the tramping costume enabled him to move seamlessly among a foreign population. As an

American abroad, London assumed the role of the tramp in order to pass through the British slums and observe them without suspicion: 'No sooner was I out on the streets than I was impressed by the difference in status effected by my clothes', he writes. 'Presto! In the twinkling of an eye, so to say, I had become one of them' (*People* 6). Orwell in turn restages this scene and takes advantage of the opportunity for participant observation it provides him.[7] In his case, the change is also immediate: 'My new clothes had put me instantly into a new world', he explains. 'Everyone's demeanour seemed to have changed abruptly' (*Down and Out* 129). As this juxtaposition indicates, the American author London provides an especially visible point of reference for the British Orwell's narrative. At the same time, Orwell's restaging of Jack London's tramp raises an immediate question about which 'world' it is that these authors are entering. The tramp's costume is akin to a passport, guaranteeing a freedom of movement that would otherwise 'be denied the average American abroad', London writes (*People* 7). In his words, London tramps in order to meet 'the English lower classes face to face' (*People* 7) – and as the previous chapter explained, to distinguish them from their American counterparts.

Orwell's own foray into the slum speaks to a very different form of class solidarity than what London imagines in his work. In *The People of the Abyss*, the American tramp is exceptionally mobile; his ability to move easily among the British poor is proof of his versatility, which is all the more apparent when compared with the typical American tourist of the time. In contrast, Orwell's own turn in the British slum is not a trip abroad but, in the context of the book, a homecoming after his sojourn in Paris. In London's case, the tramp's mobility reflects his exceptional powers of movement and adaptation, while in Orwell's it locates him among the larger degradation of the working poor in interwar Britain (Newsinger 28). To be sure, Orwell's tramp performance does provide him with a semblance of solidarity with the people he observes. His middle-class upbringing meant that he rarely had prolonged contact with the urban poor despite his professed concern for this group across his literary corpus. The fact that his tramp costume immediately grants him entry to this milieu is a source of enthusiasm for him. For example, he recalls, 'I helped a hawker pick up a barrow that he had upset. "Thanks, mate," he said with a grin. No one had called me mate before in my life – it was the clothes that had done it' (*Down and Out* 129). At the same time, the sense of comradery that Orwell observes between the hawker and the tramp should come as some surprise. The familiarity he registers here does not mark the tramp as a singular threat – as when he glimpses his own image in the shop window – but rather as one among social equals. The ease with which he enters into communion with the working classes in the guise of the tramp suggests that poverty affects the lives of a large swathe of the population. In other words, the tramp here is not an outlier – he is neither social outcast nor criminal – but something more representative of a significant portion of the country.

The transformation in the state of vagrancy evident in Orwell's work adds much-needed context to the factory scene in Chaplin's *Modern Times* with which this chapter opened. From his first Little Tramp film in 1914, Chaplin undeniably contributed to the hypervisibility of tramping figures that Orwell registers in his text. By the 1930s, the British actor's tramp films had made him not only one of the most popular film stars of the time but 'one of the most important people in the world' (Maland 132). However, the sense of normalisation attached to tramps that Orwell articulates forcefully is evident even for Chaplin by the middle of the decade. The Little Tramp's final appearance on the screen in *Modern Times* specifically evokes these institutional forces: he does not place just any character inside the factory machine, after all, but one immensely famous the world over and, consequently, thoroughly familiar to his audience. The heavy symbolism in this juxtaposition – the irascible tramp on the one hand and the machine cogs on the other – gives the film an especially sharp critical edge, which pokes at everything from the nature of the film industry to the greed of industrial society more generally (Potter 79). When viewed alongside contemporary sources like Orwell and Priestley, *Modern Times* reinforces the sense that the tramping figure has moved from society's margins to a position that is subject to disciplinary power.

By locating the tramp among the working classes, moreover, Orwell and Chaplin both anticipate to different degrees the policy arc of the British welfare state. In both cases, the archetypal tramp no longer embodies an uncontrollable mobility but instead reflects systems of control. In the case of *Modern Times*, the tramp moves from the factory floor to the jailhouse before working a number of odd jobs. The film also stresses that all of this effort to earn a living unfolds so that Chaplin's tramp might provide a stable life for himself and his love interest, a young homeless woman referred to simply as 'The Gamin' (or street urchin). At the same time, there is no indication that the character is able to leave this condition. The film concludes on a note that is at once hopeful in tone and thoroughly precarious in its implications. The Little Tramp turns to the despairing Gamin and encourages her with words that appear in a title card: 'Buck up – never say die. We'll get along!' (*Modern Times* 85:55–8). Encouraged by these words, the Gamin and the Little Tramp walk hand in hand down an empty road towards an uncertain future. As George Potter points out, the concluding scene is deeply ambiguous: the audience is uncertain whether the characters happily accept their fate because they plan to struggle against the oppressive forces they have encountered or because 'they are resolutely returning to the industrialist system' (81). If there is some doubt about what is in store for the characters, we can be certain what became of the Little Tramp. Rather than imperil the public's image of the character – by having him either perform in 'talkies' or toil along in factories – Chaplin removes the character from the public eye entirely. His narrative possibilities seemingly exhausted, Chaplin marks the end of *Modern Times* by retiring for good the Little Tramp from cinema.

Orwell's Ambivalent Critique of the State

Down and Out in Paris and London raises questions about both the cultural legacy of tramping and the socio-economic conditions shaping poverty at the time of his writing. What does it mean that the tramp, long the embodiment of irrepressible mobility in popular culture, is in Orwell's text more akin to a representative of working-class poverty?[8] Moreover, what societal changes occur between this text and *The Road to Wigan Pier* that might have led Orwell to distance himself from the tramp archetype he so eagerly assumed for himself? As noted above, Orwell was not alone in registering within his tramp narrative the wider transformations in governance and the state. Chaplin also offers a glimpse of the institutions that police both vagrants and the working poor alike and hints at what type of society these forces might create. As the final scene in *Modern Times* attests, once the tramp is subject to disciplinary power – whether in a prison cell or a psychiatric ward – there is little reason to expect he will be able to escape it. In contrast, Orwell's description of contemporary British tramps moves him to discuss not only the notional deterioration of this population – its disappearance from sensationalist headlines and popular fiction – but also its deterioration in the most literal, physical sense.

Governmental policies in turn remove any vestige of the archetypal, free-roaming tramp in *Down and Out in Paris and London*.

Orwell not only documents the conditions inside the spike and its effects on its inhabitants, he also calls attention to the longer legal process that led to these conditions. In particular, he vociferously criticises the Vagrancy Act, whose broad definition of criminal vagrancy had, as explained in the Introduction of this book, also served as the basis for anti-vagrancy laws in the US. 'Under the Vagrancy Act', Orwell writes, 'tramps can be prosecuted for smoking in the spike – in fact, they can be prosecuted for almost anything' (*Down and Out* 153). If the Vagrancy Act gave police officers wide powers to arrest just about anyone, Orwell demonstrates how this level of scrutiny does not end once one enters the spike. Instead, tramps are subject to extreme squalor and humiliation at the hands of its administrators (*Down and Out* 146–8). If previous tramp-writers like London stressed the tramp's creative powers, Orwell's presentation of the tramp's institutionalisation underscores how the state institutions that shape poverty have made this figure a more governable subject. While Orwell carries over into his text a sense of the tramp's more archetypal features, they are largely superficial: one can easily put on the costume of the tramp, he suggests, but the initial excitement one feels when doing so quickly gives way to an internalised sense of shame regarding the degraded situation, as Orwell puts it, in which tramps find themselves.

The fact that Orwell writes specifically about tramps in the English section of his text does nothing to narrow the scope of his social criticism. Indeed, the violence he observes being meted out against tramps brings into focus the power regimes governing precarious life – not only vagrants but the poor and out of work – at that time. In his telling, the tramping population here suffers harm owing to a general shift in governance towards a heightened regulation of public health. The sense that the tramp became normalised during this period assumes more than one level of meaning: in the sense both that the tramp was institutionalised and that the medical and legal oversight of once-extraordinary vagabond figures became more applicable to a broader portion of the population. Scholarship in the areas of history and criminology supports this last point. Historian Paul Lawrence shows, for instance, that the Vagrancy Act – far from applying only to tramps and vagabonds – was in fact 'a key aspect of police practice' during the turn of the century in Britain (526). The fate of the tramp, in short, is directly tied to the wider direction of social welfare. The following pages therefore situate Orwell's presentation of the physical harm suffered by tramps amid the debate going on at the time over changes to the workhouse system in Britain.

As indicated previously, British social policies enacted in the early post-war years were largely an extension of previous progressive legislation that began much earlier in the century. The sociologist and historian W. G. Runciman notes that from 1914 (and the immediate years following) wartime reforms in the fields of health, housing, education and unemployment essentially defined the British state's role in social policy in a manner that remained consistent until at least the 1980s (56–7). The previous chapters of this book have situated the emergence and literary codification of the tramp character within the long timeline of welfare development that Runciman, as well as other historians of social policy, brings into focus. These preceding chapters argued that the appearance of the tramp posed a governmental problem that existing institutions were ill-equipped to handle; in this respect, it is safe to say that the tramp – a highly visible and border-crossing figure who embodied the limits to the state's powers to monitor, regulate and detain its underclasses – factored into the social reforms that started in earnest at the turn of the century on both sides of the Atlantic. But in contrast to the US, Britain was already at the leading edge of state-managed welfare controls well before World War II.[9]

Orwell's tramp through London thus does different work than did Jack London's in the same city nearly thirty years earlier. To be sure, Orwell's relatively late entry into the field of tramp writing meant that he wrote with the benefit of precedents and literary examples from the preceding decades. Luke Seaber makes this point in relation to British 'incognito social investigation texts', a literary tradition that has *Down and Out in Paris and London* as both its best and last canonical example (1, 63). As Seaber also explains, reforms in the area of social welfare – especially in regard to workhouses and casual wards – meant that this literary tradition could not continue in the form it once did (74). Simply put, the interwar years marked a period of reckoning between long-standing relief institutions and more modern ones. By characterising Orwell's text as an innovation in tramp writing, then, I mean to call attention not only to the conventions of this literary field but also to the social policies and institutions that have, in every case, shaped the production of tramp writing. While an exhaustive overview of British welfare governance in the first half of the twentieth century is outside the scope of this book, I focus on the specific manifestations of social policy that appear – either directly or indirectly – through the lens of Orwell's tramping literature.

The treatment of tramps within the relatively robust British welfare infrastructure in the 1930s system calls attention to the moralism – centred on the sanctity of work and productivity – that nonetheless carried over from the nineteenth century. The unemployment insurance developed in Britain during this time was contingent upon distinguishing the so-called deserving poor from groups deemed too irresponsible or undesirable to be worth the state's largesse. According to these standards, anyone accused of vagrancy undoubtedly fell into the latter category. The policies enacted in the first decades of the twentieth century therefore precluded vagrants from receiving any amount of support. After its initial introduction in 1911, unemployment insurance in Britain expanded dramatically over the course of the 1920s with the passage of four separate Acts of Parliament (B. Harris 204–5). The legislation provided qualifying labourers with a stipend with which they could support themselves (in theory) while out of work in the short term. At the same time, the policy by design imposed strict standards for who could apply for this support in the first place: applicants were required to produce proof that they were 'genuinely' seeking work, a provision whose guidelines were subject to change and revision over subsequent pieces of legislation and across succeeding governments (Cross 382). The Means Test, which established who was eligible for support, met with considerable controversy and was the subject of various critiques – such as in Walter Greenwood's immensely popular 1933 novel, *Love on the Dole* – that highlighted its cruel disregard for the well-being of those the government was ostensibly protecting. Although the particulars of the Means Test changed over time, none altered the central premise of the test itself: that one must be genuinely in search of work in order to qualify for welfare benefits.

The country's population of tramps and vagrants were thus consigned to the casual-ward system, the institution meant to account for citizens who failed the standard means-tested insurance and had no fixed residency. Developed in the nineteenth century, workhouses and casual wards, much like tramps themselves, were becoming something of an anachronism alongside the rapid modernisation of the British government's welfare initiatives. A product of the 1834 Poor Law, the workhouse system had attempted to reduce the social problem associated with beggarism by connecting the distribution of poor relief – namely, shelter and food – to hard labour. The law thus enshrined the notion that the distribution of social welfare breeds dependency in the poor and therefore made the process of receiving support as unpleasant as possible (Englander 8). But as was the case in the US, the boom-and-bust economy that characterised the concluding years of the century meant that the population of vagrants at times swelled beyond the capacity of the existing framework (Vorspan 64). Until its reform in the twentieth century, the Poor Law operated on the basis that local parishes would form the heart of the system's administration (Charlesworth 139). By 1930, however, it was clear that this local approach was no longer feasible. Inconsistent standards across the workhouses meant that some went bankrupt due to expenditures while others imposed draconian measures to avoid giving support at all costs (Finlayson 251–2).

The preponderance of wandering unemployed – tramps, hobos and all manner of people on the move – completely disrupted the local orientation of the system, which stressed that relief must be distributed on the basis of one's settlement within a given parish. As a result, the government passed the Local Government Act in 1929, which abolished the previous system of administration altogether and passed power on to civil councils (B. Harris 203). Furthermore, by 1934 Parliament had set up an Unemployment Assistance Board to take over from these local bodies, funded directly by the British Treasury (Finlayson 252). In the span of a few years, the workhouses went from being a relic of the Victorian period to a prominent casualty of the centralised state's growing powers of oversight. Casual wards, on the other hand, continued on into the 1960s (designated as 'reception centres') according to the new oversight system created in the wake of the previous reforms (Seaber 74). As this short history of workhouse reforms demonstrates – and as *The American Vagrant in Literature* has stressed throughout – focusing on the management of vagrants over a long enough timeline reveals first the call for and then the development of more robust state power.

The sense of the British regulatory state's rapid expansion, as evident in the preceding overview, is also apparent in Orwell's memoir, albeit not where one might expect it. His recollection of his time in Paris, after all, not only removes him from England but also has little to do on the surface with tramps at all. Unlike American tramp-writers in the preceding decades, such as Josiah Flynt, Orwell does not observe the impoverished classes overseas in order to try to fix the problem of vagrancy back home. On the contrary, his comparative treatment of vagrancy in England and France serves a less obvious goal than the policy-minded writings of tramp ethnographers who, as Chapter 1 detailed, looked abroad for laws and governmental institutions to incorporate domestically. Instead, what Orwell communicates via the international comparison at the heart of *Down and Out in Paris and London* is a sense that in contrast to France, Britain is rather over-developed in terms of its regulatory infrastructure and policies. This point has implications not only for the shape of the text itself, which is divided between these two societies, but for Orwell's overarching understanding of the welfare state in Britain.

Indeed, it is with this comparison that Orwell expands on the wider implications of the normalisation of the tramp in Britain. In the British model, he argues, individual expressions of autonomy take a backseat to the state's protection of public health. In contrast, he locates in Paris a residual form of the individualism that is absent from the governing institutions he observes at home. Such impressions are especially evident in his recollections of arriving back in London: 'It was queer after Paris; everything was so much cleaner and quieter and drearier. One missed the scream of the trams, and the noisy, festering life of the back streets, and the armed men clattering through the squares' (*Down and Out* 134). The appeals to individualism that run throughout the text are at the forefront of this comparison of Paris with London. The French social model produces a 'fierce individuality and malice', which Orwell contrasts with the 'crowds' of people in England who are 'milder and more alike' (*Down and Out* 134). Orwell's nostalgia for the dangerous subjectivity he locates in Paris (with its 'armed men' and 'festering' street life) and embodies in the vagabond stands uneasily alongside his more pragmatic acknowledgement that this kind of Parisian figure would no longer thrive in the 'cleaner and quieter' modernity he associates with the English social model.

As this point suggests, Orwell's attachment to the tramp archetype runs parallel to and helps to clarify the narrative structure in *Down and Out in Paris and London*. He both romanticises the tramp while also registering his personal dismay at the shameful condition of tramps in the present day. The tension between a residual idealisation of an outdated subject position on the one hand and a clear understanding of its limited application to the present day on the other is not unique to this text in his oeuvre. Orwell is famous today for his fierce criticisms both of systems of power and of conventional wisdom. He is less known for his idealisation of hard work, which unfolds in a manner that calls to mind the Victorian ethos of the previous century. As Rob Breton explains, Orwell tended towards an 'anti-revolutionary' interpretation of labour that is at odds with his espoused economic philosophy (8). It is no mistake that Orwell himself takes on the role of the tramp in England and the *plongeur* in France, a person employed to wash dishes and perform menial labour in dining establishments: both call to mind pre-industrial – or in the tramp's case, anti-industrial – subject positions (Breton 8). Accordingly, for Orwell, who celebrates the 'moral individualism' he locates in the pre-industrial past, Paris represents an escape from the modernity associated with Britain (Breton 15). To be sure, it is clear throughout *Down and Out in Paris and London* that neither society provides adequate support for its vulnerable population of homeless and working poor. Nonetheless, the minimal substance that the British version provides motivates Orwell to depict nostalgically the bare individualism he associates with the *plongeur* model.

But if Orwell celebrates the Parisian model for its individualism, he also reiterates the sense that it is definitely a thing of the past. His comparison is therefore not interested in offering Paris as a place with laws or infrastructure that can be put to use in his home country; in Orwell's eyes, Paris exists firmly behind the times with respect to Britain. Instead, the atavistic features he outlines in Paris bring into relief the distinctly British policies and institutions he wishes to critique. This formulation extends the nationalist imagination in the tramp-writing tradition in the Jack London mould while revising it according to Orwell's own distinct interpretation of British social politics. The subject of the preceding chapter, W. H. Davies's presentation of American exceptionalism in *The Autobiography of a Super-Tramp*, provides a useful point of reference for elaborating on this continuity. Both Orwell and Davies offer an overview of British society by comparing their experiences abroad with the social and political conventions back home. For Davies, the 'extraordinary' expanses of the US set the stage for performing his own form of exceptional individualism as a tramp (*Autobiography* 20). Orwell parallels Davies to the extent that both use superlative language to characterise the populations and cultures they observe abroad. When Orwell writes of the 'Paris slums', for example, he foregrounds the 'eccentric people' who live there: 'people who have fallen into solitary, half-mad grooves of life and given up trying to be normal or decent' (*Down and Out* 7). In this instance, Orwell's presentation of the slum hinges on a sustained and implicit contrast with British social practices, which constitute in his words the 'normal or decent' standard against which he evaluates his Parisian neighbours.

At the same time, Orwell's vivid recollection of the shabbiness of this environment already signals a departure from the type of exceptionalism Davies associated with the US. Instead, Orwell stresses the continuities that tie together the Parisian slum and the poverty he is more familiar with back home:

> I am trying to describe the people in our quarter, not for the mere curiosity, but because they are all part of the story. Poverty is what I am writing about, and I had my first contact with poverty in this slum. The slum, with its dirt and its queer lives, was first an object-lesson in poverty, and then the background of my own experiences. It is for that reason that I try to give some idea of what life was like there. (*Down and Out* 11)

For previous authors like Davies and London, the act of tramping overseas reflected in part their personal embodiment of the exceptional powers within the discursive framework of liberal individualism. The comparative structure of Orwell's text reiterates the international lines of mobility that appeared in these previous works. If previous vagabond narrators looked abroad for social and political institutions for appropriation, however, Orwell sees in the foreign slum a preview of what he will later observe in a more austere and organised form in Britain. In the passage above, Paris is the scene of his 'first contact' with poverty – a phrasing whose teleological construction already anticipates his presentation of London as the ultimate site for understanding poverty in its modern permutation.

Orwell's international tramping thus features Paris as a specific version of poverty that predates the social situation in England not only narratively but also developmentally. Orwell makes this point especially clear upon his return to London halfway through his narrative: 'One seemed to breathe a less feverish air than in Paris. It was the land of the tea urn and the Labour Exchange, as Paris is the land of the *bistro* and the sweatshop' (*Down and Out* 135). Where one is the site of uninhibited madness, the other – albeit less desirable from Orwell's point of view – is the site of restraint and conformity. This division plays out along familiar lines: the reference to the tea urn and French bistro in particular reinforces a conventional sense of each country's respective social structure, contrasting the entrenched formality of British custom with that of the 'feverish' French model. The great detail with which Orwell explains the codification of vagrancy in Britain – as a result of the institutions and policies stemming from the Vagrancy Act, as explained above – further stresses the distance, both politically and temporally, between his native country and France on the subject of welfare oversight.

To be sure, the shades of difference Orwell finds between Paris and London with respect to welfare policies do little, in his telling, to rescue the poor from the worst effects of poverty. In both locations, the marginalised social classes are anything but free from the attenuating effects of poverty on the one hand and anti-poverty governance on the other. In the Paris section of the text, Orwell goes so far as to characterise the French *plongeur* as 'one of the slaves of the modern world' (*Down and Out* 116). As this claim makes clear, the relatively hands-off approach to poverty in France does not produce more independent labourers. Describing the *plongeur*, Orwell remarks:

> His work is servile and without art; he is paid just enough to keep him alive; his only holiday is the sack. He is cut off from marriage, or, if he marries, his wife must work too. Except by a lucky chance, he has no escape from this life, save into prison . . . One cannot say that it is mere idleness on their part, for an idle man cannot be a *plongeur*; they have simply been trapped by a routine which makes thought impossible. (*Down and Out* 116)

The picture of the labourer trapped within a prescriptive social system is especially evocative of Orwell's representation of poverty not only in France but also in Britain. In the British context, the tramp is likewise locked into a system that determines his movements. 'A tramp tramps', he explains, 'not because he likes it, but for the same reason as a car keeps to the left; because there happens to be a law compelling him to do so' (*Down and Out* 201). The comparison between the tramp and the *plongeur* adds further clarity to the contrast at the heart of Orwell's text. The *plongeur* performs 'stupid and largely unnecessary work', Orwell reasons, 'because of a vague feeling that he would be dangerous if he had leisure' (*Down and Out* 121). In his telling, the French model perpetuates useless work to entrap labourers, while the British model imposes strict laws and policies that literally determine the habits of the country's most precarious citizens. In both cases, what might appear to outside observers as an expression of idleness – the *plongeur*'s menial tasks and the vagrant's wanderings – are instead the direct result of institutional factors that restrict any attempt at productive labour in the conventional sense.

Slow Death: Tramping and Biopower

Orwell's apparent criticism of the British social-policy model reflects, I argue, a fundamental ambiguity in his thinking about the welfare state more generally. According to Orwell, the case of the vagrant in London showcases the human costs of the social mandate upholding public health. Having moved under the auspices of the state, the tramp withers to the point of death. In this rendering of physical deterioration, Orwell delineates the link between social upliftment and population control, a move that anticipates aspects of everyday life that are starkly apparent in the neoliberal era. In doing so, he identifies the big state of the early century – rather than only the enervated one of latter half of the century – as a primary force in normalising the type of debilitating poverty that he documents in his text. Orwell's presentation of a vagrant known as Paddy, who the book stresses is the embodiment of the 'typical tramp', brings into focus not only the institutionalisation of tramps but also the general harm brought upon the population that passes through the casual-ward system (*Down and Out* 150). Paddy shows nothing of the assertive individualism associated with the archetypal vagabond. 'There was something in his drifting style of walk, and the way he had of hunching his shoulders forward, essentially abject', Orwell writes. 'Seeing him walk, you felt instinctively that he would sooner take a blow than give one' (*Down and Out* 150). If Paddy represents the typical tramp in Orwell's account, then it is especially telling that Orwell encounters him not on the open road but inside the spike. From this initial point of contact, he is careful to link Paddy's thoroughly abject disposition to his time spent in the care of the state. In other words, Paddy is an archetype for tramping *because* he is thoroughly institutionalised rather than in spite of this condition.

In this case, Orwell connects state-directed efforts to improve public health (with respect to poverty and homelessness) to actual harm aimed at specific segments of the population. The tramp's physical deterioration in the 1930s, at the hands of institutions ostensibly set up to provide aid, thus anticipates more modern critiques of biopower in the post-Fordist era – most notably, Berlant's theorisation in *Cruel Optimism* of the 'feedback loop of trauma and compensation' that characterises precarious life (18). As Berlant explains, Michel Foucault's account of biopower stresses not so much the power over life and death so much as the power to compel life according to specific rules. Biopower regimes demonstrate, Berlant writes, the 'power to make something live or to let it die, the power to regularize life, the authority to force living not just to happen but to endure and appear in particular ways' (97). Serving the collective good – by protecting, for instance, public health – means in this context to subject particular segments of the population to administration, oversight and scrutiny.

The logic of demographic management that undergirds this protection of public health is everywhere evident in the English section of *Down and Out in Paris and London*. As Orwell puts it, the law requires vagrants to sleep in shelters not only because it prevents individuals from dying but also because this intervention improves the collective health of society. 'According to the law in London, you may sit down for the night, but the police must move you on if they see you asleep', he writes. 'This law is evidently a piece of wilful offensiveness. Its object, so it is said, is to prevent people from dying of exposure' (*Down and Out* 208). At once, Orwell points to the law's unreasonable standards (a man who is dying of exposure will do so 'asleep or awake', he argues) as well as the implicit moralism that shapes the ordinance (*Down and Out* 209). 'In Paris there is no such law', he continues. 'There, people sleep under the Seine bridges, and in doorways, and on benches in the square, and round the ventilating shafts of the Metro, and even inside the Metro stations . . . It does no apparent harm' (*Down and Out* 209). The contrast between these two cases stresses the relatively robust demographic ordering that is at work in the London example. By prohibiting the public spaces of the city, the law directs rough sleepers into the governmentally sanctioned spaces of the casual wards. The British model of governance that emerges from this scenario hinges relegating groups of people to certain spaces. For some, this is the home; for others, it is the shelter. Above all, the law seeks to improve overall public health by requiring everyone to reside somewhere, even if the letter of this policy only really targets vagrants.

Although the spike ensures that the tramp will avoid starvation, it provides little more than the most minimal forms of nourishment. Consequently, Orwell doubts Paddy's ability to become productive in any conventional sense. 'Two years of bread and margarine had lowered his standards hopelessly', he notes. 'He had lived on this filthy imitation of food till his own mind and body were compounded of inferior stuff. It was malnutrition and not any native vice that had destroyed his manhood' (*Down and Out* 153). To be sure, Paddy's degradation speaks to the text's immediate criticism of the appalling conditions that the workhouse system imposed upon its subjects. At the same time, Orwell's presentation of this system considers subjects like Paddy as an essentially subservient class to the public-health institutions that in effect created them. Orwell's conflation of Paddy's lost 'manhood' with his labour should indicate how extensively his criticism of policy ultimately derives from its valorisation not only of liberal individualism but of the homosocial and masculine sense of identity that undoubtedly intersects with this concept.

In effect, Orwell's concern for Paddy's absent virility reproduces the same coupling of productive economic activity and biological reproduction that Berlant describes. It is important for Berlant that slow death plays out not in outright violence (such as open warfare or genocide) but in the realm of 'ordinariness itself', in which 'everyday activity; memory, needs, and desires . . . are brought into proximity' (100). Orwell similarly casts the deleterious effects of anti-vagrancy policies into this ordinary sphere inasmuch as he brings the minute consequences of British regulation to the foreground of his narrative. The initial enthusiasm for tramping when Orwell first dons the costume gives way when he witnesses the degraded status of actual tramps in modern Britain. Rather than adventuring on the road, these tramps are concerned with the beds, teacups, bugs and porters that compose the country's nascent welfare institution. Similarly, the most potent evidence of the state's attenuation of this demographic group is the 'bread and margarine' on which the vagrant subsists rather than outright physical violence (*Down and Out* 153). At the same time, Orwell's conflation of productivity with masculinity is a clear point of departure between his critique of power and Berlant's. Life on the dole has, according to Orwell, sapped the tramp of his ability to contribute to economic production or, as the allusion to virility implies, social reproduction. His enshrinement of masculinity in these terms no doubt factors in his ambivalent rendering of welfare policy in his text.

Orwell's rather direct criticisms of how vagrants suffer in the casual ward provides renewed insight into his thoughts on social-welfare politics more generally, a topic that has been under considerable debate among studies of the author. Part of the difficulty in assessing Orwell's views on the development of British social welfare before Beveridge stems from the relatively higher attention his post-war writing, especially *Nineteenth Eighty-Four* and *Animal Farm*, receive compared with his interwar work. As Matthew Hart explains, the ubiquity of these latter texts on standardised English syllabi and high-school campuses has in turn led to a relative lack of interest among leading literary critics in Orwell's politics – at least, in comparison with the modernist authors who wrote during the same period. Orwell's propensity to articulate conflicting viewpoints across his body of writing is a further source of consternation for his critics. Raymond Williams, in *Culture and Society*, famously highlighted Orwell's vexed reception among the political left in the decades since the author became an icon of the British literary establishment. Simply put, Orwell is a 'paradox' (Williams 286). Referring to the second half of *The Road to Wigan Pier*, for example, Williams writes that Orwell 'was a socialist, who popularized a severe and damaging criticism of the idea of socialism and of its adherents' (286). Bernard Crick similarly acknowledges the author's vexed politics, which he describes as a brand of 'English socialism' (4). As the preceding pages argued in relation to Orwell's presentation of vagabondage, this political vision tends to meet a clear concern for the plight of the poor and interest in the working classes with an abiding individualism and a deep suspicion of the state (Crick 4).

In contrast with his vociferous critique of vagrancy policy and the administration of casual wards, Orwell self-consciously avoided any extended comment on the dramatic transformations under way in British welfare administration after the war. By the time he had published his most famous texts, the British government in the aftermath of the Beveridge Report had reached a consensus on the need for an expansive welfare state. By 1944, Orwell writes in 'The English People', 'the only discussion that arises' on the subject of Beveridge's welfare state 'is about whether it will adopted in whole or in part' (14). As this brief allusion suggests, Orwell's suspicion of the state – as well as his pointed critiques of vagrancy law – does not correspond to advocating for or against policy changes under way at the time of his writing. He elaborates on this stance in 'Writers and Leviathan', which considers 'the position of the writer in an age of State control' (407). Rather than meditate on the merits of this system, however, his essay presents the big state as a matter of fact. The writer's job, he concludes, involves separating artistic output from political affiliation. 'When a writer engages in politics he should do so as a citizen, as a human being, but not as a *writer*' ('Writers' 412). Orwell makes this distinction, he insists, to spare the artist from the inherently degrading world of governance. As Matthew Hart and Jim Hansen explain, 'For Orwell ... the state exists as a category of analysis in a largely negative sense. The state is overpowering, it demands conformity, and its power marks the failure of liberal principles of autonomy and free association' (492). Orwell's account of vagrant life in *Down and Out in Paris and London* reiterates this formulation, inasmuch as it acknowledges the residual autonomy present in the Parisian system and expresses disdain for the collectivism of the British one.

I have turned to these literary debates not to repeat well-worn claims about Orwell's political inscrutability but to reiterate how his vagrancy writing – indeed, how the field of tramp literature more generally – clarifies his most prescient critique of state power. To be sure, Berlant is much less concerned with explicitly state-managed institutions than either Foucault or Orwell. Nonetheless, the concept of slow death calls attention to the long temporality involved in subjecting certain demographic groups to biopower: meted out over decades, the harm suffered by vulnerable portions of the population becomes at once extreme (in terms of its effects) and thoroughly ordinary as a result of careful habituation (Berlant 96). My account of *Down and Out in Paris and London* has taken this theorisation of slow death as a point of departure. Most immediately, it supplements the timeline of biopower as outlined above, since neither Foucault in *Society Must Be Defended* (which discusses the origins of biopower in the eighteenth century) nor Berlant (whose case studies appear largely after the 1990s) considers the particularly stark expression of power in the interwar period. There is a further parallel between this slow violence and the gradual institutionalisation of the vagrant population, a process that – in view of sources from Twain and Flynt to Davies to Orwell – extended from the late nineteenth century into at least the 1930s.

But the continuities between Orwell and Berlant found here should come as some surprise given the radically different moments of governance each is addressing. After all, the rise of neoliberalism is typically seen as directly tied to the decline of the welfare state.[10] David Harvey provides perhaps the most axiomatic explanations of this timeline, which foregrounds the pro-market forces in and outside of government that dismantled welfare safety nets in both the US and Western Europe. Harvey locates this shift in the 1970s, when neoliberalism became 'hegemonic as a mode of discourse' (3). In the context of Britain, he argues, the neoliberal turn entailed 'dismantling or rolling back the commitments of the welfare state' and other 'institutions and political ways ... that had been consolidated in Britain' immediately after the Beveridge Report (22–3). Neoliberal economists, bankers and politicians over the course of the final decades of the twentieth century ultimately led the charge to refashion the very idea of welfare from a guarantor of basic equity in liberal society to an obstacle to '[i]ndividualism, freedom, and liberty' (56).

The consequences of this shift, which at once made self-care incumbent on marginalised groups while removing the resources necessary for making this care possible, are at the foreground of accounts of precarity and the precariat by Berlant as well as Judith Butler. According to Berlant, precarity refers specifically to a state of being in which the resources one depends on for survival are 'in someone else's hands' (192). While theorists such as Butler have stressed the radical potential of precariousness – which may generate a robust solidarity on the basis of shared vulnerability (Butler 28) – it is clear that certain groups are dramatically more exposed to harm than others (Berlant 192). This exposure is evident in the governmental responses to vagrancy that Orwell documents: such anti-vagrancy policies nominally protected the vagrant's life (as from 'exposure', in the preceding example) even as this management directly harmed this population by placing them in the casual ward.

By locating a version of slow death in interwar Britain, I am assigning a more active role to the state in manufacturing this so-called ordinary violence than what appears in Berlant's text. To be clear, in making this distinction I am not diminishing the destructive practices associated with neoliberalism by uncovering some equivalent form of harm in the early twentieth century. Instead, I wish to locate historical case studies to shed light on the cultural and legal practices that constitute what Berlant terms the 'the elongated *durée* of the present moment' (195). To read *Down and Out in Paris and London* is to gain an appreciation of the various hardships faced by tramps and the working poor at the time Orwell is writing. But reading this text in full view of the tradition of tramp writing, as this chapter has done, opens up further frames of reference: we see how Orwell's book fleshes out a much longer drive towards containing, disciplining and diminishing a very specific portion of the population.

What does it mean, then, that the relatively expansive state Orwell observes generates the type of population attenuation that Berlant locates in the post-welfare era? Historians and economists who have taken up this question bring renewed scrutiny to the continuities as well as discontinuities between government in the early twentieth century and the neoliberal period in Western Europe and North America. For example, economists Pierre Dardot and Christian Laval's refreshed account of neoliberalism's origins in *The New Way of the World* assigns a much more active role to the state in piloting policies and programmes that would eventually dismantle the welfare infrastructures it had previously constructed. Dardot and Laval identify the 1880s to 1930s as a period when social reformers and policy makers fought over the limits to individual freedom in liberal societies such as the US, UK and Germany (21). Most immediately, this long 'crisis of liberalism' should disrupt any sense of a monolithic liberalism well before the dismantling of post-war welfare infrastructures during the 1970s and 1980s. Moreover, this timeline demonstrates how the ideological basis for neoliberalism – namely, its heavy emphasis on individual choice over collective responsibility – runs throughout a complex network of political thought from the turn of the century. In this light, Orwell's ambiguous understanding of the state should not be taken as wholly anomalous but rather as an expression – by one of Britain's most famous literary figures – of the larger crisis of liberalism at a time of profound economic and social unrest.

To be sure, the account of neoliberalism and its historical permutations offered here is brief and incomplete. By glossing this scholarship, I gesture to the ongoing socio-economic debates that Orwell's text can address when it is read as an account of vagrancy concerning a specific time and place and also as a commentary on governmentality more generally. In other words, his striking portrayals of poverty in London indicate that the enfeebled population he sees is the result of a governmental and cultural project that has unfolded slowly over time. His self-conscious adoption of the tramp-literature template makes this slow process (*pace* Berlant) evident only when we recognise the disparity between Orwell and his tramp-writing predecessors: in Orwell, the tramp's institutionalisation might be obvious, but when read comparatively we can also appreciate the processes that precede and create this situation. As *The American Vagrant in Literature* has argued throughout, the codification of tramps in literature and their management in government – both of which are at the forefront of Orwell's text – provide considerable insight into welfare governance that extends well beyond the specific matters of vagrants and vagrancy laws.

Suffering from their own version of slow death, tramps – as Orwell sees them – lose their currency in more ways than one. Most immediately, the literal withering away of this population suggests that their time as archetypes of super-criminality and heroic mobility is past. But perhaps the more profound change for Orwell is the sense that tramps no longer provide the artistic insight he had once craved as a young writer. The literary tradition stretching back to at least Twain, as explained in Chapter 1, characterised tramps as possessing profound powers of social critique. This understanding of the tramp as essentially an artist-critic was no doubt on Orwell's mind when he set out to write *Down and Out in Paris and London*. But as his later work proves, even this appreciation for the tramp's usefulness as a social observer changes in response to the transformed condition of vagrants in Britain. *The Road to Wigan Pier* thus conspicuously avoids any prolonged discussion of this population. Instead, the limited usefulness of the tramp is manifestly clear to Orwell by this point. Recalling his time writing his tramping book, Orwell strikes an apologetic note: 'But unfortunately you do not solve the class problem by making friends with tramps' (*Wigan* 154). He continues, 'Tramps, beggars, criminals and social outcasts generally are very exceptional beings and no more typical of the working class as a whole, than, say, the literary intelligentsia are typical of the bourgeoisie' (*Wigan* 155). At first glance, Orwell's characterisation of tramping in this instance appears to contradict a central premise of *Down and Out in Paris and London*, where vagrancy reflected on the status of the working classes as a whole. But given the reckoning that is everywhere apparent in Orwell's tramping narrative – which among other things documents his own process of understanding the tramp's slow slide into cultural irrelevancy – the change should come as no surprise.

Orwell's reference to the fractious 'class problem' in *The Road to Wigan Pier* already hints at the overarching transformation in the political value of vagabondage between the two texts. The earlier book associates tramping with individualism, even as it found both in short supply as a result of the interwar version of slow death Orwell identifies. Once Orwell expands his study to include different impoverished groups in *The Road to Wigan Pier*, his nostalgia for the tramp as a relic of the past, and the homosociality he associates with this archetype, is clearly visible. On the subject of life among tramps, Orwell reflects, 'It is a sort of world-within-a-world where everyone is equal, a small squalid democracy – perhaps the nearest thing to a democracy that exists in England' (*Wigan* 155). The homogeneity of the tramping world is adaptable and democratic in this telling, while the real world is divided into regional, ethnic and class differences. The homosocial depiction of tramping thus gives way to a picture of a fractured working class. Orwell is conspicuously aware of the shortfalls inherent in his conversations with members of this expansive demographic group: 'I liked them and hoped they liked me', he writes, 'but I went among them as a foreigner, and both of us were aware of it' (*Wigan* 156). The fantasy of tramping no longer provides Orwell with the tools for investigating the lived conditions among the working classes.

Ultimately, Orwell's time writing his vagrancy narrative demonstrates that the tramp is not a subject position with a future. *The Road to Wigan Pier* in turn sets out to correct the mistake in his thinking by focusing on working-class families – a group whose ensured reproducibility overcomes the problem inherent in the homosocial communities Orwell observed among tramps. This turn towards thinking about the future of the nation state is embedded in *The Road to Wigan Pier* inasmuch as Orwell here relegates tramps to the past and excludes them entirely from his investigative writing. Along with contemporaneous sources such as Chaplin and Priestley, Orwell used the vagrant to mark not freedom from governance but the extent of the state's expanding oversight of public health. But if the tramp has lost his dangerous subjectivity along these lines, that does not mean that the values these sources celebrated with the vagabond archetype disappear. As the final chapter will argue, the features associated with tramps – not only mobility and individuality but also masculinity and whiteness – come increasingly to the foreground once the tramp ceases to be a perceived threat. Orwell helps to inaugurate this nostalgic turn to the extent that he locates the tramp in the past, unfit for the modern society that *Down and Out in Paris and London* both acknowledges as unavoidable and greets with disdain. As is clear, Orwell shows little interest in mobilising the tramp as a radical figure, even if he places great value in the tramp's expression of individualism. For greater insight into what this figuration might resemble – the vagabond as a hero of a strong, regulatory nation state – the following chapter will turn back across the Atlantic, to the US.

Notes

1. Lawrence Howe, for instance, argues that Chaplin's presentation of the factory reflects his own ambiguous relationship with the Hollywood system of cultural production. In another case, George Potter takes up Adorno's conception of the culture industry to evaluate Chaplin's ability to stage a critique of cultural production from within the film, itself a product of this industry.
2. The economist William Beveridge issued his reform agenda, the 'Report of the Inter-Departmental Committee on Social Insurance and Allied Services', to great fanfare in and outside government. The rapid adoption of the report's recommendations – resulting not only in the formation of the NHS but several other reforms in national insurance, pensions and rent control – should indicate the broad consensus supporting collectivist governance during the interwar period. See Owen's 'From Poor Law to Beveridge Report' for a contemporary example of sources reading the proposals in view of the outdated casual-ward system Orwell describes.
3. In *Cruel Optimism*, Berlant focuses on the so-called 'obesity epidemic', which emerges in part after the 'neoliberal shift' in the US government's organisation of recommended nutrition regimens (109).
4. The similarities between Orwell and Priestley are not entirely

coincidental given that they shared the same publisher, Victor Gollancz, a prominent promoter of socialist politics at the time. The relative popularity of both authors and their mutual ties have in turn led several literary critics to read them together as rivals. See John Baxendale's *Priestley's England* and Bernard Schweizer's *Radicals on the Road* for studies on both Orwell and Priestley in particular and this literary context more generally.

5. In his overview of British vagrancy literature, Alistair Robinson parallels this point about the tramp's ambivalent position within the casual-ward system. Although spikes were clearly designed with the intent of monitoring vagrant populations, the wide inconsistency between individual sites in terms of management and amenities nonetheless 'offered vagrants a degree of choice' (Robinson 104). Orwell showcases the process of information sharing amongst vagrants in the passage cited above.

6. Stephen Ross makes this point in regard to the discrepancy between scenes in *The Road to Wigan Pier* and Orwell's recollection of these events in his personal journal.

7. Pittenger identifies such scenes of extended costume changes as hallmarks of undercover social investigation literature, a genre that stretches back to the Victorian period in Britain (24). At the same time, Orwell's self-conscious engagement with London adds further context to the scene in *Down and Out in Paris and London*, which establishes Orwell's bona fides as both an undercover investigator and, more importantly for my study, an archetypal tramp.

8. Orwell offers a different account of the tramp's relationship to the working class in *The Road to Wigan Pier*. The contradiction between these two sources is at the forefront of the final pages of this chapter.

9. Although broad characterisations of the interwar period as wholly progressive in terms of policy are subject to debate, most scholars nonetheless agree that welfare institutions across the board went into decline almost immediately after the establishment of the de jure welfare state following World War II. For more specific takes on this issue, see M. A. Crowther's *British Social Policy 1914–1939*, which echoes Runciman's sentiments above. For a less positive interpretation of this era's legislation, see Rodney Lowe's *Adjusting to Democracy*.

10. There are numerous worthy accounts of the neoliberal reformulation of welfare across various states that apply to the international context I am discussing here. For example, Maria Bordas creates a comparative study of late twentieth-century welfare states in Europe and the US. The scholarly essays collected in *The Welfare State in Post-Industrial Society* produce a similar account of neoliberal practice in anglophone states such as Australia, in addition to the US and Britain (Powell and Hendricks).

Chapter 4

Steinbeck's Migrants: Families on the Move and the Politics of Resource Management

As perhaps the most widely read account of poverty and migration in the US, John Steinbeck's *The Grapes of Wrath* has exerted a powerful influence over the discourse of migration politics since its publication in 1939. Much has been written on the specific aspect of domestic migration that Steinbeck portrays – the Okies fleeing both the Dust Bowl and the farm-tenancy system – to advocate for the expansion of the social-welfare net. That Steinbeck's novel had such an influence on welfare governance is unsurprising. Indeed, numerous critics have brought to light the extent to which literature during this period considered and repackaged emerging political platforms on behalf of the American public at large. For Michael Szalay, *The Grapes of Wrath* is an archetypal case of popular sources participating in the 'reinvention of modern governance' in the wake of the New Deal (3). Though the reception of the novel among the political left continues to shift, reviews at the time of publication likewise identified the policy-oriented focus of the book.[1] The proximity of Steinbeck's novel to the legislation of its day indicates not only the sweeping relevance of the text but also the broadly ambitious scale of New Deal governance in general. In addition to stimulating the economy, the policies enacted in the 1930s following the Great Depression did more than respond to financial crisis: champions of the New Deal both in and outside of government saw these reforms as crucial to transforming the social fabric of the US. To this end, the welfare codes crafted during this period enabled the state not only to provide for its neediest citizens but also to define the standards by which citizens were deemed worthy of support in the first place. Literary sources like *The Grapes of Wrath* played a central role in actualising the state's social policies by assisting in this project of scrutinising different segments of the population.

Steinbeck's novel also initiates a turn in the type of political activism embedded in vagrant narratives as practised by, for example, Jack London and George Orwell. Unlike the vagrancy sources explored in previous chapters of this book, Steinbeck's work depicts vagrants who embrace the domestic sphere: rather than picaresque tramps or hobos, he concerns himself in *The Grapes of Wrath* with families – men, women and children – who involuntarily find themselves on the margins of society. Steinbeck's innovation in this area reflects his sustained interest in tramping figures throughout his career. Vagabond characters are at the centre of his 1937 novella *Of Mice and Men*, for example, and Steinbeck imagines himself as a romantic 'bum' in his 1962 travel narrative *Travels with Charley* (*Travels* 3). I discuss this latter text in more detail in the Epilogue, but suffice to say that *The Grapes of Wrath* stands alone among the author's oeuvre as a book that is both immensely popular to this day and intensely studied for its direct engagement with (and influence on) social-policy making. The specific depiction of vagrancy in *The Grapes of Wrath*, moreover, warrants full elaboration because it signifies the point at which the simmering literary project involving tramps essentially breaks through into both popular and governmental discourse.

If Steinbeck found a winning formula for presenting sympathetic accounts of vagrant characters, his explicit appeals to whiteness are undoubtedly part of the equation. As this last point implies, this chapter seeks to both build on and move beyond the debate concerning the racial politics implicit in the novel's presentation of the social transformation associated with New Deal policies. Michael Denning provides the definitive version of this account of *The Grapes of Wrath* when he argues that Steinbeck's narrative, which depicts 'noble white Americans' and overlooks non-white migrant farmers, ultimately 'reinforce[s] interpretations of New Deal populism as sentimental and conservative' (*Cultural* 267, 268). Denning's comprehensive overview of this problematic populism has set the tone for subsequent studies on the novel vis-à-vis its political advocacy. To be sure, critics have revised or otherwise countered some of the most critical aspects of Denning's assessment.[2] For example, Mollie Godfrey argues that if Steinbeck emphasised the whiteness of his migrant characters, he did so not to reinforce conservative racial politics but to deliberately incorporate 'the slippages within humanist terminology and techniques to correct readers' sympathies with racist and bourgeois ideologies' (109). As this scholarship makes clear, the presentation of the deserving poor in Steinbeck's work assumes distinctly racialised forms. However, in the debate over this subject we should not lose sight of how Steinbeck uses racial discourse to introduce a new economic logic in which white nobility figures as a form of labour sufficiently exploitable and durable to be worth the state's investment. Concerned with the future of migrant labour, Steinbeck deploys this racial terminology to distinguish among different populations of people. He therefore implicitly produces a timeline during which certain populations wither while others – in this case, white migrant farmers – enter the centre of society through a combination of their own so-called natural talents and specific governmental policy. In other words, for Steinbeck the family on the move is a resource that the state must tap in order to prosper.

Viewing migrancy in these terms expands previous accounts of Steinbeck's interest in the family as a matter of social policy. For example, Szalay argues that Steinbeck's representation of the Joads' domestic drama mobilises 'populist sentiment' in order to garner readers' sympathy for an underlying brand of governmental policy (167). According to this reading, the family matters to Steinbeck inasmuch as he takes the private relationships it connotes and then abstracts them, applying them to the essentially impersonal world of governance. While this interpretation is useful for placing Steinbeck's fiction into proximity with official policy, it risks overlooking the specific forms the Joad family, as the embodiment of vagrancy, assumes throughout the novel. Whereas movement figured in previous tramping narratives as an expression of individual freedom, the migrants in *The Grapes of Wrath* move in search of steady wage labour. In the former literary model, tramps and vagabonds use their separation from the domestic sphere to become astute critics of consumption and productivity. In Steinbeck's text, the unemployed (no longer solitary in their movements) stay mobile not to avoid entering the wage economy but rather to facilitate their entrance into it. Steinbeck thus treats the Joads, and the Dust Bowl migrant class they embody, as one specific population among many competing migrant groups. He makes this concept especially clear in *The Harvest Gypsies* (later republished as *Their Blood Is Strong*), a series of essays commissioned by the *San Francisco News* in 1936 that details the conditions in migrant-labour camps in Central California.

As the basis for *The Grapes of Wrath*, these essays provide a plain look at the more polemical underpinnings of the novel. In addition to describing life inside the work camps, the essays in *The*

Harvest Gypsies also 'contain specific policy recommendations' for addressing the hardships facing migrant families (*Harvest* ix). As is the case in the novel, Steinbeck resorts here to the language of race and national types to frame the debate over migrant labour in terms of preserving the future integrity of the nation state. On the subject of migrant labour in California, he presents a scenario in which Mexicans and Filipinos are waning in numbers while white migrant workers are flooding the state (*Harvest* 21). Although this flurry of movement on both sides of the border gestures to the international breadth of the Depression, it is also indicative of a distinct transformation unfolding at home, as Steinbeck claims. Referring to the non-white labourers, he argues:

> The earlier foreign migrants have invariably been drawn from a peon class. This is not the case with the new migrants. They are small farmers who have lost their farms, or farm hands who have lived with the family in the old American way. They are men who have worked hard on their own farms and have felt the pride of possessing and living in close touch with the land . . .
> They have weathered the thing, and they can weather much more for their blood is strong. (*Harvest* 22)

At once, Steinbeck conflates race, class and nationalism to make a claim about the temporal integrity of migrant labour. By delineating the face of the 'new' migrant worker, he produces a thoroughly nostalgic vision of 'the old American way' (*Harvest* 22). Of course, this representation relies on a notion of Protestant self-reliance and other stereotypes premised on 'their blood'.[3] At the same time, Steinbeck shows readers the most contemporary aspects of what he argues is a much longer narrative, one in which the state must regulate its populations on the basis of their productivity and civil-mindedness. 'Foreign labor is on the wane in California', he writes, 'and the future farm workers are to be white and American' (*Harvest* 57). Steinbeck implies that this population's ability to move is a boon to resource management inasmuch as the national workforce has the good sense to relocate as the economy changes gears. Conversely, the picture of society in this account excludes subjects who fail in his eyes to meet certain civil and domestic standards. Simply put, he visualises a future American social structure that is akin to Jeffersonian democracy without slavery – a typology that excludes deviant types entirely.

Steinbeck's exclusion of non-white subjects is not anomalous but rather echoes the long and concerted effort at state and federal levels to restrict non-white migrants' access to the mainstream of civil life. At the onset of the Depression, for instance, the US government dramatically increased the deportation of Mexican labourers in the American Southwest. Begun during the Hoover administration and carried over into the Roosevelt era, these efforts were not limited to foreign-born workers: Americans with Mexican ancestry were subject to repatriation as well, effectively nullifying the civil rights nominally granted by citizenship altogether (Hoffman 218).[4] The setting for *The Grapes of Wrath*, California in particular was a laboratory for exclusionary policies that would eventually emerge as the subject of debate at the federal level. Published in 1939, Carey McWilliams's *Factories in the Field* makes this history especially clear, tracing the state's lengthy reliance on – and suppression of – foreign labour populations from well before the Great Depression. Recent scholarship has also brought into focus the numerous anti-immigrant legislative efforts that originated in California. For example, Mae Ngai details the federal-lobbying effort by the nativist California Joint Immigration Committee to exclude Japanese subjects from citizenship during the 1920s (47). Steinbeck's minimal representation of Japanese, Filipino and Mexican labourers in his work therefore mirrors, whether intentionally or not, the anti-immigrant policies aimed at these populations at the state and federal levels.

While Steinbeck's narrow focus on whiteness dovetails with contemporary governmental policy, his construction of migrant labour looks well beyond this immediate political context. The national fantasy that he imagines is therefore not a preservationist one per se, but rather one that both forecasts and manages the movement of labour well into the future. Like Orwell in *Down and Out in Paris and London*, Steinbeck registers the end of the tramp archetype as it was once known. As I will explain below, *The Grapes of Wrath* dramatises the disappearance of these archetypal tramps most explicitly in the case of Tom Joad, who first performs and then divorces himself from the role of the tramp: entering the narrative as a restless man with a criminal past, he exits the narrative to work on behalf of the greater good. As this brief example suggests, Steinbeck's writing facilitates the end of one era of migratory politics even as it imagines a new one. The novel thus quickly establishes a model for the political activism that will play out throughout the narrative, where the exceptional qualities of the tramping figure are writ large on families – and later, Steinbeck predicts, on whole populations. On one level, this move reflects the new reality of labour after the onset of the Depression. Arriving penniless at agricultural sites, Steinbeck explains in *The Harvest Gypsies*, migrant workers must take out debts from the landowners to keep their families intact: 'while single men are able to get from harvest to harvest on the railroads and by hitch-hiking, the man with a family will starve if he loses his car. Under this threat he goes on working' (*Harvest* 35). In this context, the family emerges in Steinbeck's novel as a point of contention for both the migrants who wish to stay together and the big agribusinesses that exploit this desire as a tool for driving down wages.

Steinbeck's call for better management of the migrant family requires the state to fundamentally refashion its tools for identifying vagrant classes in the first place. The vagrant status Steinbeck describes in the passage above contradicts what he argues should be the white migrant's exceptional status: once the cornerstone of 'the old American way', they are treated no better than 'foreign labor'. As Godfrey points out, 'white migrant workers of the period did not necessarily count as white' in the public eye (219). Anti-vagrancy laws maintained this perception to the extent that they empowered local governments to disrupt the migrant family's productive labour. More robust intervention in the arena of vagrancy law, Steinbeck implies, would not only end this harassment but also elevate the status of white migrants by helping to facilitate their mobility. Only when the state can refigure the vagrancy policies that ensnare the exceptional form of vagrancy that the Joads embody, Steinbeck posits, can society benefit from this population's inherent talents: the Depression has made them migrants and big farming has kicked them off their land, but the state can turn them into assets. The intimate pictures of getting by in Steinbeck's novel therefore coexist and move in tandem with the government's dream of managing its populations along biological as well as economic lines.

Tramp Literature and the Depression

Steinbeck's representation of vagrancy, which centres on whole migratory families, is a clear point of distinction among vagrancy narratives from the turn of the century. In the context of the US, the literary consensus regarding the tramp's dangerous embodiment of individualism continued to generate popular interest well into the 1920s. For example, Jack Black's *You Can't Win*, a non-fictional account of the former hobo's criminal exploits, became a massive hit after its publication in 1926.[5] The picaresque exploits detailed in *You Can't Win*, as well as in contemporary tramping memoirs such as Jim Tully's 1924 *Beggars of Life*, extended the tramping template established by stories published in the nineteenth century. The vagabond authors of these texts present themselves as exemplary criminals able to sustain themselves on society's margins through their deft wits and physical endurance. During this same period, prominent authors of American fiction such as John Dos Passos and Ernest Hemingway elaborated on the tramp's familiar qualities. The form of the tramping narrative established in this book's earlier chapters – largely involving single men on the road – continued to persist after the economic crash, when even the most privileged readers could hardly escape scenes of poverty in their daily lives. At the same time, any lingering romanticisation associated with vagabondage is, by and large, absent from tramping texts in the wake of the Depression. As Christine Photinos points out, the swelling ranks of homeless and unemployed people precipitated a turn in tramp writing, which stressed bleak assessments of life lived on the road and under constant hardship ('The Tramp' 5). In the years prior to the Depression, texts like Black's therefore reflected something of a swan song for the criminal-tramp narrative as it appeared in the Gilded Age.

Tramp stories during the 1930s helped to facilitate this shift in the representation of vagrancy in popular culture. Like George Orwell in *Down and Out in Paris and London*, American sources still recognised the tramp archetype (and its associations with whiteness and masculinity) even as socio-economic conditions around homelessness and vagrancy changed. If the tramp emerged in the aftermath of the Panic of 1873, then the Great Depression inaugurated the end of this figure's heyday. Dos Passos acknowledges this turn in his presentation of the tramp as a figure that society has left behind. He concludes his 1936 novel *The Big Money* – the final instalment in his *U.S.A.* trilogy – with 'Vag', a vignette featuring a starving tramp travelling vainly for better opportunities 'down the road' (447). Here, the vagabond's formerly exceptional features are rendered useless when commuters pass him by in luxury cars or comfortably fly overhead in planes.

Alongside these examples, other texts published around the time of the Depression scrutinised more closely the racial associations of the tramp figure. Published in 1925, Hemingway's 'The Battler' reiterates the masculine framing of tramping stories while also noting the tramp's vexed embodiment of whiteness. In the short story, Nick Adams, Hemingway's fictional alter ego, is thrown off a train for attempting to ride the rails. In a nearby hobo camp, he encounters two tramping characters: Ad, a 'crazy' former boxer, and

Bugs, whom the narrative describes simply as 'a negro' (*In Our Time* 56, 57). Bugs eventually confides to Nick that travelling with Ad affords him a sense of mobility that would otherwise be denied him. Hemingway's story thus touches on the relative forms of privilege afforded to white vagrants that otherwise forms the unacknowledged subtext to many of the narratives considered thus far in *The American Vagrant in Literature*. While all three men take advantage of the freedom that the road provides them, Bugs's access to this rugged autonomy is viable only through his association with Ad, 'the little white man' (58). As Bugs explains, 'He likes to think I'm crazy and I don't mind. I like to be with him and I like seeing the country and I don't have to commit no larceny to do it' (61). Presenting a diverse picture of vagabondage, Hemingway's text nonetheless posits an enduring gap between Bugs's contingent relation to autonomy and Nick's relatively easy access to it.

African American writers also took note of the tramp's proximity to masculinity and whiteness.[6] Published the same year as *The Grapes of Wrath*, William Attaway's *Let Me Breathe Thunder* meditates on the danger associated with vagrant types while foregrounding the racial features attached to tramps in particular. Attaway's novel centres on two white tramps who, like Lennie and George in Steinbeck's *Of Mice and Men*, wander in the pursuit of quick cash. In both texts, the tramps' short-sightedness brings misery to the people they encounter on their travels. Hailed upon its release as 'the first novel about whites by a Negro', *Let Me Breathe Thunder* taps into the familiar literary tradition of vagrant men on the move (Rovere 26). For example, a review in the American Marxist magazine *New Masses* frets that Attaway is 'cashing in on the literary glamor of migratory labor, for which Steinbeck is largely responsible' after the success of *Of Mice and Men* (Rovere 27). In contrast to Steinbeck's work, however, Attaway is less concerned with moving the tramp out of the social margins. Instead, his depiction of vagrancy explores the limits of self-actualisation: seemingly confirming the worst prejudices regarding transient workers, *Let Me Breathe Thunder* strives to make the reader complicit in the antisocial violence that follows these figures wherever they travel.

These works attest to the potent cultural significance of the vagrant in US literature after the Depression and, more importantly, the extent to which Steinbeck diverges from the image of migratory labour he otherwise helped to establish. In the case of *The Harvest Gypsies*, he identifies the end of the archetypal bindlestiff as a useful category for discussing migratory labour in the US: no longer comprised of solitary men, the new migrant class Steinbeck depicts encompasses entire families. Moreover, the shift to a more domestic view of homelessness is embedded in the very structure of *The Grapes of Wrath*, which depicts the rehabilitation of tramp-like figures such as Tom Joad and the troubled preacher Jim Casy. The novel's earliest chapters, after all, conspicuously lack the family that is otherwise at the centre of the narrative. Instead, the text features men who, alone and out of work, roam across empty homesteads left in the wake of the Dust Bowl era. Tom's early characterisation in particular calls to mind the archetypal tramping figure that will disappear completely by the narrative's end. He is 'a man walking along the edge of the highway' with a troubled past and a criminal record (*Grapes* 5). Readers eventually learn, however, that Tom tramps not to escape the domestic sphere but as a means to return home to the confines of the family. Casy is another example of a wandering man who has transgressed social norms to some degree only to eventually re-enter the fold in order to protect the Joad family and fight against economic injustice. The novel's representation of these characters as both transients and anti-authority figures touches on the notion of vagabond criminality that the bulk of the text redirects to more socially productive outlets.

Along with his appeals to the whiteness and national character of his migrant families, Steinbeck further elaborates on how failure to protect these families will damage the nation state. The 'armed vigilantism' of local authorities, he warns, 'is an attempt to overthrow [the] system of laws and to substitute a government by violence' (*Harvest* 61). Attacks against the migrant families are, in this figuration, as dangerous to the nation state as they are to the individuals involved. At stake in this battle over migrant labour, he concludes, is the spirit of liberal democracy: 'Fascistic methods are more numerous, more powerfully applied and more openly practiced in California than any other place in the United States. It will require a militant and watchful organization ... to fight this encroaching social philosophy' (*Harvest* 62). Steinbeck here borrows from and inverts the rhetoric of anti-labour campaigns inasmuch as he frames this debate around the idea of protecting American values against foreign influence; in this case, it is the owners rather than the labourers who import tactics from overseas. According to this logic, the state of agricultural labour threatens to topple the ideological status quo in the US. In making this assertion, Steinbeck frames the political reform he is seeking – more federal oversight of the wages and working conditions of migrant labour – around the moral issue of preserving America's spiritual identity. In making this case, however, Steinbeck must play up the most stereotypical cultural and racial underpinnings of this identity. If reforming the migrant worker will transform government, he suggests, his readers can take comfort in knowing that workers like the Joads represent the most familiar segments of the US population.

While *The Grapes of Wrath* lacks the direct appeals contained in *The Harvest Gypsies*, it nonetheless constructs a similar picture of homespun American democracy. The novel consistently upholds a distinction between the federal government as an institution for social reform and more localised authority figures as agents of unregulated capitalism. The repressive authorities that appear in the text are motivated by economic forces outside of their control: a laissez-faire industry that fears for its existence so long as progressive government holds power. More specifically, *The Grapes of Wrath* points to both 'widening government' and 'growing labor unity' as sources of concern for reactionary owners in the US in general and the agriculture industry in particular (150). In contrast to the deputies and local posses keeping migrants out of their small towns, big-business interests appear in the singular form of the 'monster' that 'can make men do what it wants' (*Grapes* 34). As this image makes clear, Steinbeck sees the struggle against unregulated capitalism as one that pushes back against the dehumanising aspects of both mechanised industry and the consolidation of big business itself, which compel labourers to work against the best interests of the nation state on the one hand and the working classes on the other.

For Steinbeck, the solution to anti-labour oppression lies in a truly national framework of regulation. A site of federal relief for migrants, the Weedpatch camp in *The Grapes of Wrath* supersedes the authority of local law-enforcement agencies. As a literal, bounded space, this setting provides the migrants (as well as the novel's readers) a basis for visualising the power of national sovereignty in play. One migrant farmer in the novel explains this dynamic directly: 'You know a vagrant is anybody a cop don't like. An' that's why they hate this here camp. No cops can get in. This here's United States, not California' (*Grapes* 334). The narrative suggests that the big businesses that are keeping living standards low stand to lose if the government's plan for relief comes to pass on a large scale. In addition, the government camp provides the migrants a way to organise themselves according to a properly national basis of affiliation: thrown off their land, they cohere around a form of identity that supersedes the regional or local. Governance provides the crucial nationalising element to this end. In the text, the appearance of federal authority removes the migrants from 'California' and places them squarely within the 'United States' (*Grapes* 334). The intersection of law and land in the camp provides these subjects with a clearly defined homestead where they can begin to build on the communal bonds they have forged on the road.

Steinbeck thus constructs an American type that both embodies a self-reliant work ethic and deploys this labour for the benefit of society. But while this national type may be naturally occurring, he reasons, it nonetheless requires the state to protect these traits from the unnatural interference of unregulated industry. The scenes that take place within Weedpatch exemplify what Steinbeck sees as the ideal relation between workers and a socially conscious government. At the same time, the broad humanistic appeal of the Weedpatch camp in Steinbeck's account is belied by the exclusive characteristics of the families who thrive there. His presentation of migrant labour in terms of specific national types undergirds scenes depicting the interaction between destitute Americans and the federal programmes meant to help them. In what follows, I place Steinbeck's literary depiction of these values within the context of specific components of the New Deal that endure beyond the nominal end of the welfare state. These laws, while aiming in theory to enfranchise impoverished Americans altogether, in practice often entrenched the political power of a specific type of American at the cost of others. The continuing controversy over the implementation of Social Security after 1935 in particular showcases one of the most prominent cases of ostensibly humanist political codes operating according to hegemonic social values.

Refiguring the Family: Steinbeck and Social Security

The crowning achievement of the New Deal, Social Security continues well after its inception to foment political debate on the subjects of race, class and civil responsibility in the US. Much of the scholarship on the subject has centred on the underlying racial animus that has shaped the programme's reception among the American public. A study by the Brookings Institute in 2001 found, for example, that among the US population 'race is the single most important predictor of support for welfare' (Alesina et al. 189). The study's authors claim that decades after the Roosevelt administration's reforms, 'America's troubled race relations are clearly a major reason for the absence of an American welfare state' of the likes operating in Western Europe (189). The idea that today's welfare politics intersect with an overarching debate involving race should be familiar to most observers, especially in cases where the language of racial stereotype undergirds anti-welfare rhetoric. What is less clear in the decades since the New Deal, however, is the extent to which the state designed these social programmes in order to link racial typology to welfare administration in a matter that continues into the present day.

The implicitly hegemonic politics of Social Security belie its nominally colour-blind policies. Indeed, the appeal of Social Security among New Deal proponents rested on the notion that the programme is truly universal by design, theoretically allowing nearly all Americans in need to receive welfare benefits regardless of other demographic considerations (Winter 400). The actual insurance that the programme offers, however, falls well short of the universal coverage that is characteristic of European welfare models (Schieber and Shoven 17). Instead, the original Social Security Act of 1935 established an old-age-pension fund – the largest and most publicly visible component of the legislation – as well as benefits for impoverished children and the unemployed with strict restrictions on eligibility.[7] As is the case with any regulation of public health, popular media worked with government in both creating and policing the subsection of poor Americans who met these criteria. A broadly popular text with a very specific picture of poverty, Steinbeck's novel stands out among literary sources in shaping the public's perception of the deserving poor as components of welfare reform.

Specifically, Steinbeck uses the essentialising language of family and race as shorthand for the productive workforce he believes the state can create. Rather than an oversight, the gap between his novel's universalism and its distinct typologies mirrors a governing discourse that from its earliest stages struggled to reconcile its humanist aims with its more exclusionary policies. As a result, the Social Security Act excluded nearly half of the US labour force. The bill's insurance protections originally applied only to those in 'commerce and industry', leaving domestic and agricultural workers completely excluded from the pool of beneficiaries (DeWitt 49). Because Black workers were disproportionately affected by this provision, many scholars have argued that the bill was intentionally written in such a way as to marginalise non-white Americans, especially in the South.[8] Although the programme's provisions became gradually more inclusive over time with subsequent amendments, the original exclusions speak to the overriding impulse of the US welfare state to tie relief provisions to those citizens who satisfy the state's narrow definition of the deserving poor. In his address to Congress in 1935, Roosevelt spelled out this rationale in moralising terms: 'Continued dependence on relief induces a spiritual and moral disintegration fundamentally destructive to the national fiber', he argued (qtd in Schiltz 30). In contrast, he stressed, the administration's welfare programmes would 'derive their social legitimacy from the achievements of beneficiaries' (qtd in Schiltz 30). According to this logic, charity was harmful to the nation precisely because it damaged the integrity of the individual worker. In contrast, Social Security appeared to deliver the just desserts of the hard-working citizen.[9]

Deriving from its authors' definition of social legitimacy, Social Security further entrenched the social values of certain national types in spite of its nominally universal scope. As part of this push to establish a universal standard for evaluating welfare subjects, Social Security also scrutinised the family structure – and its encompassing gender roles – as a regulatory object. Indeed, for many scholars the codification of traditional gender roles in the name of the family has been the most enduring cultural legacy of Social Security in the US. Part of this legacy extends from tax exemptions in the original legislation given to religious and non-profit organisations, employment fields whose workers were disproportionately women (Mettler 73). According to historian Alice Kessler-Harris, 60 per cent of the exempted workers were women, even though women at the time made up less than 30 per cent of the workforce (92). In addition to these initial exemptions, the marriage benefits built into Social Security also came with drastic social consequences.[10] The state's distinguishing of worthwhile from non-productive labour further underscored the reverberations of the Social Security programme outside the workplace and inside the home.

Steinbeck's interest in fostering a more radical population is likewise tethered to a logic that imposes clear divisions between groups based on demographic difference. 'Thus [the families] changed their social life', the narrator of *The Grapes of Wrath* explains, 'changed as in the whole universe only man can change. They were not farm men any more, but migrant men' (196). Steinbeck's tempered rhetoric of universalism is especially apparent in this passage, in which even the most sweeping social changes leave untouched the exceptional nature of these (thoroughly masculine) individuals. The depiction of Ma Joad – who declares she is 'takin' over the fambly' after the men fail to provide the security she craves – gestures further to how the novel revises certain family roles (*Grapes* 423). On the one hand, the rise of Ma Joad signals the novel's interest in rejecting patriarchal family models in view of migrant labour's new realities. At the same time, this implicit critique of patriarchy hinges on a generalising sense of gender identity to rationalise this change. 'Woman can change better'n a man', she explains, since a '[w]oman got all her life in her arms. Man got it all in his head' (*Grapes* 423). As this language suggests, the scope of Steinbeck's reform is more modest than it might otherwise appear. At once, he foregrounds dramatic changes in the domestic power dynamic and emphasises the inherited gender roles that helped facilitate these transformations.

Steinbeck's critics have argued that the fine line the author often constructs between conventional social norms and more radical ones derives from his interest in applying social Darwinism to the world of policy making. One version of this Darwinist thinking appears in his non-fictional text *The Log from the Sea of Cortez*, which collects observations from a marine-biology expedition alongside wide-ranging discussions of natural selection. Here, Steinbeck and Ed Ricketts, marine biologist and collaborator on the expedition, expound the concept of what they call '"is" thinking', a perspective that stresses '[n]on-teleological ideas ... associated with natural selection as Darwin seems to have understood it' (*Sea of Cortez* 112). Steinbeck and Ricketts craft a scenario wherein people must negotiate between biological impulses on the one hand and inherited social norms on the other.[11] On its face, this outlook at least nominally celebrates social change as a means for survival. But as Cyrus Zirakzadeh concludes in his account of this philosophy, it also hinges on the premise that certain communities live or die on the basis of their cultural beliefs and practices (616). For humanity to thrive, according to this reasoning, it must adapt – but not completely ignore – its inherited knowledge in order to respond to new challenges and 'avoid extinction' (Zirakzadeh 608). *The Log from the Sea of Cortez* – researched, written and published in the decade following *The Grapes of Wrath* – highlights Steinbeck's long interest in discerning the biological underpinnings of social practices. In view of his sustained engagement with this idea, my reading analyses a crucial moment in Steinbeck's thought, visible in his figuration of white migration in both *The Grapes of Wrath* and *The Harvest Gypsies*.[12] While Steinbeck might push for social reform on all fronts in these texts, he presents a scenario in which specific groups will naturally thrive where others fail. In this light, Ma Joad's embodiment of feminine strength assumes distinctly racial and cultural overtones as well.

For Steinbeck, the natural strength of these migrants comes to fruition only with the state's intervention on their behalf. In short, the government camps signify the type of persistent, vigilant oversight necessary to direct these inherited talents to their most useful outlets. What appears at first glance to be an inherent contradiction between nature and nurture is instead a key component of the social philosophy Steinbeck outlines in his work. Taken together, *The Harvest Gypsies* and *The Grapes of Wrath* present a specific population in need of relief, most immediately in the form of state intervention against exploitative labour practices. In addition, both make the case that this population embodies in more ways than one the most advantageous characteristics of American labour. Although white migrants might possess the hereditary traits that set them apart from other populations, these natural strengths still need the support of a strongly collectivist society in order to mature. In *The Harvest Gypsies*, Steinbeck outlines this plan for relief at length, explaining that the federal government will make use of the migrant's agricultural skillset by providing subsistence farms, schools and housing for labourers and their families:

> Since the greatest number of the white American migrants are former farm owners, renters or laborers, it follows that their training and ambition have never been removed from agriculture. It is suggested that lands be leased; or where it is possible, that state and Federal lands be set aside as subsistence farms for migrants. These can be leased at a low rent or sold on long time payments to families of migrant workers. (*Harvest* 58)

The vision of relief outlined in *The Harvest Gypsies* accounts only for 'white American farmers', for these are the people whom Steinbeck views as being most capable of helping themselves, owing to their particular cultural and social upbringing. For Steinbeck, the government's interest in nurturing self-sufficiency is crucial not only to help eradicate the worst effects of poverty but also to strengthen its own polity. Accordingly, the qualities that he claims make the white migrant farmer useful as a labourer – conviction in the dignity of work as well as in the traditional family structure – apply directly to his usefulness in the civic sphere as well. In view of this role, Steinbeck concludes, 'In these communities a spirit of cooperation and self-help should be encouraged so that by self-government and a returning social responsibility these people may be restored to the rank of citizens' (*Harvest* 59). Once again Steinbeck focuses on both improving the lives of migrant workers and strengthening the rule of law on a national scale. In short, the farmers in this scenario internalise the social values that will make them better citizens in the long term.

Recalling Steinbeck's position on subsistence farms in *The Harvest Gypsies*, the government camp in *The Grapes of Wrath* offers a form of relief that nurtures what he sees as the inherent dignity of the white migrant labourer. In both texts, Steinbeck is careful to distinguish the type of relief he outlines from charity; whereas the former builds self-reliance, he suggests, the latter turns workers into slavish subjects. In *The Grapes of Wrath*, Ma Joad hears a version of this argument early on in her stay at Weedpatch. A woman from the camp's welcoming committee explains that in contrast to the individualistic form of relief at Weedpatch, taking charity 'makes a burn that don't come out' (*Grapes* 316):

> 'We don't allow nobody to give nothing to another person. They can give it to the camp, an' the camp can pass it out. We won't have no charity!' Her voice was fierce and hoarse. 'I hate 'em,' she said. 'I ain't never seen my man beat before, but them – them Salvation Army done it to 'im.' (*Grapes* 316)

For Steinbeck, the federal camp fosters a form of relief that rewards self-governance, in opposition to the dehumanising effects of outright charity. His presentation of welfare along these lines succinctly makes the case for expanding the liberal state while also paying homage to the abiding sense of individual self-sufficiency. Tom's decision to become a labour organiser of sorts is therefore possible only after his experiences in the camp, which provide him with a glimpse of what could be: 'I been thinkin' how it was in that gov'ment camp, how our folks took care a theirselves, an' if they was a fight they fixed it theirself' (*Grapes* 419). Tom's imagining of collective action here explicitly resists the more oppressive aspects of governmental authority – 'Throw out the cops that ain't our people', he reasons – on the basis of communal identity (*Grapes* 419). All the same, Tom's vision of a self-sustaining community operates fully under the aegis of the government in the form of the camp in particular and welfare legislation in general. If migrants like the Joad family organise themselves according to a natural sense of democracy, the narrative suggests, the nation state can rely on them to self-regulate accordingly. In this light, Tom's decision to 'be ever'where – wherever you look' in fighting against labour oppression represents his ultimate transformation into the novel's everyman: he stands in for the generalised image of the migrant radical that Steinbeck believes will right the course of the country (*Grapes* 419).

Given Tom's prominence early in the text, this transformation further highlights the extent to which the novel has shaped the characteristics of migrancy into a specific, homogenised demographic. As I argued above, if the novel begins by focusing on tramping men like Tom and Casy, it concludes by offering the family as the model for participation in the civil sphere. Ma Joad's position at the head of the household helps to explain what is at stake in this model for both mobile families as well as the government at large. It is Ma Joad, after all, who articulates most clearly the identity under duress that once tied together family, labour and the land. 'They was the time when we was on the lan'. They was a boundary to us then', she explains. 'Ol' folks died off, an' little fellas come, an' we was always one thing – we was the fambly – kinda whole and clear. An' now we ain't clear no more' (*Grapes* 393). Throughout the novel, Ma Joad makes the case for a strong family structure buttressed by property ownership. Accordingly, her drive to get her family on stable ground with steady jobs, a large house and a big yard continually underscores the material dimensions of this domestic identity. In this light, the novel suggests that the repressive tactics of big farming business – encapsulated best by the murder of Jim Casy, the book's prototypical labour organiser – fail in a number of ways. Most immediately, owners spell their own doom by engendering greater class solidarity among the abused workers. But more implicitly, these repressive tactics merely stand in the way of what Steinbeck sees as the inherent drive for migrant workers to become useful contributors to the economy.

The Harvest Gypsies outlines the usefulness of the federal camp programme in terms of social rehabilitation: 'The success of the Federal camps in making potential criminals into citizens', Steinbeck argues, 'makes the usual practice of expending money on tear gas seem a little silly' (42–3). The opposition he constructs between 'criminals' and 'citizens' is especially telling: the migrant is in need not only of relief but also of state intervention if he is to enter civil society at all. Once he does so, he becomes a defender of both labour and liberal democracy against the forces of laissez-faire industrialism. Of course, Steinbeck's texts paint a thoroughly critical picture of authoritarian union-busting, police brutality and other displays of violence that characterised the anti-labour movement. At the same time, his formulation places the rights-affirming government camps and such repressive policies on the same governmental continuum.

Police action might reduce criminal elements, he suggests, but the camps do the same while nurturing the individual's sense of 'dignity' (*Harvest* 43). The camps offer for Steinbeck an undoubtedly more ethical form of population control, but they pursue the same end as the tear-gas approach as far as the rehabilitation of marginal subjects is concerned.

Migrancy in *The Grapes of Wrath* likewise strips social practices down to their essential cores. The families that survive the ordeal on the road strike the proper balance between self- and social preservation: in view of their own family structures, these migrants see the value in a collective form of governance that also valorises individual acts of hard work. In facing life-and-death decisions, these subjects gradually leave outdated modes of thought by the wayside. Describing the spontaneous communities formed on the road, the narrative grounds itself in a thoroughly civil-minded discourse: it showcases the process by which certain rights are identified, tested and implemented among this migrant class. Part of this process involves identifying the limits of self-government on the basis of community consensus: 'And the families learned, although no one told them, what rights are monstrous and must be destroyed', the narrator explains (*Grapes* 194). Ultimately, the migrants receive a crash course in the tenets of democratic organisation:

> The families learned what rights must be observed – the right of privacy in the tent; the right to keep the past black hidden in the heart; the right to talk and to listen; the right to refuse help or to accept, to offer help or to decline it; the right of son to court and daughter to be courted; the right of the hungry to be fed; the rights of the pregnant and the sick to transcend all other rights. (*Grapes* 194)

In this instance, Steinbeck presents a fuller account of the natural democracy he describes in *The Harvest Gypsies*: a nature that must be produced. The passage provides a particularly clear example of how his political advocacy is grounded in provincial scenes of families at work. By portraying the death, starvation and abuse of countless families, the novel shakes its readers into action against further suffering of this sort. At the same time, this depiction also brings into focus a sharper picture of what Steinbeck sees as the most crucial aspects of a stable American middle class. In addition to advocating for political change, the text suggests that these families have already been fundamentally changed by their experiences. The migrants are builders of 'worlds' – complete with 'leaders', 'elders' and 'certain physical' boundaries – that live or die depending on the cohesiveness of the makeshift community (*Grapes* 195). So long as these families are in flight across the country, the communities prove to be short-lived. Ma Joad's efforts to keep the family together therefore reflect the first step towards solidifying this demographic as both a political force and a workforce: 'They ain't gonna wipe us out. Why, we're the people – we go on' (*Grapes* 280). If these migrants are to be the future of American labour, the worlds they carry with them promise to fundamentally alter society at large.

'Defense Migration': Vagrancy after the New Deal

We see in Steinbeck's nominally inclusive notion of 'the people' the ideological reverberations of the governmental institutions coming into full force during this time. The consolidation of the US welfare state during the Depression offered a safety net for some of the country's most destitute and marginalised citizens, but in responding to this poverty crisis the state resorted to creating the very subjects it was purporting to help. Indeed, the suggestion that relief must be earned through worthwhile labour effectively pushed entire segments of the population further into the social margins. But while it is likely that Steinbeck provided the most popular example of New Deal-inspired policy finding its way into artistic narrative, he was far from alone in depicting a universalising picture of the working classes. The art projects that emanated from government-sponsored programmes were likewise invested in depicting a distinctly American sense of national identity. In particular, the emergence of the Works Progress Administration (WPA) in 1935 cemented (if only for a brief time) the government's role in shaping popular culture. Created as an employment relief programme, the WPA directly funded numerous facets of cultural production, including art, drama, music and historical research. As Jonathan Harris argues, federal initiatives such as the WPA resulted in nothing less than the 'explicit politicization of cultural (including artistic) production' during the 1930s (5). On the subject of the Federal Art Project, Harris identifies what he calls the 'hegemonizing' influence of the New Deal in the sphere of art (9). 'Culture', he notes, 'was recognized [by Roosevelt and New Deal Democrats] to be a strategically important terrain upon which could be constructed (and possibly reconstructed) people's sense of identity and of belonging to a social totality' (9).

While nominally outside the WPA, Steinbeck nonetheless portrays in his work an image of American identity and labour that is fundamentally in sync with official government accounts. Many critics have looked to the murals and sculptures installed in public buildings during this period as archetypal examples of official New Deal propaganda at work. As in Steinbeck, the farmer appears in these works as a potent symbol of the American values that undergirded the governmental policies of the era. As Marilyn Wyman notes, one WPA mural in Central California depicts white farmers standing in the foreground while '[g]rain in the field waves in an unseen breeze', all without any 'trace of migrant laborers' or the violence they faced (34). On one level, idyllic imagery such as this present an untroubled picture of workers and the machines of industry to quell public anxiety over the state of the economy. But in addition to addressing the fears of the American public, Wyman explains, these art projects also used the connotative power of the farmer as a 'marker for Jeffersonian republicanism distinguished by its faith in the virtuous yeoman (independent) farmer who owned and worked the land' (36). In contrast to these WPA works, Steinbeck's novel provides a clear view of the various hardships facing the migrant worker and of an economic system on the brink of collapse. At the same time, however, Steinbeck relies on the same fundamental motif as these projects – in particular, a nostalgic depiction of the white yeoman farmer who augers a future state of American governance. For both artists and government officials invested in this transformation, then, the migrant farmer personifies a period of transition between Jeffersonian democracy and its future realisation via governmental policy.

The valorisation of this specific form of migrant labour continues to reverberate beyond the context of the Depression. By 1939, Congress had defunded the New Deal art projects, putting an end to a period when 'America's emerging literary talents ... worked for the federal government' (Arthur 4). The period surrounding the publication of *The Grapes of Wrath* is a liminal one, encompassing at once the apex of the US welfare state and its dismantling in the build-up to the Cold War. If Steinbeck's novel agitates for an end to the oppression of the white migrant, the push for labour-industry jobs during World War II resulted in the near-complete disappearance of the problem of vagrancy from the pages of popular news media in both California and the US more generally (Wild 330). While the agricultural industry required only seasonal employees, the country's entrance into World War II produced a rapid growth of long-term jobs that employers struggled to fill. Owing in part to this dramatic economic shift, many migrants found a more welcome reception in local communities than they had before the war.

Consolidating this shifting reception of migrant labour, the federal government ended the string of anti-migration legislation enacted at state and local levels, with the passage of federal legislation in particular signalling the rehabilitation the migrant labourer had undergone since the onset of the Depression. By the early 1940s, Congress had commissioned an investigative committee to study the problem of transient populations and to offer solutions for integrating them into the civil sphere. The name of this legislative body, the Select Committee Investigating National Defense Migration, already acknowledges the nature of the state's interest in this subject. Written in response to the problem of 'Stateless people', the 1941 Congressional report on interstate migration scrutinised local anti-vagrancy laws and proposed greater federal oversight (4). The committee took specific exception to states that imposed 'higher barriers against the interstate flow of the American people' on the basis that they violated what 'the Founding Fathers had learned before 1789' – namely, 'that a free flow of commerce between the States was an indispensable element in the founding of a Federal Union' (4). The committee's findings defend the right to interstate migration by appealing both to the integrity of the federal government and to the 'Founding Fathers' as the nostalgic embodiment of American democratic principles. Of course, the committee's report is also quick to add that these migrants are 'above the average in initiative, younger on the average of the general resident population, and in search of a job and not a hand-out' (4). While interstate migration in principle is crucial for maintaining the 'Federal Union', the characteristics of the migrants in question must still be such that they provide useful labour to their respective communities.

As the committee's language implies, governmental sources after Steinbeck and the New Deal continued to strengthen in theory the position of all migrant families while actually embracing a particular version of the American labourer. In delineating this population, the committee sees itself as putting the nation state on the right footing for addressing the needs of modern industry. 'These defense migrants were in search of jobs in a rapidly expanding job market', the report explains (217). 'Prior to the defense program many of these people had been barely holding on to part-time industrial jobs or resisting the pressure to migrate for nearly hopeless farming occupations' (217). 'Defense migrants', the term the committee uses to refer to the interstate migrant population, forcefully underscores how this governing body codifies the subject of migration according to the exigencies of the state. In the same year the report was published,

Edwards v. *California* struck down local anti-vagrancy ordinances and upheld the right to free movement – but only insofar as it met 'the requirements of national defense' (Wild 330). By the time the US entered World War II, the white migrant figure had moved from the fringes of society to the centre of the security state.

Steinbeck's novel alludes to earlier versions of the Cold War model of 'defense migration'. By showing white, industrious families like the Joads on the wrong side of vagrancy laws, the text makes the case that unfettered capitalism has disrupted the natural alliance between hardworking, mobile Americans and the nation state. In *The Grapes of Wrath*, both tenant farmers and landowners alike struggle to come to terms with the economic reality fostered by this economic system. For their part, the farmers believe that their working of the land does more than enough to establish their rights over the property. In the novel, the displaced farmers articulate a notion of work that is steeped as much in family history as it is in their labour:

> And now the squatting men stood up angrily. Grampa took up the land, and he had to kill the Indians and drive them away. And Pa was born here, and he killed weeds and snakes . . . [I]t's our land. We measured it and broke it up. We were born on it, and we got killed on it, died on it. Even if it's no good, it's still ours. That's what makes it ours – being born on it, working it, dying on it. That makes ownership, not a paper with numbers on it. (*Grapes* 33)

The farmer's impassioned defence of his ownership rights stresses the value of his work in deeply personal terms. 'Ownership' of the land, as he puts it, should be determined by all aspects of work, from labouring on the land to creating and maintaining families across generations. But the scene also calls to mind the type of labour these farmers have done at the behest of the nation state. As David Chang points out, the Okie exodus portrayed in *The Grapes of Wrath* bookends decades of white migration in the region that began in earnest with the Oklahoma Land Run of 1889, when the federal government opened up over two million acres of former Indian territory to settlement. The 'covered wagon' moving into the territory and the 'jalopy' heading west, Chang explains, 'frame the story of white settlement with movement: the arrival of white settlers in 1889 and the departure of their children only forty years later' (2). In the case of the 1889 Land Run, the migrant settlers acted at the behest of the government to consolidate white American control over lands with significant non-white and Indigenous populations. The disbandment of tribal authority in preparation for Oklahoma's statehood in

1907 only further eroded non-white civil participation in the region (Chang 151). Even after the initial wave of government-backed migration, the settled farmers encoded on a local level the federal government's overarching push to colonise these lands.

The casual reference to killing 'Indians' in the preceding passage alludes to a history in which the state privileged the mobility of one population as a means for eliminating another one entirely. Louis Owens explains that the racialised language in this instance reflects another aspect of the nostalgic American frontier myth that relegates non-white inhabitants of the land to a recent yet out-of-reach past. According to Owens, Steinbeck's invocation of this frontier myth creates here and elsewhere in his work a nostalgic 'dream that remains the exclusive property of the white dreamer while excluding the Indian – in a recognizably American pattern – from any meaningful existence in the real world' (85). Once again, the white farmer in this historical cycle is the proper inheritor of the land: non-white subjects are either excluded from the narrative structure or appear in terms of this romanticised 'dream'. The land is the farmer's by right of blood – a term that should connote not so much inheritance or birth right but outright violence.

By the time of *The Grapes of Wrath*, these once-privileged migrants have lost their ally in the government. The change is particularly apparent for the anonymous farmer in the novel who, in the excerpt above, defends his blood rights to the land: 'Maybe we can kill banks', he cries, 'they're worse than Indians and snakes. Maybe we got to fight to keep our land, like Pa and Grampa did' (*Grapes* 34). But while these appeals to self-defence at one time were endorsed and aided by government officials, the farmers now find themselves at odds with these same authority figures:

> We'll get our guns, like Grampa when the Indians came. What then?
> Well – first the sheriff, and then the troops. You'll be stealing if you try to stay, you'll be murderers if you kill to stay. The monster isn't men, but it can make men do what it wants. (*Grapes* 34)

The exchange between the farmer and the landowner makes especially clear Steinbeck's interest in depicting the migrant farmer as essentially unchanging in his figuration of land, labour and property. What has changed, the narrative suggests, is instead the economic system that governs crop production and property rights. For Steinbeck, these farmers hark back to a pioneer dream of America, where hard-working citizens charted the frontier and created homesteads along the way. The transformation of these farmers into criminalised vagrants, of course, signals a turning point in the relationship between the state and this population. Steinbeck therefore crafts a narrative that not only corrects the maligned reputation of the tramping type (as in the case with Tom and Casy) but also connects this roving population to a larger history of American settlement.

The concept of 'defense migration' makes particularly clear that the rehabilitation of the white vagrant unfolds according to the needs of the state as it manages its resources on a national scale. Steinbeck's novel precipitates this shift in governance in more ways than one. Most immediately, it stages a critique of anti-vagrancy laws that presages the reasoning in such cases as *Edwards* v. *California*, which shifted the matter of migration from local to national importance. On a more implicit level, Steinbeck also anticipates the state's formulation of the 'defense migrant' in his in-text rehabilitation of vagrant groups into industrious workers. As I have argued, Steinbeck is completely invested in identifying productive labour as a prerequisite for civil participation. On a theoretical level, his texts thus close the door to the possibility of non-productive labour coexisting with the governing interests of the nation state. Along these lines, Steinbeck works very carefully to underscore how productive his migrant subjects truly are. In doing so, he picks up an argumentative thread that extends across vagrant literature. As Chapter 1 argued, Mark Twain similarly railed against class inequality in *A Tramp Abroad* while also stressing the value of productive labour. Steinbeck goes further, however, and establishes a link between specific governing practices and the type of labour they can engender.

The continuity between the state's 'defense migrant' and Steinbeck's ideal migrant should also prompt a reconsideration of the ostensible discontinuities between the progressive policies of the New Deal and those that immediately followed. Indeed, the rise of the 'defense migrant' has been read previously as a phenomenon entirely separate from the labouring population that appears in Steinbeck's novel. For example, Keith Windschuttle notes that domestic migration to California continued to shift beyond the immediate context Steinbeck captures in the novel: 'It was not the Depression of the 30s', he argues, 'but the economic boom of the 40s that caused an abnormal increase in Okie migration' to defence-industry jobs in California in particular (25). While providing a broader view of the movement depicted in *The Grapes of Wrath*, Windschuttle's claim imposes a strict division between the policy goals embedded in the novel and the governmental policies enacted during the first years of the Cold War. But as these pages have made clear, Steinbeck's push for greater control of white migrancy as a matter of national security finds policy parallels not only during the New Deal but also, even more powerfully, after the official end of this era. Simply put, the expanding movement of labourers to defence-industry jobs in California represents not a break in Steinbeck's vision of migration management but rather its logical extension.

The labourers who thus appear both in WPA art and in the guise of the 'defense migrant' signal the official counterparts to Steinbeck's narratives, all of which recognise the migrant's potential labour power insofar as his work benefits society on a truly national scale. The migrant does not disappear from these sources but in fact reappears in a form closely aligned with the governing institutions of the nation state. Of course, workers who fall outside this demographic – whether on the basis of their race or national origin – lack such official recognition. The debate over Steinbeck's exclusion of non-white migrants in his novel has helped bring to light some of the more problematic discourse undergirding Depression-era literature and progressive legislation. The transformation of white migrancy encapsulated by the emergence of the 'defense migrant' – and the security-state apparatus it evokes – indicates that this typology of mobile labour reverberates in official government accounts not only during the New Deal but also well after it.

The success of Steinbeck's novel means that, for many, it is the definitive literary treatment of vagrancy in the US during the twentieth century. When read alongside the previous vagrancy narratives considered herein, *The Grapes of Wrath* appears as nothing less than the culmination of a longer discursive project involving the rehabilitation and normalisation of errant vagrant subjects. Steinbeck's emphasis on the utility of the white vagabond dovetails with the accounts from tramp-writers in the preceding fifty years – including Twain's *A Tramp Abroad* and W. H. Davies's *Autobiography of a Super-Tramp* – that stressed the tramp's talents and contributions to the nation state. As previous chapters have argued, these texts laid the groundwork for rehabilitating the vagabond to the extent that they elaborated on tramps' potential contributions to society: masculine, autonomous and (as latter accounts especially stress) white, they embodied the desirable characteristics elsewhere writ large in popular media and enshrined in governmental policy.

Steinbeck's explicit appeals to the whiteness of the migrant farmer should therefore be interpreted in view of the larger literary timeline that this book brings into focus. His specific imagination of productive, mobile and white migrants builds on well-established literary terrain, where tramping vagrants embody not threats to the nation but the very best of a nation's essential character. The fact that Steinbeck stresses the racial characteristics of his migrant families may not come as a surprise given the extent to which even the relatively progressive legislation of the time nonetheless excluded people of colour from its provisions. When viewed alongside his vagrant-literature forebears such as Jack London and Josiah Flynt – and his overseas contemporaries, such as George Orwell – Steinbeck's dream of a specific class of migrants deployed as a resource for the nation state appears even less anomalous. Taken together, these sources reiterate the exceptional qualities of the white vagabond in ways that anticipate Steinbeck's explicit appeals for reforming vagrancy laws as a way to manage the social reproduction of productive citizens.

Notes

1. A typical example of the novel's reception among progressive critics, Granville Hicks's 1939 review praises the 'proletariat novel' for depicting how economic forces 'operate against the interests of the masses of the people' (23). Another contemporaneous review likewise commends the novel for putting readers 'in contact not with arguments, but with people' (Stevens 3–4). Published in 1997, Denning's *Cultural Front* is representative of the way more recent critics from the left take exception to the novel's representation of labour.
2. In addition to Godfrey, Kevin Hearle makes the case that the race-based essentialism of *The Harvest Gypsies* is 'one notable exception to Steinbeck's generally progressive depictions of race' (246).
3. Charles Cunningham gestures to this dynamic when he explains that Steinbeck's representation of 'Okies as quintessential American pioneers' derives from 'an ideological convention that resonated with the implicit white supremacism of Jeffersonian democracy' (1).
4. The policy of repatriation noted above of course reflects only a small sampling of the anti-migrant policies exercised during the early twentieth century. The extent to which New Deal initiatives encoded racial prejudice into welfare governance has been the topic of extensive study. For a recent and comprehensive study on the subject, see Katznelson. On the topic of housing policy, see David Freund's study on the Public Housing Administration, the Urban Renewal Administration and the Federal Housing Administration in *Colored Property*.
5. I briefly explain the features that distinguish, according to popular perception, the hobo from the tramp in the Introduction. The usage of both terms in this chapter stresses the extent to which both derive from

a shared popular and literary tradition that focused on solitary men on the road.
6. Published the year following *The Grapes of Wrath*, Richard Wright's *Native Son* describes Bigger Thomas as a 'tramp' early in the narrative (9). The stark scenes of violence in Wright's text therefore reflect not only the depths of Bigger's social marginalisation but also Wright's own turn away from anything resembling a sentimental account of poverty and vagabondage along the lines of what one reads across Steinbeck's body of fiction.
7. See Daniel Béland's *Social Security*, which usefully outlines the creation of this programme as well as its eligibility restrictions in comparison with international models of welfare insurance.
8. One argument identifies Southern Democrats as the architects of the bill's exclusionist policies. See Lieberman, as well as Alston and Ferrie, for arguments in this vein. Larry DeWitt strongly rebuffs their claims of racial bias, however. For DeWitt, an aversion to new taxes (rather than racial animus) motivated Southern Democrats to limit the bill's language. Of course, any suggestion that the programme's intent was free from prejudice does little to address the abiding sense in the US that links welfare policies to race.
9. Roosevelt's reasoning offers insight into nearly all the New Deal work initiatives he endorsed during his presidency. As Mark Wild points out, even the expansive Works Progress Administration was created in 1935 to replace a no-obligation system of relief for migrants (under the Federal Emergency Relief Agency and the Federal Transient Service) with one that ensured that beneficiaries would always have to work in order to receive payments (321).
10. As Pamela Herd explains, women are much less likely than men to benefit from welfare insurance payments owing to a 'breadwinner' system that 'best protects individuals who either have consistent lifetime work histories . . . or individuals who get married, stay married, and do no paid work, through noncontributory spousal and widow benefits' (1365–6). As a result of this beneficiary structure, women who marry and never enter the waged workforce 'reap the highest rewards from the system' (1367).
11. Brian Railsback argues along with Zirakzadeh that the concept of natural selection shapes *The Grapes of Wrath*. Hearle also makes the case that Steinbeck's work advocates a form of social Darwinism, albeit in a manner stripped of the 'supposed logic of white supremacy' (254). See also Marijane Osborne, who explains that the biological presentation of non-teleological thinking exposes 'internal contradictions' in Steinbeck's otherwise clear concern for oppressed populations (230).
12. In *The Forgotten Village*, the documentary film for which Steinbeck wrote the script following *The Grapes of Wrath*, Steinbeck turns his focus from the white migrant farmer to the rural populations of

Mexico. In both works, he advances the federal government's responsibility to integrate otherwise-marginalised populations into modern civil society. The stark diversity of the demographic subjects of these texts, released so closely together, adds further nuance to any discussion of Steinbeck's overarching racial politics.

Epilogue: Tramping's Afterlife

These concluding pages briefly explore what I term the afterlife of the tramping archetype, which continued to make its presence felt in both post-war American literature and, as I will elaborate, prominent accounts of whiteness in that period. The centre of this book's Epilogue, Jack Kerouac and like-minded artists associated with the Beat movement took tramping journeys of their own while valorising the type of rebellious subjectivity they associated with Black culture. Kerouac's artistic indebtedness to vagrancy writers such as Mark Twain, Jack London and John Steinbeck is acknowledged in other accounts of the author.[1] Rather than retread those studies, I wish to demonstrate how the literary history of tramp writing recontextualises one of the most famous examples of post-war American literature, Kerouac's *On the Road* (1957). This argument reiterates and extends the governmentality narrative running through *The American Vagrant in Literature*, which has traced how tramping literature – which codes the tramp's exceptionalism in terms of race and masculinity – counterintuitively helped to rationalise a robust liberal welfare society. In the years following the end of the Great Depression and World War II, however, the exceptional qualities once associated with tramp characters largely disappeared from the public eye (Feied 58). By reading *On the Road* as a text fully immersed in the tramping-narrative template, I add an essential prehistory to the relatively familiar subjects and aesthetic forms that stand out in Kerouac's novel – namely, his anguish over the institutionalisation of whiteness and, relatedly, his association of blackness with social rebellion.

Writing after World War II, Kerouac sustains the allure of tramping literature for a generation removed from the Great Depression and, more distantly, the tumultuous turn of the century. At the same time, he can only lament the disappearance of actual tramping types in post-war America. In 'The Vanishing American Hobo', an essay first published in *Holiday* magazine in 1960, Kerouac celebrates vagabondage as a quintessentially American identity while decrying the 'increase in police surveillance' that makes tramping impossible (164). His preoccupation with both tramping culture and the social conditions that control vagrancy already situates his work on the same spectrum of tramping artist-sociologists that includes not only London in the US but, as previous chapters established, George Orwell and W. H. Davies in the UK. At the same time, Kerouac's observations are concerned less with living examples of tramps and more with what his essay calls the 'the ghosts of hoboism' ('Vanishing' 166). In this light, I turn to Kerouac's work to elaborate briefly on what happens to the literary reception of tramping after the demise of the tramp in the public eye. As I explain in detail below, Kerouac's dual concern over the mundanity of whiteness in post-war America and his exoticisation of blackness should be interpreted not only in relation to contemporary fiction – which experimented with incorporating jazz-inspired aesthetic forms into prose and poetry, for example – but as an extension of the comparative thinking and demographic ordering I have argued underlies the tramp-writing tradition as a whole.

Post-war Tramping and Vagrancy Law

By speaking of the tramp's afterlife, I stress the connotative or evocative power of tramps as literary figures that persisted after lawmakers and journalists had moved on from the problem of itinerant white men. As the preceding chapters argued, the consolidation of the interwar welfare state in both the US and UK coincided with a marked decline in the prominence of tramp characters in the public imagination. In this transitional period, the waning public fascination with solitary vagabonds did not result in relaxed vagrancy ordinances, however. On the contrary, anti-vagrancy laws were even more deeply encoded in the operation of the post-war state and its attempted regulation of political radicals as well as Black and queer activists. Legal scholar Risa Goluboff notes that anti-vagrancy ordinances were particularly useful to US legal authorities in the 1960s, when the combination of the student-led Free Speech Movement and the Civil Rights Movement turned major urban areas into hotbeds of political activism (2). Reflecting on this era, Goluboff explains that vagrancy codes were fundamentally 'linked to a conception of postwar American society – as they had been linked to a conception of sixteenth-century English society – in which everyone had a proper place' (3). The governmentality of population management that the tramp-writers across this book diagnosed (and in some cases encouraged) continued to expand well after the de jure welfare state's inception and into the Cold War era. The subversive population that the state concerned itself with in this latter case, however, did not consist of idle white men but was rather a more diverse collection of marginalised groups.[2]

As this last point makes clear, to study the production and circulation of the tramp archetype brings into focus an overarching narrative involving innovations in state power. How, then, does the afterlife of tramping fit into this timeline? It is crucial to note that US vagabondage narratives produced in the second half of the twentieth century appeared at a time when the specific legal framework around vagrancy was in flux. Vagrancy laws themselves were effectively ruled unconstitutional in the US after a trio of Supreme Court rulings in 1971 and 1972 (Goluboff 4). The nominal end of anti-vagrancy laws came after *Papachristou* v. *City of Jacksonville*, a Supreme Court case concerning the use of overly vague vagrancy laws to justify arbitrary arrests (Ellickson 1210). Ruling against the city officials, Supreme Court Justice William O. Douglas – who elsewhere wrote about his own time among tramps in his youth (Harper 187) – cited Walt Whitman's 'Song of the Open Road' in defence of the rights of non-conformists against repressive public ordinances (Ellickson 1211). But rather than stop anti-vagrancy codes altogether, these rulings encouraged more innovative management of public spaces. Since the 1970s, local and city governments have effectively bypassed restrictions on vagrancy laws by passing new codes banning, for instance, panhandling and lying on public sidewalks.[3] The continuing reinvention of laws policing the occupation of public space reiterates the particular usefulness of vagrancy law as a case study in governmentality in ways that extend well beyond Michel Foucault's consideration of vagabonds in seventeenth-century France and into the present day.[4]

All of which is not to say that the romance of tramping – and its underlying conventions – disappeared entirely after World War II. The preceding chapter argued that the decline of tramping as documented in Orwell and Steinbeck should be seen as the culmination of the larger project of rehabilitating the white vagrant, which spanned the late nineteenth and early twentieth centuries. But if the government and the public at large no longer fixated on tramps as a pressing social problem, the underlying racial calculus that came to define the tramp remains embedded in Kerouac's *On the Road*, the most obvious post-war successor to the tramp-writing tradition from the turn of the century (Feied 61). Celebrations of tramping and tramp types appear everywhere in literature by Beat writers, including not only Kerouac but also William S. Burroughs and Allen Ginsberg, whose works mythologised the dropout vagabond for the Cold War generation.

Although there is no shortage of critiques of *On the Road*, I turn to it to conclude *The American Vagrant in Literature* for several reasons. First and foremost, the enduring popularity of Kerouac's novel ensures that literary treatments of tramping will not likely be far from the American literary canon and, consequently, popular media and university reading lists. By approaching *On the Road* as a work concerned with the legacy of tramping, moreover, I remove Kerouac from the immediate confines of the Beat movement and place him in dialogue with the discourse of tramp literature as well as, more provocatively, Steinbeck's treatment of blackness in his travel narrative *Travels with Charley* (1962). Of course, the similarities between *On the Road* and Steinbeck's earlier work are apparent. As Jason Spangler points out, *On the Road* shares with *The Grapes of Wrath* a concern for the 'price of existence paid by the individual in modern America', an existential conflict that the vagrant embodies in both texts (309). However, to focus on the immediate parallels between these two sources risks overlooking the intriguing similarities between Kerouac's novel and Steinbeck's late-career travel text. Both writers consciously frame their journeys as tramping expeditions, and both use this framing to consider what the normalisation of exceptional whiteness – as once embodied by the tramp – means for the future of the country. Ultimately, the preoccupation with blackness in both cases suggests that tramping literature continues to facilitate the discourse of racial reductionism long after the end of tramping as a popular phenomenon.

Tramping's Ghosts: *On the Road*

Perhaps the most famous road-trip novel in US literature, *On the Road* romanticises tramping while also considering the fate of literal vagrants in post-war America. Tramps and tramping-types swarm in the novel's background and motivate Sal Paradise (Kerouac's alter ego) and Dean Moriarty's travels around the country. Sal's earliest description of Dean stresses his close association with the tramping archetype as it once appeared in the pages of Steinbeck and London. As Sal puts it, Dean was 'the perfect guy for the road because he was actually born on the road when his parents were passing through Salt Lake City in 1926, in a jalopy, on their way to Los Angeles' (Kerouac, *On the Road* 7). Kerouac immediately stresses the cultural and literary legacy associated with the white Okie migrant in these early pages. Dean calls to mind, Sal explains, 'a young Gene Autry . . . with a real Oklahoma accent' (*On the Road* 8). Kerouac famously modelled the character of Dean on Neal Cassady, a major figure in the Beat movement, whose biography shapes Dean's vagabond backstory. The vagrancy timeline established throughout *The American Vagrant in Literature* sheds further light on the literary connotations implicit in this characterisation. Although Kerouac's rowdy bohemianism signals a break with the activist-minded sentimentalism of *The Grapes of Wrath*, the heavy references to tramps, vagabonds and Okies demonstrates the 'symbolic lexicon' they share (Spangler 310). Moreover, the inseparable connection of Dean's criminality with his lust for freedom recalls the distinctly bohemian vision of the tramp as laid out by sources such as Josiah Flynt, London and Davies several decades earlier.

At the same time, neither Dean nor Sal fully inhabits the tramping archetype; instead, they continually chase after it. In this light, the tramping afterlives that haunt *On the Road* assume more literal forms. Dean and Sal first hit the road in search of Dean's father, a hobo who left his family while Dean was still young. Throughout the text, Dean recalls past glimpses of his father in hobo jungles and on rail cars but never encounters him in the flesh. Dean's inability to reunite with his father mirrors the novel's characterisation of the numerous hobos and tramps who pop in and out of the road narrative. Most notably, Sal's encounter with a 'semi-respectable hobo' whom he calls 'the Ghost of the Susquehanna' highlights the simultaneously romantic and inaccessible qualities that Kerouac assigns to tramps (*On the Road* 100).[5] But Sal's reverence for the romantic ideal of the tramp conflicts with what he sees. Passing the Ghost on the side of the road, Sal remarks, 'I suddenly saw the little hobo standing under a sad streetlamp with his thumb stuck out – poor forlorn man, poor lost sometimeboy, now broken ghost of the penniless wilds' (*On the Road* 101). The figure is ghostly in more ways than one. The character's 'broken' vigour and advanced age suggest that he is a shadow of the person he once was. Kerouac also presents the character as fundamentally 'lost', left to haunt a land in which he no longer has a place.

In other words, Sal's tramp is ghostly in the sense that he continues to live even after the death, so to speak, of the world that produced tramps in the first place. Indeed, Sal comes to find that he and the Ghost inhabit two separate worlds. The two split ways after Sal and the driver of a hitched ride fail to convince the Ghost, who intends to head north into Canada, that he is walking in entirely the wrong direction. Kerouac in this moment chooses the security that comes with the car, and the geographical certainty the road signs offer, over the old tramp's directionless ambling (Lennon 163). The tramp thus disappears into the surrounding landscape, 'his bobbing little white bag dissolving in the darkness' (Kerouac, *On the Road* 101). The encounter underscores the sense that tramps for Sal assume a spectral quality, more mythical figures than the vagrants that once appeared in the pages of bestselling memoirs and early ethnographic accounts. Sal elaborates:

> I thought all the wilderness of America was in the West till the Ghost of the Susquehanna showed me different. No, there is a wilderness in the East; it's the same wilderness Ben Franklin plodded in the oxcart days when he was postmaster, the same as it was when George Washington was a wild-buck Indian-fighter. (*On the Road* 101)

The passage strikingly underscores the tramp's status as an emblem of a history that, while still visible in the 'wilderness', is emphatically past. Instead, the tramp passes into the pantheon of national and, as the passage makes clear, colonialist myths along with Franklin and Washington. Far from the expressive characters they once were, tramps in *On the Road* are apparitions of a past to which Kerouac restlessly attempts to connect.

For my purposes, *On the Road* exemplifies how tramping as a literary type endures after the social and political factors that created tramps have changed. As previous chapters in *The American Vagrant in Literature* have indicated, Kerouac was not the only observer to remark on the decline of the tramp archetype. Like Orwell in *Down and Out in Paris and London*, Kerouac in *On the Road* mourns the disarming of subversive white vagabondage by state infrastructures that monitor public health. As elaborated in Chapter 3, Orwell encounters these aspects of the British state in the draconian form of the workhouse. In contrast, the state policies that literally propel Kerouac's journey are dedicated to enabling, rather than curtailing, movement. Taken together, Orwell and Kerouac showcase contrasting methods of population management that nonetheless work to similar ends: privileging certain demographic groups and controlling others, whether by discipline or neglect. For example, Sal enrols in university on the basis of the GI Bill of Rights, which (along with his aunt's largesse) funds his travels. Second, the mid-century expansion of public-infrastructure spending – most notably in the form of the Federal-Aid Highway Act of 1956 – opened new destinations for casual travellers and labourers alike. Indeed, the emergence of the federal highway system is inseparable from the decline of tramping in popular culture: the rarefied sense of tramping disappears amid the proliferation of passenger cars and roads, which opened up travel to millions of Americans eager to be on the move (Lennon 180).

As this last point implies, this sanctified mobility was not evenly distributed in the country. Sal benefits from infrastructure that solidifies the privileges of one demographic – young white men, in this case – and forecloses this social and economic mobility to others. To adapt the literature on 'infrastructuralism', Kerouac's text demonstrates how state oversight of public health can operate in largely invisible ways alongside more austere (or, in this context, Orwellian) state landmarks such as the prison or workhouse (Rubenstein et al. 580).[6] This invisible operation of state power is everywhere in *On the Road* while the latter institutions are largely kept out of sight. Although Sal's mobility continually pushes him to the limits of the disappearing frontier, legal tactics across the country limited the movement of Black Americans on various fronts, from redlining in neighbourhoods to the debilitating inequality that shaped everyday life under segregation.[7]

The novel elsewhere embeds in its prose the governing logics that propel its protagonists' journey. Kerouac's narrative is replete with typifying language that distils the strangers he observes into ethnic, regional and sexual archetypes.[8] Sal and his crew meet hitchhikers and vagabonds, such as 'the Okie' and 'the Fag', who correspond to larger, singular types (*On the Road* 158, 194). This typifying presentation links Kerouac to vagrancy writers considered elsewhere in *The American Vagrant in Literature* who encode the language of demographic sorting throughout their texts. But unlike these writers, Kerouac proclaims his sense that the white vagabond is far from the 'tramp royal' archetype outlined in London's *People of the Abyss* (see 66). Sal elaborates on this point throughout *On the Road*, but perhaps the most explicit example appears during a sojourn in Colorado:

> At lilac evening I walked with every muscle aching among the lights of 27th and Welton in the Denver coloured section, wishing I were a Negro, feeling that the best the white world had offered was not enough ecstasy for me, not enough life, joy, kicks, darkness, music, not enough night ... I wished I were a Denver Mexican, or even a poor overworked Jap, anything but what I was so drearily, a 'white man' disillusioned ... I was only myself, Sal Paradise, sad, strolling in this violet dark, this unbearably sweet night, wishing I could exchange words with the happy, true-hearted, ecstatic Negroes of America. (169–70)

The premise of this passage – to be white is to be disqualified from 'life, joy, kicks' – resonates well beyond the specific literary legacy of tramp writing that is at the centre of *The American Vagrant in Literature*. Indeed, this presentation of racial envy is not anomalous even in the rather specific context of post-war American fiction by white male authors.[9] Kerouac's desire for the 'ecstasy' he associates with people outside 'the white world' thus invokes several overlapping critical strands – some familiar and others likely less familiar to readers of the novel – that run throughout *On the Road* as a whole. Most immediately, the passage reiterates the author's reductive invocation of blackness as a subjectivity associated with improvision (which Kerouac associates with jazz in particular) and authenticity. More generally, it exemplifies a larger sensibility in post-war fiction that decries the dual institutionalisation of artistic expression on the one hand and whiteness on the other.[10]

Alongside the literary traditions alluded to here, the conventions of tramp writing further clarify the novel's imagination of race. For Kerouac, whiteness affords a sense of privilege and security that, in his account, fundamentally divorces him from inhabiting the dangerous role once afforded tramps near the turn of the century. This reading places Kerouac into a closer, more sustained dialogue with the tradition of tramp writing than might otherwise be apparent. For example, historian Todd DePastino notes Kerouac's indebtedness to London and Twain, whose work influenced artists in the Beat movement (237). At the same time, DePastino presents the 'romance of race' in *On the Road* (as evidenced in the passage above) as a unique innovation; the suggestion being that Kerouac's preoccupation with whiteness separates him from his tramping predecessors (239). In contrast, the account in *The American Vagrant in Literature* should make it clear that the racialised framing of Kerouac's performance of vagabondage is not incidental. Rather, he is fully extending the racialised discourse that had long been encoded in tramping texts by the time he is writing. In other words, tramping and racial politics are completely intertwined; Kerouac cannot talk about tramping without resorting to the language of whiteness.

Kerouac's text thus acknowledges the extent to which tramp types – and their corresponding racial identity – have been incorporated into a regulatory state that facilities the movement of one demographic while marginalising countless others. The point I raise here is not to suggest that the tramping reflections contained in Kerouac's novel discount the points raised by the critical accounts mentioned briefly above. Instead, I offer Kerouac as a prominent case study in how the literary reception of tramping is, in many ways, inseparable from the marquee topics that have made *On the Road* such a long-lasting object of popular and academic attention: not only its explicit valorisation of vagabondage but also its celebration of autonomy and its vexed presentation of race. Kerouac may mourn his personal incorporation into the safety net afforded young white men like himself, but as the passage above suggests, his writing reifies race as an impassable barrier. Whiteness is still the hegemonic norm against which all populations are to be judged and evaluated. Kerouac emphasises the often reactionary and nationalist thinking that was embedded in tramp writing and carried over into Beat literature – both nominally anti-establishment artistic movements.

We see at play in Kerouac's text the comparative and demographic logic that is characteristic of tramping literature. Texts from Twain, London and others elaborate on national differences, they distinguish socially valuable talents from less valuable ones, and they critique social or political practices that harm the integrity of their observed subjects. The fact that these observations can assume racist valences should come as no surprise. Instead, we should question why the literary depiction of tramping in *On the Road* cannot refer to tramping without referring to matters of racial difference. By the time Kerouac writes, popular depictions of tramping have long established this type of romantic wandering as the domain of white men. At the same time, Kerouac bemoans the essential security afforded by whiteness, a position he can only describe through contrast with the people of colour he encounters on his travels. In 'The Vanishing American Hobo', Kerouac blames the proliferation of policing and surveillance for the pacification of the white vagabond. What Kerouac does not acknowledge – and what this book has been dedicated to explaining – is the extent to which this incorporation into the surveillance state was won, so to speak, by previous generations of writers who described tramps as a population worth protecting.

After Tramping: Normalising Race

The preceding pages approach Kerouac's famous novel as a text with special insight into tramping's social and political connotations after the end, so to speak, of vagabondage's heyday. At the same time, I have argued that *On the Road* is far from unique in its imagination of race and vagabondage at the time of its publication. Kerouac's novel is without a doubt the most famous celebration of bohemian vagabondage in post-war American fiction, but it shares with other prominent sources from the time its lament for the normalisation of whiteness vis-à-vis its appropriation of the tramping narrative. To expand on this shared discourse more fully, I return to the work of Steinbeck, who himself inaugurated the disappearance of the tramping type in *The Grapes of Wrath*. However, the most striking parallel between Kerouac and Steinbeck lies not in the Dust Bowl novel but in Steinbeck's late-career travelogue, *Travels with Charley*. Recounting a 1960 road trip across the US, *Travels with Charley* meditates on the health of the nation in the wake of a polarising presidential election on the one hand and the fight against racial segregation on the other. Steinbeck does not intervene in these incidents so much as he watches them from the relative comfort of his camping trailer (which he christens 'Rocinante') with his poodle, Charley, at his side. As the allusion to *Don Quixote* implies, Steinbeck's depiction of post-war white mobility plays up the romantic connotations of tramping that were largely absent from *The Grapes of Wrath*.

To different degrees, Steinbeck and Kerouac acknowledge in their travel texts the fundamental sense of security that underwrites their respective rambling journeys. Unlike the Joads, Steinbeck moves with a kind of financial and cultural stability afforded to the generation of retirees in the era of the post-war Fordist welfare state. His travels pose no threat to the communities he visits; instead, his performance of migration underscores the extent to which the connotations of white migration have changed since the Depression. Indeed, this political shift affords him a thoroughly romantic interpretation of life on the road. 'Once a bum always a bum', he quips in the book's earliest pages (*Travels* 3). Considering the scenes of poverty contained in *The Grapes of Wrath*, one should see his own 'bum' voyage across the US as a return to the subject of the solitary white wanderer. The wanderlust the author portrays here extends not from pressing financial need, however, but from the stability afforded by a lifetime of work.

Like Kerouac, Steinbeck's travels propel him to consider the future of America, a country at once buoyed by unprecedented wealth and rife with institutional discrimination and inequality. He pays particular attention to scenes of anti-Black racism, which he observes with increasing regularity near the end of his travel text. For instance, he recalls with disdain the 'Cheerleaders', a group of white protestors who attempt to physically bar – and verbally threaten and insult – Black families attempting to integrate a previously all-white school in New Orleans (*Travels* 249). Such scenes do more than highlight entrenched racism: they suggest to Steinbeck something of the collective political tenacity, in his eyes, of Black Americans. At the same time, Steinbeck was reluctant to engage at much length with the Civil Rights Movement in his writings. As Shane Lynn explains, Steinbeck's body of work demonstrates time and again an unwillingness to depict people of colour as much more than foils to the white characters who are front and centre in his stories. This reluctance extends across his most familiar works like *The Grapes of Wrath*, the subject of the previous chapter, to personal correspondence and interviews (Lynn 156).

In *Travels with Charley*, however, Steinbeck gets around his characteristic reticence by calling on anecdotes and conversations that offer provocative accounts of race. At one point, he recalls an exchange with a 'well-known and highly-respected political reporter' (*Travels* 168). Disturbed by his time covering the presidential campaigns, the reporter advises Steinbeck to watch for 'a man with guts' on his journey (*Travels* 168). The narrative in turn gives space for the journalist to elaborate at length:

> I swear to God the only people in this country with any guts seem to be Negroes. Mind you . . . I don't want to keep Negroes out of the hero business, but I'm damned if I want them to corner the market. You dig me up ten white, able-bodied American men who aren't afraid to have a conviction, an idea, or an opinion in an unpopular field, and I'll have the major part of a standing army. (*Travels* 168–9)

If Steinbeck himself does not verbalise this point, his reproduction of the quotation in full signals his interest in the journalist's sentiment. The passage also provides some context for the dismay Steinbeck elsewhere expresses for the status of the white American worker. For instance, he frets over the prospect that 'we Americans' might one day be 'overwhelmed' by 'peoples not too proud or too lazy or too soft to bend to the earth and pick up the things we eat' (*Travels* 64). Read together, these passages gesture to Steinbeck's alarm at how thoroughly white Americans have found themselves on the other side of what Foucault terms the normalisation of racist discourse: no longer waging battle against the state, they throw their lot in with the state to protect their fantasy of racial purity. The martial terms that punctuate the journalist's tirade ('a standing army') are in this context best understood as a nostalgic expression of the power that 'white, able-bodied American men' have, in his telling, given away.

In short, the travelogue registers the extent to which the Fordist welfare model provided comfort and security to some, but not all, Americans. Moreover, the normalising of whiteness that Steinbeck records in his text is incompatible with the superlative form of autonomy he and others once personified in the character of the tramp. While writers like Twain, London and Davies once equated the tramp's superlative qualities with his embodiment of whiteness, Steinbeck imagines in *The Grapes of Wrath* a political system that deploys this population to where it can most benefit the state. In contrast, *Travels with Charley* wonders if privilege and heroism, to adapt the journalist's term, are compatible with each other. *Travels with Charley* thus exemplifies the post-war moment when the state in effect erased the threat of white vagrancy and displaced its disruptive qualities onto people of colour. Whereas this latter group embodies – the racial connotations in this phrasing should be clear – subversiveness by dint of their continued marginalisation, Steinbeck as well as Kerouac characterise heroic white Americans in terms of their absence; they are ghosts who, like Kerouac's pantheon of tramping Americans, left their mark on the country but seemingly have no place in its future.

This affinity between these writers should come as a surprise – after all, no person at the time personified the literary establishment Kerouac self-consciously rebelled against more than Steinbeck, who won the Nobel Prize in Literature the same year *Travels with Charley* was released. If Kerouac and fellow Beats loosely defined themselves by their anti-conformity, then Steinbeck should have been a natural adversary. But as these pages have claimed, their shared preoccupation with the tramp archetype moves them each to reach similar conclusions regarding what they both see as the institutionalisation of white mobility. In *On the Road*, Kerouac mourns not only the passing of tramping's heyday but also the essential danger that once characterised that particular embodiment of whiteness. Kerouac's own envious equation of blackness with danger and unpredictability in his novel thus clarifies how the racialised imagination characterising tramp writing endures well after the end of nominal anti-vagrancy laws in the US. Steinbeck shares with Kerouac an abiding preoccupation with the allure of tramping, which he indulges from the relative comfort of 'Rocinante'. From this sheltered perspective, he assesses the conformity that whiteness demands – in terms of both its intersection with the discourse of the state and its marginalisation of non-white groups. Taken together, these sources epitomise the extent to which not only tramping but also state-sanctioned forms of mobility were, and continue to be, tied to an overarching racial discourse. By referring to the literary history of tramping, these final pages of *The American Vagrant in Literature* reframe some of the most familiar texts in the American canon around their shared contributions to the discourse of race, mobility and social-welfare politics.

As this last point suggests, I turned to *Travels with Charley* and *On the Road* here in large part owing to their widespread popularity and their authors' place in the literary canon. In doing so, I place their romantic treatment of vagabondage among wider social and literary turns in the second half of the twentieth century. As was the case in *The Grapes of Wrath*, Steinbeck's travel narrative assesses the health of the nation state and worries about the integrity of the white worker. Reading the latter as a text at least in part about tramping is not meant to minimise the dramatic economic and political transformations that separate 1939 from 1960, the New Deal from the Cold War, or the displaced migrant from the comfortable retiree. Rather, the literary history established in this book helps make the points of divergence between these contexts, as well as their often-surprising points of intersection, all the more apparent. As Steinbeck and Kerouac both articulate, the literary archetypes associated with tramping become thoroughly nostalgic once tramps essentially disappear from popular media in the 1940s. The nostalgia for tramping is invariably tied to a distinct longing for a particular category of whiteness that is mythical in stature: wildly autonomous, completely mobile, and at once widely admired and thoroughly feared. Kerouac and Steinbeck acknowledge to different degrees the infrastructures and state policies that nurture their own performance of vagabond mobility, though in the end they can only decry the institutionalisation that comes along with these privileges.

When read alongside one another, the sources in this book demonstrate how literature about tramping involves more than describing one's travels and destinations; it also involves testing and scrutinising the legal institutions and social policies in place that assist movement for some and restrict it for others. Kerouac finds in his text that he can move free from restraint, but less because he is exceptional in the sense of Davies's 'Super-Tramp' and more because US legal and social structures – which map onto and reinforce racial differences – facilitate his movement. To return to the point raised in the opening pages of this Epilogue, Kerouac finds himself in a structural position that also includes Steinbeck in his retiree phase, who waxes nostalgic about the 'bum' even as he documents discriminatory violence from a safe distance. The comparison of Kerouac and Steinbeck is not meant only to say that both benefit from the structural privileges doled out to them by a society in which masculinity and whiteness are both synonymous with privilege. The comparative framing between these texts and, indeed, the interdisciplinary sources that appear throughout *The American Vagrant in Literature* ultimately reveal the enduring legacy of tramp writing as a literary form that facilitates the discourse of state building – demographic sorting, international comparison and the proliferation of nationalist archetypes – in ways that are written into the social policies that endure in the present.

Notes

1. DePastino's history of hobo culture notes that Kerouac was 'profoundly influenced by Jack London and John Dos Passos as well as by Walt Whitman and Mark Twain' (237). Kerouac's personal and artistic interest in the legacy of the Dust Bowl and John Steinbeck's fiction is the subject of Spangler's 'We're on a Road to Nowhere'.
2. Vagrancy laws in the Southern US, for instance, enforced Jim Crow segregation by providing police with wide powers to arrest literally anyone. Michael Klarman explains that law-enforcement agencies used this intentionally broad language to coerce Black labourers to work for free as part of incarcerated chain gangs (44). Goluboff also elaborates on the history of vagrancy law in the South as a tool for segregation (see 115–27).
3. For a thorough account of the timeline linking anti-vagrancy law to modern ordinances regulating homelessness, see 'From Vagrancy Law to Contemporary Anti-Homeless Policy' in Leonard Feldman's *Citizens without Shelter*.
4. Foucault, in *Security, Territory, Population*, points to vagrancy laws as an origin point for understanding the link between geographical location and civil status. Brenna Bhandar places Foucault's sense of

vagabondage in the context of colonial administration and biopolitical experimentation in *Colonial Lives of Property*.
5. 'The Ghost' hobo reoccurs across Kerouac's body of work. For an overview of this specific character, see Norma Goldstein's 'Kerouac's on the Road' and John Lennon's *Boxcar Politics*.
6. David Alworth offers another account of the infrastructure that enables the narrative in *On the Road*. Alworth points to the road itself as an actor (in the sense advocated by scholars in the field of actor-network theory) that helps to 'facilitate a bond between the two men' in the story (78).
7. Although generally used to describe instances of racial discrimination in the housing market, redlining originally referred to colour-coded maps (devised by the US government) that rated neighbourhoods on the basis of their worthiness for investments, home loans and insurance. Residents of largely Black and non-white areas were in turn subject to loan denials from banks and insurers. In this light, Adrienne Brown explains that redlining was a key tool for protecting the 'category of whiteness' after the economic and social tumult of the early twentieth century (27). As noted previously, there is a large body of scholarship about race (especially as it relates to masculinity) in Kerouac's narrative. Rather than retread the insights these previous accounts offer, I turn briefly to this line of criticism to demonstrate how Kerouac mobilises the racialised logic that (as previous chapters have argued) has always undergirded the tramp narrative.
8. See Kerouac's presentation of race and masculinity figures in DePastino's study of post-war hobohemia in *Citizen Hobo*. The reactionary subtext to both Kerouac's and Beat fiction's presentation of race and masculinity is the subject of Manuel Luis Martinez's *Countering the Counterculture*. Ed Morales expands on Kerouac's presentation of Latinx subjects and Mexico as a space for his own self-exploration in *Latinx*.
9. For example, Norman Mailer's widely read explication of the hipster in 'The White Negro' appeared the same year as *On the Road*. Brendon Nicholls explains that the 'sociohistorical correlation' between the two sources is evident in their shared exotification of blackness (542).
10. This allusion draws from two influential accounts of post-war American fiction. The first is Mark McGurl's *Program Era*, which elaborates on the standardisation of creative-writing programmes and university courses and its attendant effects on cultural production. The second is Andrew Hoberek's *Twilight of the Middle Class*, which argues that the instances of racial appropriation in *On the Road* typify the 'historical amnesia' characterising post-war writing that wished for alternatives to the conformity of the middle class (69).

Works Cited

Alesina, Alberto, et al. 'Why Doesn't the United States Have a European-Style Welfare State?' *Brookings Papers on Economic Activity*, no. 2, 2001, pp. 187–277.
Alston, Lee J., and Joseph P. Ferrie. *Southern Paternalism and the American Welfare State: Economics, Politics, and Institutions in the South, 1865–1965*. Cambridge University Press, 1999.
Alworth, David J. *Site Reading: Fiction, Art, Social Form*. Princeton University Press, 2016.
Anderson, Benedict. *Imagined Communities: Reflections on the Origin and Spread of Nationalism*. Verso, 1991.
Anderson, Nels. *The Hobo: The Sociology of the Homeless Man*. University of Chicago Press, 1923.
Anderson, Nels, and Raffaele Rauty. *On Hobos and Homelessness*. University of Chicago Press, 1998.
Arthur, Jason. *Violet America: Regional Cosmopolitanism in U.S. Fiction since the Great Depression*. University of Iowa Press, 2013.
Auerbach, Jonathan. *Male Call: Becoming Jack London*. Duke University Press, 1996.
Bailey, Quentin. *Wordsworth's Vagrants: Police, Prisons and Poetry in the 1790s*. Ashgate, 2011.
Battat, Erin Royston. *Ain't Got No Home: America's Great Migrations and the Making of an Interracial Left*. University of North Carolina Press, 2014.
Baxendale, John. *Priestley's England: J.B. Priestley and English Culture*. Manchester University Press, 2007.
Beck, Hermann. *The Origins of the Authoritarian Welfare State in Prussia: Conservatives, Bureaucracy, and the Social Question, 1815–70*. University of Michigan Press, 1995.
Beier, A. L., and Paul R. Ocobock. *Cast Out: Vagrancy and Homelessness in Global and Historical Perspective*. Ohio University Press, 2008.
Béland, Daniel. *Social Security: History and Politics from the New Deal to the Privatization Debate*. University Press of Kansas, 2007.
Bellesiles, Michael A. *1877: America's Year of Living Violently*. New Press, 2010.

Berlant, Lauren. *Cruel Optimism*. Duke University Press, 2011.
Berliner, Jonathan. 'Jack London's Socialistic Social Darwinism.' *American Literary Realism*, vol. 41, no. 1, 2008, pp. 52–78.
Betensky, Carolyn. 'Princes as Paupers: Pleasure and the Imagination of Powerlessness.' *Cultural Critique*, vol. 56, 2004, pp. 129–57.
Bhandar, Brenna. *Colonial Lives of Property: Law, Land, and Racial Regimes of Ownership*. Duke University Press, 2018.
Bliss, William Dwight Porter. *The Encyclopedia of Social Reform; Including Political Economy, Political Science, Sociology and Statistics*. Funk & Wagnalls, 1897.
Bordas, Maria. 'Social Welfare Reform: Comparative Perspectives on Europe and the United States.' *International Journal of Public Administration*, vol. 24, no. 2, 2001, pp. 225–33.
Brandon, David. *Stand and Deliver! A History of Highway Robbery*. The History Press, 2001.
Breton, Rob. *Gospels and Grit: Work and Labour in Carlyle, Conrad and Orwell*. University of Toronto Press, 2005.
Brown, Adrienne. *The Black Skyscraper: Architecture and the Perception of Race*. Johns Hopkins University Press, 2017.
Busby, Mattha 'Homeless Households in England Rise by 23% in a Year.' *The Guardian*, 18 December 2019, https://www.theguardian.com/society/2019/dec/18/homeless-households-in-england-up-by-23-in-a-year-official-figures.
Butler, Judith. *Frames of War: When Is Life Grievable?* Verso, 2009.
Chance, Sir William Bart. *Vagrancy: Being a Review of the Report of the Departmental Committee on Vagrancy, 1906, with Answers to Certain Criticisms*. P. S. King & Son, 1906.
Chang, David A. *The Color of the Land: Race, Nation, and the Politics of Landownership in Oklahoma, 1832–1929*. University of North Carolina Press, 2010.
Charlesworth, Lorie. *Welfare's Forgotten Past: A Socio-Legal History of the Poor Law*. Routledge, 2010.
Chatterjee, Partha. *The Politics of the Governed: Reflections on Popular Politics in Most of the World*. Columbia University Press, 2004.
Christensen, Tim. 'The Unbearable Whiteness of Being: Misrecognition, Pleasure, and White Identity in Kipling's "Kim".' *College Literature*, vol. 39, no. 2, 2012, pp. 9–30.
Clifford, James, et al. *Writing Culture: The Poetics and Politics of Ethnography*. University of California Press, 1986.
Cordella, Peter, and Larry J. Siegel. *Readings in Contemporary Criminological Theory*. Northeastern University Press, 1996.
Courtwright, David T., and Shelby Miller. 'Progressivism and Drink: The Social and Photographic Investigations of John James McCook.' *Journal of Drug Issues*, vol. 15, no. 1, 1985, pp. 93–109.
Cresswell, Tim. *The Tramp in America*. Reaktion, 2001.

Crick, Bernard. 'Orwell and English Socialism.' *George Orwell: A Reassessment*, edited by Peter Buitenhuis and Ira B. Nadel. Palgrave Macmillan, 1988, pp. 3–19.
Cross, Rodney. 'How Much Voluntary Unemployment in Interwar Britain?' *Journal of Political Economy*, vol. 90, no. 2, 1982, pp. 380–5.
Crowther, M. A. *British Social Policy 1914–1939*. Macmillan Education, 1988.
Cunningham, Charles. 'Rethinking the Politics of the Grapes of Wrath.' *Cultural Logic: An Electronic Journal of Marxist Theory and Practice*, vol. 5, 2002.
Dardot, Pierre, and Christian Laval. *The New Way of the World: On Neo-Liberal Society*, translated by Gregory Elliott. Verso, 2017.
Davies, Jude. 'Naturalism and Class.' *The Oxford Handbook of American Literary Naturalism*, edited by Keith Newlin. Oxford University Press, 2011, pp. 307–21.
Davies, Luke Lewin. *The Tramp in British Literature, 1850–1950*. Springer, 2021.
Davies, W. H. *The Autobiography of a Super-Tramp*. A. C. Fifield, 1908.
—. *Beggars*. Duckworth & Co., 1909.
Dawson, William Harbutt. *The Vagrancy Problem: The Case for Measures of Restraint for Tramps, Loafers, and Unemployables*. P. S. King & Son, 1910.
Denning, Michael. *The Cultural Front: The Laboring of American Culture in the Twentieth Century*. Verso, 2010.
—. *Mechanic Accents: Dime Novels and Working-Class Culture in America*. Verso, 1987.
DePastino, Todd. *Citizen Hobo: How a Century of Homelessness Shaped America*. University of Chicago Press, 2003.
DeWitt, Larry. 'The Decision to Exclude Agricultural and Domestic Workers from the 1935 Social Security Act.' *Social Security Bulletin*, vol. 70, no. 4, 2010, pp. 49–68.
Dos Passos, John. *The Big Money*. Houghton Mifflin, 2000.
Eliot, T. S. *The Varieties of Metaphysical Poetry: The Clark Lectures at Trinity College, Cambridge, 1926, and the Turnbull Lectures at the Johns Hopkins University, 1933*, edited by Ronald Schuchard. Faber and Faber, 1993.
Ellickson, Robert C. 'Controlling Chronic Misconduct in City Spaces: Of Panhandlers, Skid Rows, and Public-Space Zoning.' *The Yale Law Journal*, vol. 105, no. 1165, 1996, pp. 1167–248.
Englander, David. *Poverty and Poor Law Reform in Britain: From Chadwick to Booth, 1834–1914*. Addison Wesley Longman, 1998.
Esping-Andersen, Gøsta. *The Three Worlds of Welfare Capitalism*. Polity Press, 1990.
Esty, Jed. *Unseasonable Youth: Modernism, Colonialism, and the Fiction of Development*. Oxford University Press, 2012.

Feied, Frederick. *No Pie in the Sky: The Hobo as American Cultural Hero in the Works of Jack London, John Dos Passos, and Jack Kerouac*. Citadel Press, 1964.
Feldman, Leonard C. *Citizens without Shelter: Homelessness, Democracy, and Political Exclusion*. Cornell University Press, 2004.
Finlayson, Geoffrey B. A. M. *Citizen, State, and Social Welfare in Britain 1830–1990*. Clarendon Press, 1994.
Fleissner, Jennifer. *Women, Compulsion, Modernity: The Moment of American Naturalism*. University of Chicago Press, 2004.
Flynt, Josiah. *The Little Brother: A Story of Tramp Life*. The Century Company, 1902.
—. *My Life*. Outing Publishing Company, 1908.
—. *Tramping with Tramps: Studies and Sketches of Vagabond Life*. 1899. Patterson Smith, 1972.
The Forgotten Village. Directed by Herbert Kline and Alexander Hammid, written by John Steinbeck, narrated by Burgess Meredith. Arthur Mayer & Joseph Burstyn, 1941.
Foucault, Michel. *Abnormal: Lectures at the Collège de France, 1974–1975*, edited by Valerio Marchetti and Antonella Salomoni, translated by Graham Burchell. Picador, 2003.
—. *Discipline and Punish: The Birth of the Prison*. Vintage, 1995.
—. *Security, Territory, Population: Lectures at the Collège de France 1977–1978*, edited by Michel Senellart, translated by Graham Burchell. Picador, 2009.
—. *Society Must Be Defended: Lectures at the Collège de France, 1975–1976*, edited by Mauro Bertani and Alessandro Fontana, translated by David Macy. Picador, 2003.
Freund, David M. P. *Colored Property: State Policy and White Racial Politics in Suburban America*. University of Chicago Press, 2007.
George, Henry. *Social Problems*. Clarke & Co., 1883.
'A Girl Murdered by Tramps.' *Daily State Gazette*, vol. 34, 3 November 1880.
Glass, Loren Daniel. *Authors Inc.: Literary Celebrity in the Modern United States, 1880–1980*. New York University Press, 2004.
Godfrey, Mollie. '"They Ain't Human": John Steinbeck, Proletarian Fiction, and the Racial Politics of "the People".' *Modern Fiction Studies*, vol. 59, no. 1, 2013, pp. 107–34.
Goldstein, Norma Walrath. 'Kerouac's on the Road.' *The Explicator*, vol. 50, no. 1, 1994, pp. 60–2.
Goluboff, Risa Lauren. *Vagrant Nation: Police Power, Constitutional Change, and the Making of the 1960s*. Oxford University Press, 2016.
Gordon, Bowker. 'Orwell's Library.' *New England Review*, vol. 26, no. 1, 2005, pp. 56–61.
Great Britain, Parliament. Vagrancy Act (5 Geo. 4. c. 83). 21 June 1824.
Great Britain, Departmental Committee on Vagrancy and John Lloyd

Wharton. *Report of the Departmental Committee on Vagrancy*. Her Majesty's Stationery Office, 1906.

Harding, Jason. 'Non-Modernists.' *The Cambridge Quarterly*, vol. 36, no. 2, 2007, pp. 178–84.

Harper, Douglas. *Good Company: A Tramp Life*. 1982. Routledge, 2016.

Harris, Bernard. *The Origins of the British Welfare State: Society, State and Social Welfare in England and Wales, 1800–1945*. Palgrave Macmillan, 2004.

Harris, Jonathan. *Federal Art and National Culture: The Politics of Identity in New Deal America*. Cambridge University Press, 1995.

Harrison, Gary Lee. *Wordsworth's Vagrant Muse: Poetry, Poverty and Power*. Wayne State University Press, 1994.

Hart, Matthew. 'The Measure of All That Has Been Lost: Hitchens, Orwell, and the Price of Political Relevance.' *Postmodern Culture*, vol. 13, no. 3, 2003.

Hart, Matthew, and Jim Hansen. 'Introduction: Contemporary Literature and the State.' *Contemporary Literature*, vol. 49, no. 4, 2008, pp. 491–513.

Harvey, David. *A Brief History of Neoliberalism*. Oxford University Press, 2005.

Hearle, Kevin. 'These Are American People: The Spectre of Eugenics in *Their Blood Is Strong* and *The Grapes of Wrath*.' *Beyond Boundaries: Rereading John Steinbeck*, edited by Susan Shillinglaw and Kevin Hearle. University of Alabama Press, 2002, pp. 243–54.

Hellwig, Harold H. *Mark Twain's Travel Literature: The Odyssey of a Mind*. McFarland, 2008.

Hemingway, Ernest. *In Our Time*. 1924. Scribner, 2003.

Hennock, E. P. *The Origin of the Welfare State in England and Germany, 1850–1914: Social Policies Compared*. Cambridge University Press, 2007.

Herd, Pamela. 'Reforming a Breadwinner Welfare State: Gender, Race, Class and Social Security Reform.' *Social Forces*, vol. 83, no. 4, 2005, pp. 1365–93.

Hicks, Granville. 'Steinbeck's Powerful New Novel.' *The New Masses*, 1939, pp. 22–3.

Hitchcock, David. *Vagrancy in English Culture and Society, 1650–1750*. Bloomsbury Academic, 2016.

Hoberek, Andrew. *The Twilight of the Middle Class: Post-World War II American Fiction and White-Collar Work*. Princeton University Press, 2005.

Hoffman, Abraham. 'Stimulus to Repatriation: The 1931 Federal Deportation Drive and the Los Angeles Mexican Community.' *Pacific Historical Review*, vol. 42, no. 2, 1973, pp. 205–19.

Howarth, Peter. *British Poetry in the Age of Modernism*. Cambridge University Press, 2005.

—. 'The Simplicity of W. H. Davies.' *English Literature in Transition, 1880–1920*, vol. 46, no. 2, 2003, pp. 155–74.

Howe, Lawrence. 'Charlie Chaplin in the Age of Mechanical Reproduction: Reflexive Ambiguity in Modern Times.' *College Literature*, vol. 40, no. 1, 2013, pp. 45–65.

Hsu, Hsuan L. *Sitting in Darkness: Mark Twain's Asia and Comparative Racialization*. New York University Press, 2015.

Ignatiev, Noel. *How the Irish Became White*. Routledge, 1995.

'In Dreams He Sees an Army.' *The New York Times*, 25 March 1894.

Jones, Gavin Roger. *American Hungers: The Problem of Poverty in U.S. Literature, 1840–1945*. Princeton University Press, 2008.

Kaplan, Justin. *Mr. Clemens and Mark Twain*. Harper & Brothers, 1966.

Katznelson, Ira. *Fear Itself: The New Deal and the Origins of Our Time*. Liveright, 2013.

Kelly, Edmond. *The Elimination of the Tramp by the Introduction into America of the Labour Colony System Already Proved Effective in Holland, Belgium, and Switzerland*. G. P. Putnam's Sons, 1908.

Kerouac, Jack. *On the Road*. 1957. Penguin, 1998.

—. 'The Vanishing American Hobo.' *Lonesome Traveller*. 1960. Panther Books, 1972, pp. 164–74.

Kessler-Harris, Alice. 'Designing Women and Old Fools: The Construction of the Social Security Amendments of 1939.' *U.S. History as Women's History: New Feminist Essays*, edited by Linda K. Kerber, Alice Kessler-Harris and Kathryn Kish Sklar. University of North Carolina Press, 1995, pp. 87–106.

Kipling, Rudyard. *Kim*. 1901. Dover Thrift, 2005.

Klarman, Michael J. *Brown v. Board of Education and the Civil Rights Movement: The Supreme Court and the Struggle for Racial Equality*. Oxford University Press, 2007.

Kusmer, Kenneth L. *Down and Out, on the Road: The Homeless in American History*. Oxford University Press, 2002.

Langan, Celeste. *Romantic Vagrancy: Wordsworth and the Simulation of Freedom*. Cambridge University Press, 1995.

Lawrence, Paul. 'The Vagrancy Act (1824) and the Persistence of Pre-Emptive Policing in England since 1750.' *The British Journal of Criminology*, vol. 57, no. 3, 2017, pp. 513–31.

LeMaster, J. R., and James D. Wilson. *The Routledge Encyclopedia of Mark Twain*. Routledge, 2011.

Lemke, Thomas. *Foucault's Analysis of Modern Governmentality: A Critique of Political Reason*, translated by Erik Butler. Verso, 2019.

Lennon, John. *Boxcar Politics: The Hobo in U.S. Culture and Literature, 1869–1956*. University of Massachusetts Press, 2014.

Lesjak, Carolyn. *Working Fictions: A Genealogy of the Victorian Novel*. Duke University Press, 2006.

Lieberman, Robert C. 'Race, Institutions, and the Administration of Social Policy.' *Social Science History*, vol. 19, no. 4, 1995, pp. 511–42.
London, Jack. *The People of the Abyss*. 1903. Pluto Press, 2001.
—. *The Road*. 1907. Seven Treasures Publications, 2008.
—. 'These Bones Shall Rise Again.' *No Mentor but Myself: Jack London on Writers and Writing*, edited by Dale L. Walker and Jeanne Campbell Reesman. Stanford University Press, 1999, pp. 65–72.
Lowe, Rodney. *Adjusting to Democracy: The Role of the Ministry of Labour in British Politics, 1916–1939*. Clarendon, 1986.
Lye, Colleen. *America's Asia: Racial Form and American Literature, 1893–1945*. Princeton University Press, 2005.
Lynn, Shane. '"A Room of Experience into Which I Cannot Enter": John Steinbeck on Race.' *Steinbeck Review*, vol. 12, no. 2, 2015, pp. 149–58.
McCook, J. J. 'A Tramp Census and Its Revelations.' *The Forum*, August 1893, pp. 753–66.
McGurl, Mark. *The Program Era: Postwar Fiction and the Rise of Creative Writing*. Harvard University Press, 2009.
McKee, Patricia. 'Travel in *The Ambassadors*.' *Arizona Quarterly*, vol. 62, no. 3, 2006, pp. 105–27.
McWilliams, Carey. *Factories in the Field*. Little, Brown and Company, 1939.
Maland, Charles J. *Chaplin and American Culture: The Evolution of a Star Image*. Princeton University Press, 1989.
Martinez, Manuel Luis. *Countering the Counterculture: Rereading Postwar American Dissent from Jack Kerouac to Tomás Rivera*. University of Wisconsin Press, 2003.
Messent, Peter. 'Tramps and Tourists: Europe in Mark Twain's "A Tramp Abroad".' *The Yearbook of English Studies*, vol. 34, 2004, pp. 138–54.
Mettler, Suzanne. *Dividing Citizens: Gender and Federalism in New Deal Public Policy*. Cornell University Press, 1998.
Metzler, Mark. *Lever of Empire: The International Gold Standard and the Crisis of Liberalism in Prewar Japan*. University of California Press, 2006.
Miller, Peter, and Nikolas S. Rose. *Governing the Present: Administering Economic, Social and Personal Life*. Polity, 2008.
Modern Times. Directed by Charlie Chaplin, performances by Charlie Chaplin, Paulette Goddard, Henry Bergman, Tiny Sandford and Chester Conklin. United Artists, 1936.
Monteiro, George. 'The Jungle Out There: Nick Adams Takes to the Road.' *The Hemingway Review*, vol. 29, no. 1, 2009, pp. 61–72.
Morales, Ed. *Latinx: The New Force in American Politics and Culture*. Verso, 2018.
Murray, Hannah Lauren. *Liminal Whiteness in Early US Fiction*. Edinburgh University Press, 2021.

Neider, Charles. 'Introduction.' *A Tramp Abroad* by Mark Twain. Harper & Row, 1977, pp. ix–xxiv.
Newsinger, John. *Orwell's Politics*. Macmillan, 1999.
Ngai, Mae M. *Impossible Subjects: Illegal Aliens and the Making of Modern America*. Princeton University Press, 2004.
Nicholls, Brendon. 'The Melting Pot That Boiled Over: Racial Fetishism and the Lingua Franca of Jack Kerouac's Fiction.' *Modern Fiction Studies*, vol. 49, no. 3, 2003, pp. 524–49.
Nicolazzo, Sal. *Vagrant Figures: Law, Literature, and the Origins of the Police*. Yale University Press, 2021.
Orwell, George. *Down and Out in Paris and London*. 1933. Harcourt, 1961.
—. 'The English People.' *As I Please, 1943–1945: The Collected Essays, Journalism and Letters of George Orwell*, vol. 3, edited by Sonia Orwell and Ian Angus. D. R. Godine, 2000, pp. 1–38.
—. *The Road to Wigan Pier*. 1937. Harcourt, 1958.
—. 'Writers and Leviathan.' *George Orwell: The Collected Essays, Journalism and Letters*, vol. 4, edited by Sonia Orwell and Ian Angus. D. R. Godine, 2000, pp. 407–13.
Osborn, Marijane. 'Participatory Parables: Cinema, Social Action, and Steinbeck's Mexican Dilemma.' *A Political Companion to John Steinbeck*, edited by Cyrus Ernesto Zirakzadeh and Simon Stow. University Press of Kentucky, 2013, pp. 227–46.
Owen, A. D. K. 'From Poor Law to Beveridge Report.' *Foreign Affairs*, vol. 21, no. 4, 1943, pp. 743–55.
Owens, Louis. '"Grampa Killed Indians, Pa Killed Snakes": Steinbeck and the American Indian.' *MELUS*, vol. 15, no. 2, 1988, pp. 85–92.
Park, Robert Ezra, et al. *The City*. University of Chicago Press, 1967.
'The Pathology of the Tramp.' *British Medical Journal*, vol. 2, no. 2544, 1909, pp. 999–1000.
Paul, Ronald. 'Beyond the Abyss: Jack London and the Working Class.' *Nordic Journal of English Studies*, vol. 9, no. 3, 2010, pp. 25–40.
Pearce, Philip L., and Gianna M. Moscardo. 'The Concept of Authenticity in Tourist Experiences.' *Australian and New Zealand Journal of Sociology*, vol. 22, no. 1, 1986, pp. 121–32.
Photinos, Christine. 'The Figure of the Tramp in Gilded Success Narratives.' *The Journal of Popular Culture*, vol. 40, no. 6, 2007, pp. 994–1018.
—. 'The Tramp in American Literature, 1873–1939.' *AmeriQuests*, vol. 5, no. 1, 2008.
Pittenger, Mark. *Class Unknown: Undercover Investigations of American Work and Poverty from the Progressive Era to the Present*. New York University Press, 2012.
Plotz, Judith, A. 'The Empire of Youth: Crossing and Double-Crossing Cultural Barriers in Kipling's *Kim*.' *Children's Literature*, vol. 20, 1992, pp. 111–31.

Potter, George. 'The Tramp & the Culture Industry: Adorno, Chaplin, and the Possibility of Progressive Comedy.' *Arizona Quarterly*, vol. 69, no. 1, 2013, pp. 73–90.

Pound, Ezra. *The Selected Letters of Ezra Pound, 1907–1941*, edited by D. D. Paige. Faber and Faber, 1971.

Powell, Jason L., and Jon Hendricks, editors. *The Welfare State in Post-Industrial Society: A Global Perspective*. Springer, 2009.

Priestley, J. B. *English Journey. Being a Rambling but Truthful Account of What One Man Saw and Heard and Felt and Thought during a Journey through England during the Autumn of the Year 1933*. 1934. William Heinemann, 1949.

Railsback, Brian. 'Searching for "What Is": Charles Darwin and John Steinbeck.' *Steinbeck and the Environment: Interdisciplinary Approaches*, edited by Susan F. Beegel et al. University of Alabama Press, 1997, pp. 113–26.

Ranney, Joseph A. *In the Wake of Slavery: Civil War, Civil Rights, and the Reconstruction of Southern Law*. Praeger Publishers, 2006.

Reti, Steven P. *Silver and Gold: The Political Economy of International Monetary Conferences, 1867–1892*. Greenwood Press, 1998.

Robinson, Alistair. *Vagrancy in the Victorian Age: Representing the Wandering Poor in Nineteenth-Century Literature and Culture*. Cambridge University Press, 2021.

Rodden, John. *George Orwell: The Politics of Literary Reputation*. Transaction Publishers, 2001.

Rodgers, Daniel T. *Atlantic Crossings: Social Politics in a Progressive Age*. Harvard University Press, 1998.

Roediger, David R. *The Wages of Whiteness: Race and the Making of the American Working Class*. Verso, 1991.

Roggenkamp, Karen. *Narrating the News: New Journalism and Literary Genre in Late Nineteenth-Century American Newspapers and Fiction*. Kent State University Press, 2005.

Roosevelt, Franklin D. 'Annual Message to Congress, January 4, 1935.' *The American Presidency Project*, https://www.presidency.ucsb.edu/documents/annual-message-congress-3.

Ross, Dorothy. *The Origins of American Social Science*. Oxford University Press, 1991.

Ross, Stephen. 'Authenticity Betrayed: The "Idiotic Folk" of *Love on the Dole*.' *Cultural Critique*, vol. 56, 2003, pp. 189–209.

Rovere, Richard H. 'First Novel (Review).' *The New Masses*, 18 July 1939, pp. 26–7.

Rubenstein, Michael, et al. 'Infrastructuralism: An Introduction.' *Modern Fiction Studies*, vol. 61, no. 4, 2015, pp. 575–86.

Runciman, W. G. 'Has British Capitalism Changed since the First World War?' *British Journal of Sociology*, vol. 44, 1993, pp. 53–67.

Said, Edward W. *Culture and Imperialism*. Vintage, 1994.

Schieber, Sylvester J., and John B. Shoven. *The Real Deal: The History and Future of Social Security*. Yale University Press, 1999.

Schiltz, M. E. *Public Attitudes toward Social Security: 1935–1965*. Government Printing Office, 1970.

Schuster, David G. 'The Rise of a Modern Concept of "Health".' *A Companion to the Gilded Age and Progressive Era*, edited by Christopher M. Nichols and Nancy C. Unger. Wiley Blackwell, 2017, pp. 255–68.

Schweizer, Bernard. *Radicals on the Road: The Politics of English Travel Writing in the 1930s*. University of Virginia Press, 2001.

Seaber, Luke. *Incognito Social Investigation in British Literature: Certainties in Degradation*. Palgrave Macmillan, 2017.

Seelye, John. 'The American Tramp: A Version of the Picaresque.' *American Quarterly*, vol. 15, no. 4, 1963, pp. 535–53.

Shaw, George Bernard. 'Preface.' *The Autobiography of a Super-Tramp* by W. H. Davies. A. C. Fifield, 1908, pp. vii–xiv.

Shelden, Michael. *Orwell: The Authorized Biography*. HarperCollins, 1991.

Shumsky, Neil L. *Homelessness: A Documentary and Reference Guide*. Greenwood, 2012.

Siegel, Larry J. *Criminology: Theories, Patterns, and Typologies*, 11th edition. Wadsworth Cengage Learning, 2013.

Simpson, David. *Wordsworth's Historical Imagination: The Poetry of Displacement*. Methuen, 1987.

Sinclair, Andrew. *Jack: A Biography of Jack London*. Weidenfeld and Nicolson, 1978.

Smith, Sidonie, and Julia Watson. *Reading Autobiography: A Guide for Interpreting Life Narratives*. University of Minnesota Press, 2010.

Spangler, Jason. 'We're on a Road to Nowhere: Steinbeck, Kerouac, and the Legacy of the Great Depression.' *Studies in the Novel*, vol. 40, no. 3, 2008, pp. 308–27.

Steinbeck, John. *The Grapes of Wrath*. 1939. Penguin, 2006.

—. *The Harvest Gypsies: On the Road to the Grapes of Wrath*. 1936. Heyday Books, 1988.

—. *The Log from the Sea of Cortez*. 1951. Penguin, 1995.

—. *Travels with Charley: In Search of America*. 1962. Penguin, 1980.

Steinbrink, Jeffrey. *Getting to Be Mark Twain*. University of California Press, 1991.

Stevens, George. 'Steinbeck's Uncovered Wagon.' *The Saturday Review of Literature*, vol. 19, no. 25, 1939, pp. 3–4.

Suleri, Sara. *The Rhetoric of English India*. University of Chicago Press, 1992.

Szalay, Michael. *New Deal Modernism: American Literature and the Invention of the Welfare State*. Duke University Press, 2000.

Tichi, Cecelia. 'Canonizing Economic Crisis: Jack London's *The Road*.' *American Literary History*, vol. 23, no. 1, 2011, pp. 19–31.

Tocqueville, Alexis de. *Democracy in America, Volumes I & II*, translated by Henry Reeve. 1840. The Floating Press, 2009.

'A Tramp's Revenge. He Burns up $10,000 Worth of Property Because He Was Refused a Meal.' *Wheeling Register*, vol. 18, 20 October 1880.

Twain, Mark. *Mark Twain's Notebooks and Journals, Volume II: 1877–1883*, edited by Frederick Anderson, Lin Salamo and Bernard L. Stein. University of California Press, 1976.

—. 'To the Editor of the Hartford Courant, February 2, 1879.' *Mark Twain on Potholes and Politics: Letters to the Editor*, edited by Gary Scharnhorst. University of Missouri Press, 2014, pp. 113–17.

—. *A Tramp Abroad*. 1880. Dover, 2002.

United States, Congress, Select Committee Investigating National Defense Migration. *Interstate Migration: Report of the Select Committee to Investigate the Interstate Migration of Destitute Citizens, House of Representatives, Pursuant to H. Res. 63, 491, 629 (76th Congress) and H. Res. 16 (77th Congress) Resolutions to Inquire into the Interstate Migration of Destitute Citizens, to Study, Survey, and Investigate the Social and Economic Needs and the Movement of Indigent Persons across State Lines*. Government Printing Office, 1941.

United States, Department of Housing and Urban Development. 'Secretary Carson Certifies Annual Data: Homelessness Ticked Up in 2019, Driven by Major Increases in California.' https://archives.hud.gov/news/2019/pr19-177.cfm. Press release.

Urry, John. 'The Consumption of Tourism.' *Sociology*, vol. 24, no. 1, 1990, pp. 23–35.

Vorspan, Rachel. 'Vagrancy and the New Poor Law in Late-Victorian and Edwardian England.' *English Historical Review*, vol. 92, no. 362, 1977, pp. 59–81.

Wiegman, Robyn. 'Whiteness Studies and the Paradox of Particularity.' *boundary 2*, vol. 26, no. 3, 1999, pp. 115–50.

Wild, Mark H. 'If You Ain't Got That Do-Re-Mi: The Los Angeles Border Patrol and White Migration in Depression-Era California.' *Southern California Quarterly*, vol. 88, no. 3, 2001, pp. 317–34.

Williams, Raymond. *Culture and Society, 1780–1950*. Columbia University Press, 1983.

Windschuttle, Keith. 'Steinbeck's Myth of the Okies.' *The New Criterion*, vol. 20, no. 10, 2002, pp. 24–32.

Winter, Nicholas J. T. 'Beyond Welfare: Framing and the Racialization of White Opinion on Social Security.' *American Journal of Political Science*, vol. 50, no. 2, 2006, pp. 400–20.

Woodbridge, Linda. *Vagrancy, Homelessness, and English Renaissance Literature*. University of Illinois Press, 2001.

Wordsworth, William. 'Beggars.' *Poems of William Wordsworth, Volume 1: Collected Reading Texts from The Cornell Wordsworth*, edited Jared Curtis. Humanities-Ebooks, 2011, pp. 619–20.

Wright, Richard. *Native Son*. 1940. Harper Perennial, 2005.
Wrigley, Richard, and George Revill. *Pathologies of Travel*. Rodopi, 2000.
Wyman, Marilyn. 'Affirming Whiteness: Visualizing California Agriculture.' *Steinbeck Studies*, vol. 16, no. 1–2, 2007, pp. 32–55.
Youngs, Tim, editor. *Travel Writing in the Nineteenth Century: Filling the Blank Spaces*. Anthem Press, 2006.
Ziff, Larzer. *Return Passages: Great American Travel Writing, 1780–1910*. Yale University Press, 2000.
Zirakzadeh, Cyrus Ernesto. 'John Steinbeck on the Political Capacities of Everyday Folk: Moms, Reds, and Ma Joad's Revolt.' *Polity*, vol. 36, no. 4, 2004, pp. 595–618.

Index

Anderson, Nels, 10, 15
Attaway, William, 130
Autobiography of a Super-Tramp (Davies)
   critical reception, 87–8
   critique of British social welfare policies, 73–4
   Davies as a tramp-writer, 69–70, 78, 85
   influence on Orwell's work, 98
   racial identities and vagrancy, 26–7, 62, 63–4
   the urban poor in Davies's writing, 72–3
   US-British comparison, 13, 26–7, 63, 70–2, 73–4, 110

Beat movement, 151, 154; see also Kerouac, Jack
Bellesiles, Michael, 4, 5–6, 38
Berlant, Lauren, 95, 113, 115, 117–18
Beveridge Report, 93, 115, 116, 117
Black, Jack, 128–9
Breton, Rob, 109
Burroughs, William S., 154
Butler, Judith, 117–18

Cassady, Neal, 155
Chance, William, 83
Chang, David, 144
Chaplin, Charlie
   Little Tramp films, 10, 103, 121
   Modern Times, 92–3, 94–5, 97–8, 103–4
Churchill, Winston, 86
Civil Rights Movement, 152–3, 161
class
   cultural images of the working classes, 141, 147
   impact on the British tramp figure, 62
   Jack London's undercover narratives of urban poverty, 65–7
   race, class and nationalism in Steinbeck, 126–7, 131–3, 147–8
   racial categories and, 9, 10
   tramps within the working-class poor in Orwell, 101, 102–3, 119–20
   the working tramp in *Modern Times* (Chaplin), 92–3, 97–8, 103–4
   working-class families in Orwell, 95–6, 98–9, 119–20
Clifford, James, 44
Crane, Stephen, 55
Cresswell, Tim, 4, 6, 35
Crick, Bernard, 116
criminality
   expansion of disciplinary and surveillance institutions, 5, 56
   imprisonment of the tramp, 92, 93, 103
   as an inherited trait, 50–1
   tramps as figures of, 5–6, 46–7, 99–100, 128–9

Dardot, Pierre, 118
Davies, W. H.
   Beggars, 13, 81, 86
   within the international nexus of tramp writing, 12, 14, 85–6
   racial identities and demographic sorting, 26–7, 64
   vagrancy as a reflection of national character, 81–2, 85–6, 87, 88–9, 100
   the vagrant as a distinct demographic group, 26–7, 64, 78, 87
   valorisation of the individualism of American tramps, 70–2, 81
   see also *Autobiography of a Super-Tramp* (Davies)
Dawson, William Harbutt, 82
demographics
   demographic difference in Steinbeck, 135–6, 139–41, 147
   demographic ordering by the state, 79–82, 87, 113–15, 117
   deserving vs undeserving poor, 79–80
   racial identities and demographic sorting, 9–10, 26–7, 61, 62, 64, 65, 67, 157–9, 164
   state control of the vagrant population, 17–18
   the vagrant as a distinct demographic group, 3–4, 15–16, 17–18, 49–51, 54, 57, 78, 79–80, 87, 157, 157–9, 159, 164

the vagrant as a social threat, 1–2, 3–7, 8–9, 16, 34–5, 57
Denning, Michael, 4, 36, 44, 124
Dickens, Charles, 75
Dos Passos, John, 129
Douglas, William O., 152
Down and Out in Paris and London (Orwell)
  biopower and the vagrant subject, 95, 112–15, 116–17
  British social policy, 94, 97–8, 115–16
  the comparative imagination in, 94, 97
  comparison between France and the UK, 94, 108–12, 116
  distinction of public/private spaces, 18, 114
  impact of the Vagrancy Act of 1824 (UK), 17–18, 105
  individualism of the *plongeur* model, 109–10, 112
  institutionalisation of the vagrant, 93, 94–6, 97–8, 105, 112–13, 117, 156
  Jack London's influence on, 94, 98, 101–2
  medical oversight of vagrants, 93
  mobility and infrastructure inequalities, 157
  nostalgia for the tramping archetype, 98, 99–100, 101, 109, 120
  Orwell as a tramp-writer, 93, 94, 95, 99–100, 101–3, 120
  Orwell's critique of state policy, 95–6, 104–12, 119
  patterns of tramp movements, 97–8, 112
  physical deterioration of tramp bodies, 113, 114–15, 119
  policing of vagrants, 93
  shame of the tramp persona, 99–100, 105
  state power over British vagabondage, 94–5
  tramping as an expression of national identity, 100–1
  tramps within the working-class poor, 101, 102–3, 119–20
  as an undercover social investigation text, 106
  workhouses (the spike), 17–18, 93, 97–8, 113–14
Dupouy, Roger, 16

Eliot, T. S., 87

Flynt, Josiah
  ethnographic studies, 10, 33, 45
  figure of the tramp in the works of, 45
  importation of overseas vagrancy social policies, 46
  Jack London's debt to, 65
  The Little Brother: A Story of Tramp Life, 45

  Twain's influence on, 33, 44, 49–50
  as an undercover writer, 55
  the vagrant as a distinct demographic group, 49–51, 54, 57
Foucault, Michel
  biopower, 9, 17, 18, 113, 117
  disciplinary power, 56
  normalisation of racist discourse, 162
  public spaces/state power over, 153
  scientific racism, 64, 83–4
Free Speech Movement, 152–3

George, Henry, 1, 2, 4, 12, 17
Germany, 45, 49, 52–5
Gilded Age, 1, 4, 36, 128–9
Ginsberg, Allen, 154
Godfrey, Mollie, 124, 128
Goldman, Emma, 15
Goluboff, Risa, 152, 153
governance
  civil responsibility discourses, 86–7, 88
  consolidation with law and medicine, 17–19
  disciplinary power, 5, 56
  international networks of exchange, 12–13
  linking of individualism and civic responsibility, 56
  literature's influence on, 123–4
  New Deal, 3, 123, 124, 133, 141
  problem of the urban poor, 72–3
  race and anti-vagrancy legislation, 8, 11–12
  state relations with migrant farmers, 142–7
  see also welfare codes; welfare institutions; welfare state
Grapes of Wrath, The (Steinbeck)
  defense migration model, 144, 146–7
  disappearance of the archetypal tramp, 127, 131, 163
  influence on welfare governance, 123–4, 136
  the migrant family, 19–20, 124, 128, 131–2, 135–6, 139–41
  migrant settlers and the frontier myth, 144–6
  need for national labour regulation, 123–4, 132
  On the Road's parallels with, 154
  presentation of post-Depression labour, 127–8
  problematic populism of, 124
  state relations with migrant farmers, 142–7
  tenant farming system, 144
  value of federal camps, 138–40
  value of state investment in migrant labour, 21, 124, 128, 131–3, 137–9, 147

Grapes of Wrath, The (Steinbeck) (*cont.*)
  whiteness of vagrant characters, 124–5, 126–7, 147–8
Great Britain (GB)
  British vagabond literature, 60
  categories for welfare assistance, 79–80
  imperialism in *Kim* (Kipling), 64, 76–7
  racial identity and vagrancy, 9–10, 12
  tramp population, 7, 79
  transatlantic discourses on the tramp, 4, 5, 12, 21–2, 30–1, 33, 43, 61–2
  urban poor, 65–7, 72–4, 79, 82
  Vagrancy Act (1824), 13, 17–18, 105
  welfare reform, 19–20, 82–3, 86–7, 89, 106–8
Great Depression (1873)
  figure of the British tramp, 48
  and the rise of the tramp, 4–5, 38
  stock-market crash, 36–7, 38
Great Depression (1929)
  consolidation of the US welfare state, 133–41
  figure of the tramp, 4, 129–30
  formation of the welfare state, 19–20
Greenwood, Walter, 107

Hart, Matthew, 115, 116
Harvest Gypsies, The (Steinbeck)
  migrancy as productive for the nation state, 21
  the migrant family, 128, 130–1
  natural democracy, 140
  race, class and nationalism of migrant labour, 126
  role of the federal camps, 139–40
  vision of social reform, 125–6, 136–7
Hemingway, Ernest, 129–30
highwaymen, 29 n.9
homelessness
  the figure of the tramp and, 2, 4
  public spaces and, 12, 18, 114, 153
  romance of the tramp narrative, 36
  in Steinbeck's works, 19–20
Howells, William Dean, 38
Hsu, Husan, 11–12, 35

Ignatiev, Noel, 9

James, Henry, 43
Joffroy, Alix, 16

Kelly, Edmond, 6–7, 46, 55
Kerouac, Jack
  affinity with Steinbeck, 154, 160, 162, 164
  exoticisation of blackness, 152, 158, 162–3
  the mundanity of whiteness in post-war America, 152, 158–9
  within the tramping-narrative genre, 151, 152

'The Vanishing American Hobo,' 152, 159
  see also *On the Road* (Kerouac)
Keynes, John Maynard, 94
Kim (Kipling)
  British imperialism and, 64, 76–7
  exceptional mobility, 64, 76–7
  Kim as governmental asset, 64, 76, 77
  white vagabondage in, 64, 76–8
Kipling, Rudyard
  as a literary source for London, 75–6, 78
  'These Bones Shall Rise Again' (London), 75–6

labour
  and categories of unemployment, 79–80
  defense migrants of World War II, 142, 143–4, 146–7
  mobile labour of the tramp, 5, 6, 8, 57
  need for national labour regulation, 123–4, 132
  non-white migrant labour, 8, 126–7
  Orwell's idealisation of hard work, 109–10
  the rehabilitated tramp as, 6, 16, 17, 21
  state measures for the maintenance of, 94
  Steinbeck's migrant families, 20, 21, 125, 128, 131–2, 135–6, 139–41
  tenant farming system, 144
  the tramp within the industrialist system, 92–3, 97–8, 103–4
  Twain's equation of artistry with work, 31–2, 119
  visibility of in Victorian fiction, 25–6
  see also migrants; unemployment
Laval, Christian, 118
legislation
  alongside academic research, 47
  anti-vagrancy legislation, 8, 11–13, 19, 30–1, 33, 82, 152–3
  consolidation with governance and medicine, 17–19
  Edwards v. *California*, 143–4, 146
  end of anti-vagrancy laws, 152
  English Poor Laws, 80, 107–8
  Jim Crow segregation, 8, 164 n.2
  legal codifications of vagrancy, 5, 12
  Papachristou v. *City of Jacksonville*, 152
  public spaces and vagrancy laws, 12, 18, 114, 153
  race and anti-vagrancy legislation, 8, 11–12
  Social Security Act, 134–5
  Vagrancy Act of 1824 (UK), 13, 17–18, 105
Lesjak, Carolyn, 25–6
literature
  'Beggars' (Wordsworth), 60–1
  British vagabond literature, 60

cultural creation of the tramp figure, 36, 43–4
figure of the tramp, 5
influence on welfare governance, 123–4
international nexus of tramp writing, 11, 12, 14, 85–6
nature of ethnographic texts, 44
post-war figure of the tramp, 152, 153
undercover social investigation texts, 55, 65–7, 84, 102, 106
vagrancy in Beat literature, 151, 154
vagrancy in Romantic literature, 60–1, 85
Lloyd George, David, 86
Lombroso, Cesare, 50–1
London, Jack
  debt to Flynt, 65
  international nexus of tramp writing, 12, 62, 85–6
  Kipling as a literary source for, 75–6, 78
  masculinity and whiteness of tramping, 8, 75–6
  The Road, 65
  'These Bones Shall Rise Again,' 75–6
  time with Kelly's Army, 8
  as a tramp-writer, 11, 62, 65, 85, 94
  vagrancy as a reflection of national character, 68–9, 100
  see also *People of the Abyss, The* (London)

McCook, John James, 46, 55, 56, 57
medicine
  biological framing of vagrancy, 16–17
  biopower, 9, 17, 18, 113, 117
  biopower and the vagrant subject in Orwell, 95, 112–15, 116–17
  consolidation with governance and legislation, 17–19
  physical deterioration of the tramp, 113, 114–15, 119
  regulation of public health by the welfare state, 16–17, 20, 92, 105, 112–14, 121
  slow death (Berlant), 95, 115, 119
  vagrancy as a medical condition, 16
Messent, Peter, 31, 42
migrants
  and citizenship rights, 8, 127
  defense migrants of World War II, 142, 143–4, 146–7
  figure of the migrant farmer, 142
  migrant settlers and the frontier myth, 144–6
  US restrictions on non-white migrant labour, 126–7
  see also labour
Miller, Peter, 3, 17, 18, 56, 87
mobility
  on the American railroads, 35, 79
  infrastructuralism in Kerouac, 157
  international mobility of white vagabondage, 25, 52, 75, 78–9

in *Kim* (Kipling), 64, 76–7
mobile labour of the tramp, 5, 6, 8, 57
non-white migrant labour in Steinbeck, 125–7
patterns of tramp movements, 96–8, 112
racial restrictions on, 157
social commentary through, 65, 68
Steinbeck's migrant families, 20, 21, 125, 128, 131–2, 135–6, 139–41
US-British comparisons, 32–3, 63, 65–7, 70–2, 73–4
of white vagabondage, 8, 10, 35–6, 63–4, 76–8
see also migrants

nationalism
  cultural depictions of the working classes, 141–2, 147
  exceptionalism of American tramps, 62–3, 67–9, 72, 78, 81, 84, 110
  imperialist framing of *Kim* (Kipling), 64, 76–7
  race, class and nationalism in Steinbeck, 126–7, 131–3, 147–8
  in travel writing, 74–5
  vagrancy as a reflection of national character, 81–2, 85–6, 87, 88–9, 100
neoliberalism
  slow death (Berlant), 95, 115
  and the welfare state, 117, 118–19
New Deal, 3, 123, 124, 133, 141–2
Ngai, Mae, 8, 127

On the Road (Kerouac)
  demographic sorting of vagrant types, 157
  figure of the tramp, 3, 154–7, 163
  the mundanity of whiteness in post-war America, 152, 158–9
  parallels with *The Grapes of Wrath*, 154
  racial difference in, 157–9, 162–3
  within the tramping-narrative genre, 151–2
Orwell, George
  Animal Farm, 115
  critique of state policy, 95–6, 104–12, 119
  'The English People,' 116
  idealisation of hard work, 109–10
  Nineteenth Eighty-Four, 115
  within the tramp writing tradition, 11, 12, 98–9
  views on British social welfare, 17–19, 115–16
  'Writers and Leviathan,' 116
  writing on working-class families, 95–6, 98–9
  see also *Down and Out in Paris and London* (Orwell); *Road to Wigan Pier* (Orwell)
Owens, Louis, 145

People of the Abyss, The (London)
  adaptability of the exceptional tramp, 78
  British literary sources in, 75
  exceptionalism of American tramps, 62–3, 67–9, 72, 78, 81, 84, 110
  influence on Orwell's work, 98, 101–2
  London as a tramp-writer, 62, 65, 67–8, 78, 101–2
  social commentary on the urban poor, 65–7, 84, 102
  US-British comparison, 65–7, 72, 74
Pittenger, Mark, 41, 67
policing
  of vagrancy, 12, 50–1, 82, 92, 93
  under the Vagrancy Act, 13, 17–18, 105
  see also criminality
Pound, Ezra, 87
poverty
  biological framings of, 72–3
  British urban poor, 65–7, 72–4, 79, 82
  Davies's critique of British welfare policies, 73–4
  the deserving poor, 6, 79, 107
  empirical observation of, 55
  English Poor Laws, 80, 107–8
  following the 1873 crash, 38
  governance and the problem of, 72–3
  Jack London's undercover narratives of urban poverty, 65–7, 84, 102
  the poor as indolent, 5–6
  public perceptions of via vagabond accounts, 11
  tramps within the working-class poor in Orwell, 101, 102–3, 119–20
  the urban poor in Davies' writing, 72–3
  vagrants as the non-deserving poor, 79, 107
  see also People of the Abyss, The (London)
Priestley, J. B., 94, 96–7, 121
Progressive reforms, 46, 55, 84

race
  anti-vagrancy legislation, 8, 11–12
  the figure of the white (male) tramp, 1, 3, 7–8, 10, 20–1, 25, 26, 36, 62, 75–7, 78–9, 129–30
  international migrancy in vagrancy narratives, 25–6
  Jim Crow segregation, 8, 164 n.2
  Kerouac's exoticisation of blackness, 152, 158, 162–3
  migrant settlers and the frontier myth, 144–6
  non-white vagrancy, 8–10
  and the post-Depression tramping figure, 129–30
  and the post-war figure of the tramp, 154
  race, class and nationalism in Steinbeck, 126–7, 131–3, 147–8
  racial categories and social rehabilitation, 9, 10
  racial difference in *On the Road* (Steinbeck), 157–9, 162–3
  racial identities and demographic sorting, 9–10, 61, 62, 64, 65, 67, 157–9, 164
  racial identities and vagrancy in *Autobiography of a Super-Tramp*, 26–7, 62, 63–4
  racial identities and vagrancy in Twain, 35–6
  scientific racism, 55–6, 64, 83–4
  in *Travels with Charley* (Steinbeck), 154, 160–3
  and US welfare provision, 133–4
  whiteness and the exceptional tramp, 61, 62, 63–4, 72
  whiteness of Steinbeck's vagrant characters, 124–5, 126–7, 147–8
  whiteness studies, 9
rehabilitation
  economic needs of the state, 144, 146
  federal camps, 138–40
  labour camps, 5, 6–7, 46
  the labour potential of tramps, 6, 16, 17, 21
  and the nascent welfare state, 2–3, 6–7, 8–9, 10, 86
  for the public health, 16
  racial categories and social rehabilitation, 9, 10
  social reform movements, 46, 55, 153–4
  tramp-citizen template, 64–5
  workhouses (the spike), 17–19, 80–1, 82, 93, 97–8, 107–8, 113–14
Reitman, Ben, 14–15
Revill, George, 1–2
Ricketts, Ed, 136
Road to Wigan Pier (Orwell)
  British social policy, 115–16
  Jack London's influence on Orwell, 98–9
  reflections on Orwell as tramp-writer, 99
  on working-class families, 98–9, 119–20
Robinson, Alistair, 9, 12, 19, 43–4
Rodgers, Daniel, 3, 12–13, 46, 53
Roediger, David, 9
Romanticism, 60–1, 85
Roosevelt, Franklin D., 20, 135, 141
Rose, Nikolas, 3, 17, 18, 56, 87

Said, Edward, 77
scientific racism, 55–6, 64, 83–4
Select Committee Investigating National Defense Migration, 143
Shaw, George Bernard, 63, 87–8
Shelden, Michael, 101
Sherwood, Margaret, 55
slow death (Berlant), 95, 115, 119
social policies *see* welfare codes

Steinbeck, John
  The Forgotten Village, 149 n.12
  Kerouac's affinity with, 154, 160, 162, 164
  The Log from the Sea of Cortez, 136
  Of Mice and Men, 124, 130
  migrancy as productive for the nation state, 20–1
  the migrant family, 20, 21
  on non-white migrant labour, 126–7
  race in *Travels with Charley* (Steinbeck), 154, 160–3
  representations of homelessness, 19–21
  social Darwinism, 136
  vagabond characters, 124
  vision of social reform, 136–9
  see also *Grapes of Wrath, The* (Steinbeck); *Harvest Gypsies, The* (Steinbeck)
Szalay, Michael, 123, 124

Tocqueville, Alexis de, 71
Tramp Abroad, A (Twain)
  audience for, 44
  critique of modernity, 42–3
  critique of the materialistic American tourist, 10, 21–2, 32–3, 39–42
  Europe contrasted with the US, 21–2, 30, 33, 43, 47, 53
  explorations of idleness, 21–2, 33, 38, 41–3
  influence on Flynt's *Tramping with Tramps*, 33, 44, 49–50
  pre-modern Europe, 42–3
  state's approach to social problems, 33–4
  the tramp-as-artist formulation, 31–2, 119
  Twain as a tramp writer, 35, 36, 38–9, 42
Tramping with Tramps (Flynt)
  criminality and the policing of vagrancy, 50–1
  Europe contrasted with the US, 21–2, 33
  explorations of idleness, 21, 33
  figure of the American tramp, 48–9
  Flynt as a tramp-writer, 48, 54
  Flynt's debt to Twain, 33, 44, 49–50
  German social-welfare system, 33, 53–5
  international frames of comparison, 47–9
  social reintegration of the tramp, 21, 50–4, 56
  on social-welfare policies, 33–4
  vagrancy as an international problem, 46–7, 56–7
  vagrants as a criminal class, 46–7
tramps
  and the Anglo-American liberal subject, 10, 11
  exceptionalism of American tramps, 62–3, 67–9, 72, 78, 81, 84, 110
  figure of, 1–4, 25, 128–9
  of the inter-war period, 92–3
  as masculine and white, 2, 3, 7–8, 10, 20–1, 25, 26, 36, 62, 75–7, 78–9, 129–30
  origin stories, 1, 5
  post-war figure of, 152, 153
  as privileged observers, 10, 19, 27, 32
  public debates on social policies and, 2–3, 5
  as romantic figures, 15, 16, 36, 155
  Romantic vagrancy, 60–1, 85
  shame of the tramp persona, 99–100, 105
  social threat of, 1–2, 3–7, 8–9, 16, 34–5, 57
  subgroups of, 14–15
  the tramp-as-artist, 15, 31–2, 61, 119
  transatlantic discourses on, 4, 5, 12, 21–2, 30–1, 33, 43, 61–2
  whiteness and the exceptional tramp, 61, 62, 63–4, 72
  see also vagrancy
travel writing
  international frames of comparison, 47–8
  nationalism in, 74–5
  of Twain, 37–8, 47, 49–50
  see also *Tramp Abroad, A* (Twain)
Travels with Charley (Steinbeck), 124, 154, 160–3
Tully, Jim, 129
Twain, Mark
  on anti-vagrancy legislation in Hartford, Connecticut, 30–1
  figure of the tramp in the works of, 31, 35, 43–4
  Huckleberry Finn, 35–6
  The Innocents Abroad, 37
  within the international nexus of tramp writing, 12, 30–1
  The Prince and the Pauper, 41
  racial identities and vagrancy, 35–6
  Roughing It, 37
  the tramp as social observer, 10
  the tramp-as-artist formulation, 31–2
  travel writings, 37–8, 47, 49–50
  white, mobile tramps, 11–12
  see also *Tramp Abroad, A* (Twain)

unemployment
  Coxey's Army march, 7–8
  the figure of the tramp and, 1, 4
  following the 1873 crash, 38
  migrant vagrants, 4
  post-Great Depression (1873), 4–5
  and public spaces, 12, 114
  tramps adoption of, 6, 16, 17
  unemployment insurance, 107
  see also labour
United Kingdom (UK) see Great Britain (GB)
United States of America (USA)
  American exceptionalism, 71
  the American 'road' narrative, 79

United States of America (USA) (*cont.*)
American students at German universities, 45
anti-vagrancy legislation, 12–13
emergence of the welfare state, 19–20, 34
exceptionalism of American tramps, 62–3, 67–9, 72, 78, 81, 84, 110
federal highway system, 157
importation of overseas social policies, 12–13, 46
Progressive reforms, 46, 55, 84
racial identity and vagrancy, 8, 12
railroad network, 35, 79
restrictions on non-white migrant labour, 126–7
Select Committee Investigating National Defense Migration, 143
Social Security Act, 134–5
transatlantic discourses on the tramp, 4, 5, 12, 21–2, 30–1, 33, 43, 61–2
Works Progress Administration (WPA), 141–2, 147

vagrancy
biological framing, 16–17, 19
categorisation of, 9–11, 13, 14–16, 79–80
as an international problem, 4–5, 46
of the inter-war period, 92–3
legal codification, 5, 12
as a medical condition, 16
as a pathological threat to national health, 16–17
racial identity and, 8, 9–10, 26–7, 35–6
reforms and welfare policies, 2–3
unemployment as the trigger for, 1

welfare codes
adoption of European social programmes, 46
biopower, 9
categories for welfare assistance, 79–80
under the English Poor Laws, 80, 107–8
the individual vs the social good, 17, 18
international networks of exchange, 6–7, 12–14, 62
under the New Deal reforms, 123, 124, 133, 141
racial categories and social rehabilitation, 9, 10

and the rehabilitation of the tramp figure, 2–3, 6–7, 8–9, 10
tramp-citizen template, 64–5
unemployment insurance, 107
US Social Security, 133–5
US-British comparison in Davies's works, 73–4

welfare institutions
concept, 3
German social-welfare system, 52–5
intersection with the medical profession, 16–17
of the inter-war period, 92
moral responsibility, 5
policy based on scientific observation, 55–6
reforms of the inter-war period, 106–8
regulation of public health, 20, 92, 105, 112–13
state control of vagrancy, 17–19, 82–3, 86–7, 89
in the UK, 19–20, 82–3, 86–7, 89
in the US, 19–20, 34
workhouses (the spike), 17–19, 80–1, 82, 83, 93, 97–8, 107–8, 113–14

welfare state
Beveridge Report, 93, 115, 116, 117
in Britain, 93–4
British social policy in Orwell, 17–19, 94, 97–8, 104–12, 115–16, 119
post-Depression consolidation of, 133–41
precarity of the individual, 117–18
race and support for in the US, 133–6
and the rehabilitation of the tramp figure, 2–3, 6–7, 10, 86, 89
and the rise of neoliberalism, 117, 118–19
Steinbeck's influence on welfare governance, 123–4, 136
White, Andrew Dickson, 46–7, 53
whiteness studies, 9
Whitman, Walt, 152
Willard, Frances, 45
Williams, Raymond, 115–16
Wordsworth, William, 60–1, 85
Works Progress Administration (WPA), 141–2, 147
Wyckoff, Walter, 55

Ziff, Larzer, 37, 47

www.ingramcontent.com/pod-product-compliance
Lightning Source LLC
LaVergne TN
LVHW010325200525
811683LV00031B/315